The Hamburg Rules

An appreciation of the cause and effect of the amendments to the Hague Rules and the Hague-Visby Rules

Fairplay Publications

Published and distributed by
FAIRPLAY PUBLICATIONS LTD
52/54 Southwark Street, London SE1 1UJ
Telephone 01-403 3164
Telex 884595 FPLAY G

ISBN 0 905045 31 9

Printed by Page Bros (Norwich) Ltd.,
Mile Cross Lane, Norwich, Norfolk NR6 6SA.

About the Author

The author is well known in the world of marine insurance and shipping for his work in relation to the adjustment of claims, as between shipowners and carriers of goods by sea and marine insurers, arising out of the question of liability in respect of cargo loss and damage occurring during the course of the carriage of goods by sea. He was for many years the examiner to the Chartered Insurance Institute on this subject and is presently a marine consultant in this and other fields relating to cargo loss and damage. He is a past member of the Royal Institute of Navigation and Institute of Transport, and is also the author of "Shipowners, Cargo Liabilities and Immunities".

In 1980, Fairplay published "Shipping and the Law" which discusses the Hague Rules in detail and provides a practical review of their effect and interpretation. A companion volume, "Hague Rules Law Digest", was published in 1981, providing a ready reference to all cases involving the Hague Rules and the Hague-Visby Rules.

When the report by the Secretariat of the United Nations Conference on Trade and Development on Bills of Lading and proposals for the amendment of the Hague Rules was considered at the Geneva Conference, the author was quoted from time to time, and his book "Shipowners, Cargo Liabilities and Immunities" was privileged to be included in the Select Bibliography contained in the report.

The author has many years' experience in the adjustment and settlement of claims arising under the Hague Rules and his studies have kept him fully appraised of the events leading to the introduction of the Hamburg Rules. It is hoped that this book will be of interest to shipowning and cargo interests and their insurers, as well as maritime lawyers and others, providing as it does a concise guide to the cause and effect of the amendments to the Hague Rules and the Hague-Visby Rules as embodied in the Hamburg Rules.

Author's Preface

All those concerned with seaborne commerce will be appreciative of the in-depth study carried out by the UNCTAD Shipping Committee's Working Group on International Legislation, and the report of the Secretariat, leading to the Final Act of the United Nations Conference on the Carriage of Goods by Sea, upon which the author has leaned heavily in the production of this volume and hereby expresses his acknowledgments.

The author also wishes to express his thanks to Phyllis Gorton for her expertise in the checking of the many drafts, texts and proofs and for her invaluable help and encouragement. The author's thanks are also due to his many friends in the world of shipping and marine insurance who encouraged and in fact persuaded him to embark upon this treatise.

Preface

The amendments to the Hague Rules brought about by the Hamburg Rules have indeed been drastic and as and when the maritime nations begin to adopt the Hamburg Rules and introduce them into their own statute books or codes thus giving them the effect of law, so will the concept of cargo insurance and protection and indemnity insurance come under change. In fact the Hamburg Rules may seriously affect the distribution of the risks borne by cargo and their insurers and the risks borne by shipowners and other carriers by sea and their insurers. On the one hand those risks borne by the cargo and their insurers may be reduced whilst the risks borne by the carrier of goods by sea and his insurers will be increased.

However, it has to be remembered that the allocation of risks in the carriage of goods by sea has not been constant almost from the time when the ocean transport of goods commenced. For a long time before the eighteenth century the carrier of goods by sea bore most of the risks, but in the nineteenth century and in the earlier years of the twentieth century, the distribution of risks changed to the disadvantage of cargo owners with the exception of certain countries who introduced governing legislation following upon the example set by the United States in the passing of the Harter Act in 1893. In fact it was quite a common practice for shipowners, exercising their rights of freedom of contract in the absence of any legislation covering the carriage of goods by sea, to insert in their bill of lading such wide clauses of exemption from liability as to make them virtually immune from any liability in respect of cargo loss or damage during the transit of the goods.

It was this situation that gave rise to the birth of the Hague Rules which, by incorporation into the Carriage of Goods by Sea Act of the U.K. and similar legislation in other countries, imposed upon carriers certain minimum responsibilities and liabilities in respect of cargo loss or damage out of which they could not contract, and so the distribution of risks once again changed to the advantage of cargo interests.

United Nations Conference on Trade and Development make the point that the movement to again redistribute the risks of damage or loss of cargo carried under contracts evidenced by bills of lading, does not create a new situation, but is only a movement in a field in which change has been frequent and towards a situation which, in the past, worked.

However, such changes in maritime law as we are at present witnessing, affecting the distribution of risks in the carriage of goods by sea, will mean that if the shipowner carries additional liabilities his protection and indemnity cover will cost more and the result will be that the cost of claims for cargo loss or damage will be reflected in the freight charges. But whether the cost of these claims is borne by the P. & I. insurers or the cargo underwriters, or by both, the costs of cargo claims will ultimately be met by the cargo owners either in the freight charges or the premiums for the cargo insurance, or both.

Such changes as are likely to be made in the law to effect the new distribution of risks involve action (a) internationally, through conventions or amendments to conventions (b) nationally, through local legislation or regulation and (c) by wider usage of uniform contracts etc.

The purpose of this book is threefold. Firstly to present the Hamburg Rules in their final form. Secondly to present them in such a form so that the reader has before him, rule by rule, an immediate reference to the relative Hague Rule and an explanation of the nature and manner of the amendment to the Hague Rule concerned. Thirdly to provide a review of the findings of the Shipping Committee of United Nations Conference on Trade and Development after their investigations into the present modus operandi of the Hague Rules leading to the decision that the Rules required amendment. Also the author has incorporated a review of the findings of the Shipping Committee following upon their study of certain specific subjects that need to be linked with the Hague Rules and Hamburg Rules to provide a proper understanding of the manner in which seaborne commerce operates in practice under the umbrella of maritime law relative to the carriage of goods by sea.

Contents

The Hamburg Rules

INTRODUCTION

More than half a century past, on the 25th August, 1924, there took place an event that was to change maritime law history, namely the signing at Brussels of the Interntional Convention for the unification of certain rules of law relating to bills of lading. This event put the seal on the ending of the freedom of contract hitherto enjoyed by carriers of goods by sea in so far as contracts evidenced by bills of lading were concerned.

These rules of law are known as the Hague Rules which defined on the one hand the responsibilities and liabilities of the carrier and on the other hand defined the carrier's rights and immunities. Those rules have been accepted and recognised by almost every maritime nation and have now, with the exception of certain minor grievances on the part of carriers, been accepted by both cargo and shipowning interests, and their insurers, as being a fair distribution of the rights of both shipowners and cargo interests and their respective liabilities under the contract of carriage.

However, in the early 1960's it was becoming increasingly apparent that there was a need for the Hague Rules to be amended in certain respects, leading to the Stockholm Conference of the Comite Maritime International in June 1963 when the Visby Rules were adopted, to become later amended and thereafter known as The Brussels Protocol — 1968, signed at Brussels on the 23rd of February, 1968.

The first really positive moves by United Nations towards a review of the Hague Rules were not taken until April, 1969, when the Committee on Shipping of the United Nations Conference on Trade and Development, established a Working Group on International Shipping Legislation.

At its first session held at Geneva in December, 1969, the Working Group established its work programme and an order of priorities among the different items. The first priority was given to a study on bills of lading, which, it was agreed, should be considered by the Working Group at its second session, not later than February, 1971.

The topics for the programme of work on the first priority item, bills of lading, given in the work programme of the Working Group, were that the Working Group should review the economic and commercial aspects of international legislation and practices in the field of bills of lading from the standpoint of their conformity with the needs of economic development in particular of the developing countries and make appropriate recommendations as regards, amongst other things, the following subjects.

(*a*) Principles and rules governing bills of lading, including:
    (i)   Applicable law and forum including arbitration
    (ii) Conflict of laws between conventions and national legislation
    (iii) Responsibilities and liabilities in respect of carriage of goods
    (iv) Voyage deviation and delays
(*b*) Study of standard forms of documentation, including an analysis of common terms
(*c*) Trade customs and usages relating to bills of lading
(*d*) Third party interests at ports of call

This list of topics called for the examination of four distinct elements:

(*a*) General problems arising from the functioning of international legislation and practices concerning bills of lading, in particular those relating to the points listed above
(*b*) The more specifically economic and commercial aspects of these problems
(*c*) The extent to which the international legislation and practices conform with the balancing of equities between the owners and carriers of cargo, with particular concern for the position of the developing countries
(*d*) The specific provisions of the Hague Rules and associated national laws which seem to give rise to difficulties

Thereafter, at the request of the Working Group, following upon their investigations and enquiries, the secretariat of United Nations Conference on Trade and Development issued a report upon the whole situation, which will be examined later in this volume, leading to the draft Convention by United Nations Commission on International Trade law. The General Assembly of United Nations, by a resolution of December 15, 1976, convening the Conference on the Carriage of Goods by Sea, referred to the Conference, as the basis for its consideration of the carriage of goods by sea, the Draft Convention on the Carriage of Goods by Sea contained in the report of United Nations Commission on International Trade Law on the work of its ninth session, the text of draft provisions concerning implementation, reservations and other final clauses prepared by the Secretary-General, the comments and proposals by Governments and international organisations, which led finally to the Conference in 1978 when the Conference drew up the UNITED NATIONS CONVENTION ON THE CARRIAGE OF GOODS BY SEA, 1978, namely the Hamburg Rules.

SECTION I

An outline of the studies of the Shipping Committee of the United Nations Conference on Trade and Development, on the bill of lading and its function in modern commerce, an essential pre-emptible to the examination of the Hague Rules. Including an historical review of the development of the bill of lading.

The historical development of the bill of lading

Prior to making their recommendations with regard to amendments to the Hague Rules, the UNCTAD Committee made a deep study of the development of the bill of lading, and the results of this study will make interesting reading to all those concerned with seaborne commerce, cargo interests, insurers and shipowners alike.

The pattern of modern shipping and the associated law has been traced to the practice of the Italian city-states of the 11th century, and from this origin maritime law grew up under the tutelage of civil law and still bears the imprint so acquired. In the seventh century A.D., various principles were laid down and became embodied in the maritime customs of the island of Rhodes. These were approved and developed by Roman lawyers and found their way, as "Rhodian Law", into the statute books of the great Mediterranean trading cities. Some of this is the basic principle of maritime law today. For example, the "law of General Average" may be found in the Rhodian Law of the seventh century A.D. in which it is provided that "it is lawful to throw over as much of the lading as might put the ship in a position to resist the storm. And because it seldom happens that the whole lading belongs to one merchant, it is justly provided that the person whose goods are cast overboard shall not be the only loser, but that the others shall contribute towards the loss of those that were thrown overboard proportionately and not according to bulk but to value." It is felt that these facts will be of interest before passing to the results of the studies of UNCTAD into the bill of lading proper, in that the Committee have noted that, because of its origin as general law in the Mediterranean region, the developing law retained a remarkable likeness in all countries, and that even until the late 19th century "a large part of the course of maritime law applied by the Courts of various nations was regarded as supra-national". This similarity exists today, and is advanced by several widely ratified conventions applicable to various aspects of maritime law, and in many, if not most, instances the developing countries have modelled their national maritime laws on the law of the developed country, frequently that of their former metropolitan powers.

The view has been expressed by one authority on the subject that, since this more or less uniform body of maritime law has been shaped by developed nations, and most particularly by nations with shipping interests, it may be vested with a bias unsuitable to less developed nations. To the extent that maritime law favours carrier interests over cargo interests, the authority in question states that it is inimical to less developed countries because, by and large, less developed countries do not have substantial merchant fleets. In any event, those countries which do not choose to develop a substantial merchant fleet have an obvious interest in seeing that their law does not discriminate against cargo interests. In this present day and age, discussion of whether maritime law is fairly balanced between cargo and carrier interests often focuses on one central question, namely, how should losses arising from the carriage of goods by sea be borne?

This is a relatively recent question, and basically the background of the recommendations for the amendments to the Hague Rules. Records show that as late as the 19th century this question was not regarded as of pressing importance, the only available vessels being small sailing ships, and cargoes were not usually of a perishable nature. A certain amount of damage to cargo was expected as an incident of every ocean voyage and very little litigation found its way into the courts until the mid 19th century. Further, until the advent of steam, the absence of the modern need for speedy despatch of vessels in port bred tolerance of more leisurely methods of cargo handling and tallying ashore and this factor in turn afforded greater opportunity for more careful ship-side tallies than is perhaps possible today, so reducing that fertile area of disputes as to where and when any loss or damage was caused.

Historically, maritime law held the carrier of goods by sea absolutely liable for cargo loss or damage, whether or not the carrier was negligent, and regardless of the cause of the loss. The carrier could only escape liability if the loss or damage was caused by an act of God, a public enemy, inherent vice of the goods, fault of the shipper or if the goods had been appropriately made the subject of a general average sacrifice. The Committee comment that even where the loss was caused by one of these "Common law exceptions" the carrier remained liable if he had been negligent or otherwise at fault. The shipper would succeed in his claim if he proved receipt of the goods for carriage in good order and either non-delivery or delivery in bad order, provided that the carrier could not show that one of the "Common Law exceptions" had caused the loss or damage. In effect, the carrier was a guarantor of the safe arrival, and fault was immaterial. In addition to this, there were implied in all contracts for the carriage of goods by sea, in the absence of expressed stipulations to the contrary, undertakings by the carrier (a) that the carrying vessel was seaworthy, and (b) that the ship would commence and carry out the contractual voyage with reasonable diligence and without unjustifiable deviation. Cargo owners, or charterers, could repudiate the contract of carriage and claim compensation for any damage suffered as a result of the breach of these undertakings as defeating the commercial purpose of the voyage. The carrier was so liable for any loss or damage occasioned to cargo carried on his vessel if it occurred, either through his own negligence or through the unseaworthiness of the vessel, and even the exceptions implied by the law did not, it would seem, avail the shipowner unless they were expressly stipulated in the bill of lading. Therefore the shipowner's liability under both the Common Law and the civil codes was in theory strict, and until the 1880s shipowners and shippers were in apparent agreement that it was the former's responsibility to carry and deliver safely the goods entrusted to them "in like good order and condition" in which they were shipped. The bill of lading was the document which came in time to specify the goods at risk and the basis for any claim for non-delivery or damage.

The merchant did not at first need a custody-of-cargo receipt from his carrier, while his business arrangements, later referred to as his contract of carriage, remained part of the customary arrangements for dividing the expenses and the profits of the venture.

For so long as merchants travelled with the goods, particulars were merely entered in a book or register which was part of the ship's papers. When the merchant ceased to accompany his goods, the necessity arose for a separate document which was at first a receipt and later embodied the terms on which the carrier would transport and deliver the goods. At first, these were customary terms which came in time to be incorporated into the common law of England and the Commercial Codes of continental Europe, and so was born, in the twelfth century, the primitive precursor of the modern bill of lading. The "book" gave way to a "bill" in the 14th century when excerpts from it were delivered to the shipper, who received in this form what was akin to the modern bill of lading.

The advent of marine insurance in the 12th century introduced a further element of sophistication into the usages of sea carriage. Originally, marine insurance was simply a mutual protection among individual shipowners themselves and its customs became somewhat standardised before they were articulated in extant codes in the Middle Ages. The earliest codes known date from the early 15th century and these attempted to regulate the practice of marine insurances, which became established as a business by about 1600.

Reference was made to quotations from three authorities. In *Gilmore and Black* it is stated that the basic insurance policy of apparently Italian origin which came to be generally used, and has with slight changes come down to this day, originally did service for both hull, and cargo risks that were frequently insured together. *Holman* states that a contract of insurance is a contract of indemnity whereby the assured pays a certain sum, called the premium, to the underwriter, who in consideration thereof, takes upon himself the risks insured against and undertakes to make good to the assured any loss that he may sustain by reason of the named peril. A contract of marine insurance, it is stated, is a contract whereby the insurer undertakes to indemnify the assured against marine losses.

The third authority referred to in this connection is *W. D. Winter* on marine insurance, where it is stated that the procurement of marine insurance results in the sharing by the ultimate consumer of the losses that overtook property in commerce, and the reduction of uncertainty in ocean carriage. The underwriter charges a premium for the insurance of the risks that he underwrites, and this premium charge becomes one of the items in the invoice for the sale of the goods, and in the freight rate, which is also an item in the invoice, and thus it becomes indirectly included in the price of the goods and is an indirect charge on the consumer.

For centuries, a sort of maxim or fundamental principal existed in maritime commerce, that between the shipowner and the marine insurance underwriter, the goods owner ought to be kept harmless against all losses except those of the market. The rule was that once properly packed goods were placed on board a vessel so as to be fit for carriage, and were fully insured against all risks, the owner of them, by either the contract of affreightment or insurance, must be made to feel secure. This ideal for security in maritime trade presupposed, however, that the bill of lading was always in such form that, when accompanied by the insurance policy or certificate, it would be regarded by merchants and bankers as connoting possession of the goods, *i.e.* that the liabilities of the carrier and the underwriter were coterminous. The shipowner undertook to deliver the goods, accidents of navigation excepted, the underwriter making good the loss or damage to the goods by accidents of navigation.

However, not all risks were, or are, insurable, and at first underwriters would not assume any of the risks of personal injury or damage to cargo, and, as will be later described, carriers came to exempt themselves from most, if not all, of their liability by inserting specific exoneration clauses in their bills of lading. This practice served to impair the value of the bill of lading and insurance policy when taken together as evidence of the security of the goods. It was to protect themselves from uninsured risks that shipowners devised and organised mutual protection clubs, which developed into the modern type of P. & I. clubs in the 19th century. Similarly, the cargo owners sought wider cover from the marine insurance market for the risks of sea carriage. The marine insurance market responded to this need by covering new perils as commerce developed, but did not afford protection against every type of marine loss that may arise in the course of a voyage. The principal risks insured are named in the "perils" clause of the policy, and are either supplemented to cover land risks before shipment and after discharge, or restricted by further clauses.

It is generally the practice for underwriters to pay the cargo owners' losses first and then attempt later to recoup from the carrier sums paid out in respect of losses or damage for which carriers were liable. In this way, the insurer may pay for the damage to the goods caused, for example, by improper stowage, although it may be that the carrier of the goods is at the same time liable to the consignee for such damage. Cargo owners are, therefore, much attracted by the wide cover afforded by modern insurance policies, and by the speed with which most underwriters pay claims, as contrasted with what has been described as the slowness and resistance of private parties, including carriers in dealing with claims. In course of time, the bill of lading became the basic shipping document.

The Committee's study of the development of the bill of lading in so far as it is pertinent to the revision of the Hague Rules, shows that the bill of lading was originally a "straight" or non-negotiable document. In due course, however, the spread of commerce, the increasing complexity of business and the concern for speed meant that the need was felt for transferring the property in the goods before they arrived at destination, and thus arose the practice of transferring ownership of the goods by endorsing the bill of lading to the buyer. By the 18th Century, this practice was well established and the "negotiable" bill of lading was in common use. However, the early bills of lading did not contain any exceptions from liability, and the early simple form contained no indication, beyond such vague phrases as "the accidents of navigation excepted", as to what was to be done, or what the respective rights of the parties were in any of the situations that might lead to the voyage being unsuccessful. In fact the exception was taken to mean no more than the negative proposition that in the event of such accidents the shipowner was not bound to do an impossibility.

It seems that the earliest qualifications to be introduced were either of a general type, such as "dangers of the sea only excepted", or "said to be" clauses, but as a result of 18th century judicial decisions, shipowners began generally to amend their bills of lading to stipulate not only from the old common law exceptions but also to exempt themselves from liability in respect of all perils of the sea and of navigation "of whatever kind". Through such provisions inserted in their bills of lading, known as "exoneration clauses" or "negligence clauses" carriers of goods by sea began to limit contractually the strict liability imposed upon them by the maritime law. Their use of freedom of contract principles, considered by cargo interests as being more technical than real, expressed in both common law and civil law, created a situation whereby the carrier was enjoined on the one hand to strict liability by the maritime law, but could, nevertheless, contract out of almost all liability by appropriately framing the clauses in the bill of lading. The law permitted carriers to extend the principles of freedom of contract, which they did with such success that they came to exempt themselves from practically all liability for cargo loss or damage suffered during sea transport. In fact, no sooner did a court decision go against the carrier than his legal advisers would insert a fresh clause in the bill of lading to nullify this result in the future.

Bills of lading came to include stipulations to the effect that the carrier was not to be liable for the results of his own negligence or that of his employees. The reasons which originally led carriers to disclaim liability for their servants' actions relating to stowage and mis-delivery of the goods were said to be bound up with "the infancy of steam navigation". In this connection reference was made to one of the great authorities on general average, *Lowndes,* which ascribes the reasons advanced by the steamship owners for taking this action to the peremptory necessity "for steamers of quick despatch". This it was stated, was a "crude device" for shaking off responsibility for careless cargo handling. The view was expressed that these reasons were likely to lose in time most, if not all, force. From *Lowndes'* remarks, it appears that no sooner were the old deliberate ways "which served sailing ships" abandoned than the necessity for despatch led to a great deal of hurry and confusion in the loading and discharging of steamships. It seems that it was not realised sufficiently in the early years of steam that despatch was not incompatible with strict precaution against error.

Meanwhile, competition between shipowners was increasing enormously, and the volume of world trade exceeded the carrying capacity of shipping. Where exoneration clauses were upheld, the position of the carrier became virtually the reverse of that under maritime law, in that instead of the carrier being absolutely liable irrespective of negligence, he enjoyed a contractural exemption from liability regardless of negligence, and this contractural exemption became as wide as the carrier's bargaining position would allow. Generally speaking, in what might be termed "cargo oriented" countries, the views of cargo interests largely prevailed and stricter liability was imposed upon carriers than in shipowning countries where carriers continued to enjoy an almost unlimited freedom of contracting.

In view of the growing dissatisfaction of the shippers, bankers, underwriters, and others, shipowners were forced to negotiate and to meet some of the shippers' complaints about the situation. Some U.K. shipowners agreed to adopt model bills of lading which expressly stipulated that they would be relieved from liability only in cases of errors in navigation and not in the case of cargo loss or damage arising out of fault on the part of the master or crew in the care and custody of the cargo. Under other model bills of lading the shipowner was held liable for faults committed by the master or crew unless these related to navigation and to the management of the ship.

The introduction of legislation to govern bill of lading clauses

It is recorded that a "Conference Form" bill of lading was adopted at a meeting in Liverpool in 1882, which was the first to admit the concept of "due diligence" and to fix a limit to the shipowner's liability of 100 pounds sterling per package. This "Conference Form" bill of lading became the basis for the Hamburg Rules adopted in Hamburg in 1885. In Japan, the position was so strict that the shipowner could not even by express agreement exempt himself from liability for damage to the goods caused by his own fault, or bad faith, by the gross fault of his employees, or by unseaworthiness of the vessel. The Spanish Commercial Law of 1885 was also very strict in its provisions concerning the liability of shipowners.

Simultaneous developments took place in the United States and the British Dominions, the ocean trade of the Dominions depending heavily on United Kingdom shipowners, and it was in these countries that the struggle between shipowning and cargo interests came to a head, and eventually legislation was demanded "to remove the chaos and abuse produced by unlimited freedom of contract", and the demand of the shippers gave rise to the United States introducing the Harter Act in 1893, followed by Australia bringing into force a Carriage of Goods by Sea Act in 1904, a Carriage of Goods by Sea Act in New Zealand in 1908 and the Canadian Water Carriage Act in 1910.

The Harter Act, which led the way in this new legislation aimed at the protection of cargo interests, prohibited clauses exonerating the carrier or his agents from liability for faults in the care and custody of the cargo, but at the same time the Act provided that the carrier was not to be held liable for results of unseaworthiness if he had exercised due diligence to make the ship seaworthy, and if the damage caused to the cargo resulted from faults and errors in the navigation or management of the vessel. The Harter Act established an important principle which later inspired the Hague Rules and the Brussels International Convention, in that it settled the problem of the carrier's liability by making a distinction between faults in the navigation and management of the vessel and faults in the care and custody of the cargo. The Acts of the Dominions were broadly similar to the Harter Act.

It was shown that the need for further reform was generally felt but shipowning countries feared that the reimposition of liabilities upon their carriers would increase their freight charges and place them at a disadvantage by comparison with others. They did not relish the idea of abridging the principle of freedom of contract which formed a fundamental feature of their legal systems. It also came to be realised that a solution would have to be based on an international agreement in order to be of any practical value in international trade. Moves towards the reform and unification of the law, relative to bills of lading, thus began to concentrate on the creation of an international model bill of lading which would establish certain world wide minimum standards of the shipowner's liability. International conferences were held, mainly under the auspices of the International Law Association and the Comite Maritime International (CMI). The trend towards uniform legislation was, however, temporarily halted by a movement in favour of the preparation of a code of rules defining the rights and liabilities of sea carriers which would be voluntarily incorporated into bills of lading, but the project for uniform legislation was later revived. Events then came to a head when the British Government, under the pressure of the Dominions, insisted that the shipowners reach an agreement.

After considerable discussion among the leading shipowners, underwriters, shippers, and bankers of the major maritime nations, a set of rules was finally drafted by the Maritime Law Committee of the International Law Association at a meeting held at the Hague in 1921 and came to be known as the Hague Rules, but they were not immediately adopted. The Rules were drafted in the form of a uniform bill of lading in the hope that the shipping companies would adopt them voluntarily and that similar enterprises would soon follow suit. One or two shipping companies did adopt the Rules, but generally the companies were not prepared to give up their extensive immunities from liability under the then existing laws of many countries. It was soon apparent that legislation would be necessary to make the uniform Rules part of bills of lading.

Introduction of The Hague Rules

The Hague Rules were amended at the London Conference of the Comite Maritime International in 1922, and thereafter agitation for legislative action on the lines of the Rules continued and a diplomatic conference on Maritime Law was held in Brussels in 1922, when a draft convention was drawn up which was amended at the Brussels Convention in 1923. In the following year an International Convention at Brussels was signed by the major maritime nations. The Brussels Convention was not conceived as a comprehensive and self-sufficient code regulating the carriage of goods by sea, and was not meant altogether to supplant the contract of carriage but only to control on certain topics of freedom of contract, which the parties would otherwise have. It was intended, merely to unify certain rules relating to bills of lading, its most important effect being, perhaps, that the carrier could no longer contract out of certain defined responsibilities and was given specific rights and remedies.

The Convention, in fact, established minimum obligations of the carrier, the carrier's maximum immunities, and the limit of his liability. Under the Rules, the carrier was not held responsible for unseaworthiness of the ship, providing that this unseaworthiness was not caused by lack of due diligence on his part before and at the commencement of the voyage, nor for the consequences of acts, neglect or faults of the Master or his other agents in the navigation or management of the ship. The Rules then listed a series of exceptions fully exempting the carrier from liability unless proof to the contrary was provided.

Finally, if the carrier was held liable for cargo loss or damage, the amount to be payable, under the Rules, was not to exceed £100 sterling (Gold Value), unless the nature and value of the packages or units had been declared by the shipper prior to loading and stated in the bill of lading. The carrier could not lessen his liabilities under the Rules but it was provided that, if he wished to do so, he was at liberty to enlarge, in part or in whole, any of his liabilities.

The suggestion that the Rules should be re-examined arose in a report of the Sub-Committee on Conflicts of Law of the CMI (Comite Maritime International), which was considered at the Rijeka Conference of the CMI in September 1959. The Conference, after having discussed whether it was desirable to amend Article 10 of the Rules, which states that the provisions of the Convention shall apply to all bills of lading issued in any of the contracting States, adopted a resolution on its future work instructing its Sub-Committee to study other amendments and adaptations to the provisions of the International Convention.

The UNCTAD study shows that there were many divergent views among the national maritime law associations as to the desirability of amending the Hague Rules. Some delegations felt that only a limited number of amendments to the Rules would be desirable in order not to upset the agreement reached in 1924 whilst others thought that a substantial revision had become necessary after 40 years of usage. It was against this background that the suggestion was made that the Hague Rules should be amended by way of a Protocol so as not to upset its general scheme.

In the meantime, two judicial decisions in the English Courts had given rise to concern. Firstly there was the case of *The Muncaster Castle* which concerned the question of the shipowner's liability, under the Hague Rules, for the damage which was suffered by a consignment of ox tongues shipped from Sydney to London, the damage being due to the entry of seawater into the hold of the vessel by way of the vessel's storm valves. The events giving rise to the important legal issue in this case arose prior to the vessel leaving the U.K. on her outward voyage to Australia, her owners having arranged for her to be surveyed. To enable the surveyors to inspect the storm valves, the ship repair yard were instructed to remove the inspection covers. When the survey had been carried out, these covers were replaced by a fitter in the employ of the ship repair yard. This man carried out his work negligently, the nuts securing the storm valve covers being insufficiently and unevenly hardened up. Although there was no leakage on the outward voyage to Australia, water entered one of the holds due to the working and straining of the ship in conditions of heavy weather on the return voyage to the U.K., the nuts covering the storm valves working loose and so allowing seawater to enter the hold and damage the cargo. The cargo interests proceeded against the shipowners for the recovery of their loss

9

but the shipowners declined to accept liability on the grounds that they had "exercised due diligence to make the ship seaworthy" within the meaning of the Hague Rules.

Introduction of the Visby Rules

When the case came before the House of Lords for final adjudication, the Court said that the words "exercise due diligence to make the ship seaworthy" in the Hague Rules were adopted from the American Harter Act, and similar British Commonwealth Statutes, and that a carrier was responsible to the cargo owner unless due diligence in the work had been shown by every person to whom any part of the necessary work had been entrusted, no matter whether he was the carrier's servant, agent, or independent contractor. It was held, therefore, that the shipowners were liable for the negligence of a ship repairers' fitter.

Another case which gave rise to concern among shipowning and other interests, was the case of *Midland Silicones Ltd v. Scruttons*, which arose out of the loss sustained by the consignees when a drum of chemicals was dropped by the stevedores after discharge from the ship. The shipowners had for many years employed this particular firm of stevedores to discharge their vessels at London under an agreement which contained a clause stating expressly that the stevedores were responsible for any damage to goods by reason of negligence of the stevedores. However, there was, in addition, a clause in the agreement to the effect that the stevedores were to have such protection as was afforded by the terms, conditions and exceptions of the bills of lading.

The consignees brought an action against Scruttons, the stevedoring contractors, for the recovery of their loss and the stevedoring contractors sought to obtain the benefit of the provisions of the bill of lading which, by reason of the fact that the terms and conditions of the bill of lading were governed by the Hague Rules, as incorporated in the United States Carriage of Goods by Sea Act, provided that the shipowner's liability was limited to $500 per package. When the case came before the House of Lords it was held that the word "carrier" in the Rules did not include stevedores, and that the relation of stevedores to carriers in this case was that of independent contractors, and that the carriers were not contracting as agents for stevedores. Further, that the cargo owners were unaware of the relations between carriers and stevedores and there was no ground for implying a contract between cargo owners and stevedores. The Court said that it was a fundamental principle of English law that only a party to a contract could sue upon it, and that, therefore, the stevedoring contractors were not entitled to the protection of a contract made between the carriers and the cargo owners.

In 1963 the Stockholm Conference of the CMI on the matter of the revision of the Hague Rules reached an agreement on the text of the amendments to the Hague Rules that should be submitted to the

Diplomatic Conference on Maritime Law. This was a draft Protocol to amend the International Convention for the unification of certain rules of law relating to bills of lading. The main recommendation of the conference was, in effect, the overruling of these two British judicial decisions.

There were other important recommendations for amendment to the Hague Rules at the Stockholm Conference aimed at further governing of the terms and conditions, leading eventually to the Diplomatic Conference at Brussels in May 1967 and February 1968 which were considered by UNCTAD in their deliberations on amendments to the Hague Rules.

The Diplomatic Conference met at Brussels in two sessions in May 1967 and February 1968 with the draft of the 1963 Stockholm Conference before it for approval. At the first session the Conference rejected the amendment intended to overrule the *Muncaster Castle* decision. Moreover, several countries criticised the amendments relating to the carrier's liability and application of the Hague Rules, which led the Conference to postpone its deliberations for further discussions between delegations. At its second session in February 1968 the Conference reached agreement on the final text of the amendments to the Hague Rules, known as the Brussels Protocol 1968.

Amendments to the Hague Rules by the Brussels Protocol 1968

Added to Article III paragraph 4 of the Rules is a new sentence by which statements in bills of lading are to be regarded as conclusive evidence when such bills of lading have been transferred to a third party acting in good faith. Article III paragraph 6 is amended to provide that in any event there shall be no liability in respect of cargo loss or damage unless suit is brought within one year, stating also that it is permissible to extend such period should the parties so agree. A new paragraph has been added to Article III so that recourse actions may be brought after the expiration of the one year time limit, within the time limit allowed by the law of the Court seized of the case.

On the matter of the limitation of the carrier's liability, the whole of Article IV paragraph 5 of the Rules has been amended and it is provided that weight (kilo) is an alternative to package or unit as a basis for limitation, the basis giving the higher figure to be adopted. The limit of liability per package or unit is raised from £100 to Poincaré francs 10,000 and the limit of liability per kilo to Poincaré francs 30. It is also provided that the total amount recoverable is to be calculated by reference to the value of the goods at the place and time at which the goods are discharged.

The problem of the Rules in relation to goods which are palletised or carried in containers has also been dealt with, the amendments providing that where a container, pallet or similar article of transport is to be used to consolidate goods, the question as to whether limitation is based on packed in the container, then the unit basis will be adopted, otherwise itself. If packages or units are enumerated in the bill of lading as being packed in the container, then the unit basis will be adopted, otherwise the container itself will be the basis.

With regard to the "Himalaya" clause, giving stevedores and agents of the carrier the benefit of the bill of lading limitations and exemptions from liability, a new Article has been added to the Rules which provides that the servants and agents of the carrier will be entitled to benefit from the definitions and limits of liability available to the carrier. However, servants or agents of the carrier will not be entitled to avail themselves of this provision if it is proved that the loss or damage resulted from an act or omission of the servant or agent done with intent to cause damage, or recklessly, or with knowledge that damage will probably result.

With regard to the application of the Convention, Article X has been amended so that the Convention will apply to every bill of lading relating to the carriage of goods between ports in two different states if the bill of lading is issued in a contracting state, or if the carriage is from a port in a contracting state, or if the contract of carriage contained in or evidenced by the bill of lading provides that the Rules of the Convention, or legislation of any state giving effect to them, are to govern the contract whatever may be the nationality of the ship, the carrier, the shipper, the consignee, or any other interested person.

However, the Protocol provides that it shall come into force three months after the date of the deposit of ten instruments of ratification or accession, of which at least five shall have been deposited by states that have each a tonnage equal or superior to one million gross tons. The new Rules contained in the Protocol have been given effect in the Carriage of Goods by Sea Act of 1971, which enactment received Royal Assent on the 8th April, 1971. The Act, which incorporates the amendments made to the Hague Rules of 1924 by the Brussels Protocol of 1968, came into force on June 23, 1977, on the deposit of the ten instruments.

The function and purpose of the bill of lading

Prior to the recommendation being made with regard to the amendments to the Hague Rules, the UNCTAD Committee examined the matter of the bill of lading itself, and it is now proposed to deal with their deliberations on this document.

Firstly, the question to be dealt with was "What is a Bill of Lading?" In the opinion of the Committee, the words "Bill of Lading" convey the normal meaning of a document evidencing the loading of goods on a ship, although the Hague Rules do not define the meaning of "Bill of Lading".

In general, the modern form of bill of lading may be described as (a) a receipt signed by or on behalf of the carrier and issued to the shipper acknowledging that goods, described in the bill of lading, have been shipped in a particular vessel to a specified destination, or have been received in the shipowner's custody for shipment. Article III of the Hague Rules states what the bill of lading must contain. Besides stating the number of packages or pieces, quantity or weight of the goods, marks and their apparent order and condition, the carrier is not required to indicate any other particulars in the bill of lading, and that, accordingly, it is perfectly valid to state in the bill of lading that the quality, nature, value, contents and technical specification of the goods are unknown. Such a bill of lading would not thereby be regarded as otherwise than a clean bill of lading.

The bill of lading may also be described as (b) a memorandum of the terms and conditions of the contract of carriage, which will, in fact, almost invariably have been concluded much earlier than the signing of the document and (c) a document of title to the goods which enables the consignee to take delivery of the goods at their destination or dispose of them by way of an endorsement and delivery of the bill of lading. It may be said that the principal purpose of the bill of lading today is to enable the owner of the goods, to which it relates, to dispose of them rapidly, although the goods are no longer in his hands but already in the custody of the carrier. Its importance lies in its role as the foundation of overseas trade, by reference to which the responsibilities and rights of both carriers and shippers are determined, and on the basis of which is established, through bankers, the credit necessary for the financing of mercantile contracts.

Following upon their studies of the sequence of events in the "life" of a bill of lading, the Committee commented that these may be summarised as being (a) the shipper's description of the goods, with his own name and that of the consignee inserted on the carrier's form; particulars of the total gross weight and the measurement, for freight calculation purposes, and, where necessary, the f.o.b. value of the goods, are also inserted by the shipper. (b) Lodging of the bill of lading at the office of the shipowner or his agent or broker (c) the completion and checking of the contents of the bill of lading by the shipowner or broker against tallying details taken at the time of loading the cargo (d) the freight calculation (e) the signature of the bill of lading by or on behalf of the carrier or the ship's master and by such other parties as may be by law required to do so in different countries (f) the release by the shipowner or his agent of the signed bill of lading to the shipper against freight and, where appropriate, a mate's receipt or equivalent document (g) despatch of the Bill of Lading by the shipper to the buyer or consignee or its lodgment with the bank when a letter of credit is involved (h) the surrender of the bill of lading by the consignee to the shipowner's agent at the port of discharge in order that he may obtain delivery of the goods.

With regard to further particulars of the general practice relating to bills of lading the Committee comment, concerning the consignee, that bills of lading are drawn either to order, when negotiated against a letter of credit, or to the name of the party to whom the goods are consigned and who has direct claim to the goods as soon as he is in possession of a signed copy of the bill of lading. The word "order" means that the document is more than a receipt for the goods and more than a contract to carry the goods. The Committee decided that by use of the words "to the order of" a named party, the bill of lading acquires its third characteristic of a document of title, and that the legal ownership of the goods can be transferred from the named consignee to other persons and by then in turn to others. The name of the expected consignee is usually inserted on "order" bills of lading. The carrier would then usually advise the parties to be notified when their goods are due, but is not obliged to do so in some countries.

In connection with the bill of lading date, the comment is made that, whilst at present it is the date the bill of lading is usually signed, shippers, on the other hand, often require that the date should be the day on which the goods are loaded, which is earlier than the date of signature. Also, bills of lading are customarily given on an earlier date in some trades, provided that by that date the goods have been delivered alongside the vessel, which has started to load. A "received for shipment" bill of lading may be issued if the shippers require proof of delivery for shipment, and such a bill of lading may later become a "shipped" bill of lading.

In this connection reference has to be made to Article III paragraph 7 of the Hague Rules which provides that, after the goods are loaded, the bill of lading to be issued by the carrier, master or agent of the carrier, to the shipper shall, if the shipper so demands, be a "shipped" bill of lading, provided that if the shipper shall have previously taken up any document of title to such goods, he shall surrender the same as against the issue of the "shipped" bill of lading, but at the option of the carrier such document of title may be noted at the port of shipment by the carrier, master, or agent of the carrier with the name of the carrying vessel and the date of shipment, and when so noted the same shall be deemed to constitute a "shipped" bill of lading.

The bill of lading must state, how many negotiable copies have been signed and the terms and conditions of carriage. The release of the goods at destination is usually effected by issuing a delivery order to the receivers in exchange for the original bill of lading and freight, unless the freight has been paid on shipment, in which case this fact is usually endorsed on the bill of lading. The "released" bill of lading, or the delivery order, is then presented by the receivers to the authority competent to deliver the goods at the port, and surrendered to that authority in exchange for the goods. In practice, the shipper reserves space on the vessel and is instructed by the carrier when and where to deliver the goods at the dock. A receipt will be issued to the shipper, and, as from this point, the carrier usually has the charge of the goods, and issuing, in place of the receipt, a bill of lading. This document then serves as written evidence of the terms of the contract of carriage and becomes a document of title. By virtue of this fact, the bill of lading plays a vital part in international commerce and in the financing of the sale of the goods, and is usually forwarded through a bank to the buyer together with a draft for the price of the goods shipped, and the insurance policy. On buying or accepting the draft the buyer obtains the other papers. However, as has been disclosed in various legal actions, the bill of lading is not itself the contract of carriage but is evidence of its terms after it has been accepted by the shipper. The actual contract usually comes into being when shipping space is reserved before the bill of lading is signed by the carrier, and its terms must be inferred from the carrier's sailing announcements and arrangements made before the goods are shipped. For example a carrier has been held liable for damage to cargo during loading, under the provision of the Carriage of Goods by Sea Act, which incorporates the Hague Rules, despite the fact that no bill of lading had, at the time of the damage, been issued.

Besides being a receipt for the goods, the bill of lading is also a negotiable document, by which the goods described in it may be transferred from the shipper to the consignee. For all practical purposes, order bills of lading are usually treated as fully negotiable and the shipper, consignee and all intervening parties holding negotiable order bills of lading are wholly dependent upon them for the accuracy of the loading tally, the correctness of the apparent good order and condition of the goods as described in the bill of lading and the correctness of the date of loading.

However, goods are not always delivered in the same apparent good order and condition as described in the bill of lading, and sometimes the carrier fails to deliver the quantity described in the bill of lading.

The Committee made a useful examination of the manner in which cargo claims arise, and the processes and issues involved in their settlement or rejection, and no doubt the deep investigation into this matter had some considerable bearing upon the recommendations of UNCTAD over amendments to the Hague Rules.

A review of cargo claims procedure

Generally speaking the cargo owner, or his representative, collects his goods from the shipowner, or his agent, on arrival of the carrying vessel at the port of destination. In practice he collects the goods from a public or privately owned wharf, a port authority or some other depository into whose custody the ship will have delivered the goods under local laws. For reasons of convenience, the term "warehouse" was used by the Shipping Committee in their report, and will continue in this review.

If, on taking delivery, the consignee finds that his goods are not available, either in whole or in part, through perhaps misdelivery, theft etc., or they are damaged, the consignee has a duty, under the Hague Rules, to give notice of loss or damage to the carrier. The warehouse will usually issue an out-turn report, or a certificate purporting to state the condition of the goods as received from the vessel, or certifying their short landing. This document, either alone, or together with the survey report, will create the general basis upon which the consignee may seek redress for his loss from the carrier and the basis of his claim for compensation. The basis of the claim against the carrier, under the Hague Rules, will be that a clean bill of lading has been issued showing the apparent good order and quantity of the goods shipped, whereas the goods have not been discharged in the same apparent good order and condition. From this point matters of procedure arise, and the Committee commented that the usual procedure in regard to a situation in which cargo has been discharged in bad order, is that the cargo owner will obtain a bad order certificate from the dockside warehouse or Port Authority and on obtaining this "bad order" or "short landing" certificate, will claim for the loss of his goods against the carrier.

The cargo owner must usually furnish 'prima facie' proof that the loss or damage took place whilst the goods were in charge of the carrier by establishing that clean bills of lading were issued and that defective receipts were granted on discharge. The Committee comment that it may take many months before any kind of definite answer to the location and condition of the goods can be given to the cargo owner, by reason of the practice of the carrier to institute general enquiries as to whether the goods were shipped at all, whether they were mistowed on the vessel, landed at earlier ports of call or over carried to subsequent ports. However, the Committee comment that the nature of the contract of carriage is such that the carrier would be entitled to make investigations and searches before agreeing to consider the claim, but the cargo owners should expect a reasonable period of time, consonant with modern methods of communication, to be consumed in this process.

It has to be remembered, however, that once the cargo claimant establishes a 'prima facie' case against the carrier, the onus of proof shifts to the carrier to contradict, if he can, the case made out against him by the statements in the bill of lading as to the good order of the goods, receipts, and other evidence brought forward by the cargo claimants as to the bad order on discharge. It was found that the burden of proof "shifts" back and forth between the claimants and the carriers, and may often be decisive in settlement of the claim.

In the ordinary course of events, when loss or damage is discovered on discharge of the goods, the cargo owners, acting in compliance with the requirements of their insurance certificates, will either notify their insurers of their loss or, in the cases of deliveries abroad, will notify the parties named in the insurance certificates to survey the loss or damage.

The survey report which is subsequently issued forms the basis, together with the ships' outturn report, for any critical examination of a particular dispute about a claim.

The Committee comments that it is essential for the purpose of establishing liability to determine the cause and time of loss or damage, and that most of the differences and misunderstandings between cargo owners and shipowners arise at this point because it is difficult to establish where, how and when the loss or damage occurred and assess the burden of proof on the parties, all vital considerations for establishing liability. From the cargo receiver's point of view, if goods are short landed, or damaged, he has suffered a loss whilst they were entrusted to the care of the carrier. The enquiries of the Committee disclose that the cargo owner is not usually readily amenable to the carrier's explanations as to why he cannot obtain immediate relief, particularly when it is argued that the loss or damage occurred when the goods were not in the carrier's custody or arose from negligence in the management of the ship, or in the navigation of the ship, or from perils of the sea etc., included in the exceptions contained in the Hague Rules. When cargo owners are faced with such arguments, which the shipowners may validly advance under the Hague Rules, as incorporated into the Statute books of the maritime nations, they may tend to take the view that it should be no concern of theirs that the shipowner has parted with the custody of the goods in such a manner as to prevent the cargo owner from exercising his rights, or has negligently managed his business and employed mariners who failed to care for the goods or were unable to cope with the perils of the sea and navigation risks. The enquiries show that cargo owners are of the opinion that carriers, who are directly concerned with the business of ship management and the craft of seamanship and navigation, should well be able to cope with all the situations arising in the course of transport without having to shelter behind the immunities in the Hague Rules.

As the Hague Rules presently stand, the shipowner has the benefit of a large number of exceptions and immunities from liabilities which carriers are perfectly justified in raising when the facts appear to bring an incident, giving rise to cargo loss or damage, within these exceptions, such as loss or damage arising out of perils of the sea, neglect or fault in the navigation or management of the ship, etc. However, the point was made that the party against whom the claim is made, namely the carrier, is, initially, the sole judge as to whether he should or should not plead exemption from liability and if he does so on slender grounds, whilst his misjudgment may be corrected by any subsequent litigation, he has meanwhile injured the cargo owner by delaying the settlement of the claim.

The enquiries also disclosed that the cargo owner becomes frustrated, if, having claimed against the carrier, the only party with whom he understands himself to be in legal relationship, he is told instead to apply to a third party, the warehouse, to which the carrier, under local regulations, has delivered his goods. He is then usually faced with the answer of the warehouse that it is protected by its own bye-laws and regulations, either exempting or limiting its liability or imposing unreasonably short time limitations. Another source of frustration found was the shipowner's insistence on a full set of original claim papers, *i.e.* invoice, bill of lading, certificate of origin or of value, insurance certificate, etc., and tallying documents appropriate to a particular port, cargo owners often finding great difficulty in presenting this complete set of papers quickly to shipowners in support of a claim.

Procedural complications

To pass on to the findings on procedural complications, it was found that the cargo owner, when faced by such substantive and procedural complications, often stops pursuing a claim further against the carrier and either absorbs the loss or claims against his insurers, it being found that it is usually much easier and quicker for the cargo owner to recover a claim from his insurer than from the carrier, against whom he must also establish liability.

Many cargo interests complained in response to the UNCTAD questionnaire that, in consequence of the lengthy procedure in the pursuit of claims against a carrier, with its acknowledged further result of blurring the cogency of evidence or lightening its weight, claims often become barred by the expiry of the statutory period of twelve months, as provided for in the Hague Rules for the commencement of proceedings against a carrier. It was found readily apparent that in order to establish his case the cargo owner, like any other claimant, faces the hurdle of procedural laws of the country in which he prosecutes his claim. All questions of procedure, including ordinarily those regarding evidence, are usually decided according to national law of the court in which the proceedings are brought. The rules relating to burden of proof are generally considered to be in an intermediate position, forming part of both the substantive and procedural laws, although they are almost invariably treated in text books as part of procedure. The Committee in this connection, said that the amendment of the Hague Rules will not *per se* resolve all the claimant's difficulties.

Generally, the order of procedure is (a) the claimant must first prove his loss (b) the carrier must then prove the cause of the loss, that due diligence was exercised to make the vessel seaworthy to guard against the loss, and that he is not responsible by virtue of at least one of the exemption provisions contained in the Rules. (c) the claimant must then put forward any relevant arguments in rebuttal. (d) finally, there is the middle ground where both parties may produce various additional proofs. Initially the burden is on the claimant to prove (a) that he is the owner of the goods and/or the person entitled to make the claim (b) the contract or the tort/delict, *i.e.* either that a contract of carriage existed, or the negligence of the person sued. In this connection it should be mentioned that most jurisdictions take the position that the existence of the contract with the carrier excludes the action in tort, *i.e.* for damages, against the carrier. Some jurisdictions, however, have allowed the claim in contract to be joined with the claim in tort in the same action. An action in tort is, however, usually brought against the carrier's servants, agents or independent contractors with whom the claimant has no direct contractural relationship. Also, the burden is on the claimant initially to prove (c) that the person against whom the claim is made is the responsible person, and in this connection, it has to be mentioned that the claimant sometimes has difficulty in deciding whom to sue, particularly in the case of contracts of carriage involving charter-parties. (d) that the loss or damage occurred while the goods were in the carrier's possession: usually the claimant will attempt to prove the condition of the goods when they were received by the carrier and the condition at the time of the discharge of the goods from the ship. (e) the physical extent of the damage or the loss. (f) the actual monetary value of the loss or damage.

In order to avoid liability, the carrier will need to prove (a) the cause of the loss (b) the exercise of due diligence to make the vessel seaworthy at the beginning of the voyage, that is in the event of the loss or damage arising out of unseaworthiness, and to guard against the loss. (c) his right to invoke one of the valid immunities stipulated in the bill of lading, as may be appropriate in different jurisdictions. It is then up to the cargo claimant to allege, amongst other things, such matters as negligence at loading, negligence in stowage, failure to take proper care of the cargo, negligence in handling or in discharge etc.

The Committee took the view that cargo interests should not ordinarily find it too difficult to establish loss or damage in a straight forward case against a "reasonable" carrier if he can produce clean bills of lading and unqualified "bad order" discharge receipts. The cargo owner should then, in the ordinary course of events, secure compensation unless his claim was barred by a valid limitation or exemption clause in the bill of lading or warehouse deposit conditions. It was pointed out, however, that should the burden of proof shift back to the cargo owner he would normally face very great difficulty in trying to establish how, where and when the loss or damage occurred, as most of the necessary supporting information would be in the possession of either the carrier or the warehouse, or would be unavailable. In the case of pilferage or unobserved specific acts of negligence or default on the part of anyone, the claimant's position becomes difficult. Special reference was made to these difficulties because they illustrate the practical difficulties usually faced by a cargo owner when he attempts to establish his claim. Ordinarily the production of a clean bill of lading, with evidence of apparent loss on discharge, should be sufficient to establish a *prima facie* claim against the carrier, but it was pointed out that under modern trading conditions it is seldom possible to carry out a careful physical shipside tally.

Further the tally after discharge, which also serves as the tally for entry of the goods into the warehouse, is often prepared several days after the discharge of the goods from the vessel. The further comment is made that specific reservations are frequently inserted on tally sheets or outturn reports about the quantity, quality or condition of the goods. These "speak" against the ship, even though the ship may have discharged the goods in sound condition and they were lost or damaged before the warehouse tally took place.

The period of the liability of the carrier would seem, therefore, to be extended beyond the discharge period as defined in the Hague Rules, and the cargo owner should be able in such cases to hold the carrier 'prima facie' responsible unless the carrier can produce incontrovertible evidence that, in fact, the goods had been discharged in sound condition and that the loss occurred later. However, in most cases the carrier will draw attention to exonerating clauses in the bill of lading which may provide that his liability ceases as soon as the goods have passed over the ship's rail, or after they have been "discharged". When this happens, the cargo owner must then either go to the extreme of litigation or else claim against the warehouse. The warehouse, particularly if it is administered by a public authority, will usually have such stringent exoneration clauses, and limitation of time clauses, in its conditions of deposit, that the cargo owner can proceed no further except to collect his loss from his insurer.

When the "in tally" sheets of the warehouse contain indeterminate observations and qualifications as to the quantity or the condition of the goods, the cargo owner is again facing the dilemma of not being able to obtain compensation, either from the ship or the warehouse. Replies to questionnaires on this subject show that this vagueness has been a recurrent source of complaint by cargo interests and that there is a pressing need to ensure that uniform local regulations and practices should exist in ports to make the cargo owner's position secure, and enable him to obtain recompense for loss or damage from either the carrier or the warehouse without undue strict limitation and exonerating clauses barring or delaying the settlement of his claim. Such a solution, it was thought, would equally assist carriers, as the line of demarcation between their responsibility and that of the warehouse would be more effectively drawn, and a clearer definition of risks should ordinarily tend to reduce insurance rates in the long run. Alternatively, the carrier alone should be made responsible to the cargo owner for the care of the goods until delivery, and any loss or damage which occurred after discharge from the vessel and before delivery to the cargo owner could be settled between the warehouse under separate agreements between them.

To be considered in conjunction with these proposals are examples of bills of lading clauses to which reference was made. These will be discussed later, but for the present, it is proposed to look at a clause captioned "Liability of the Carrier during Transport". This provides that the liability of the carrier commences when the hook of the ship's loading tackle engages in the goods to be shipped and ends at the precise moment that they are disengaged from the hook of the tackle after unloading. If loading and unloading operations are carried out by means of hooks, cranes, derricks or other devices which are not those appertaining to the ship, the carrier shall not be liable for any damage or loss which the goods may undergo during handling, unless the winches, cranes, derricks or other devices were used on the initiative of the carrier and in his own exclusive interest.

Another clause to which reference was made is captioned "Liability of the Carrier Before and After Actual Transport". Under the provisions of this clause, it is provided (a) Before the goods are loaded and after they are unloaded, (in the exact circumstances defined in the clause referred to above), and until the goods are received by the addressee, providing that the latter duly complies with all his obligations under this bill of lading, the carrier shall be liable for the goods while he has them in his effective material custody and under his effective material control. Section (b) of the clause provides that any delivery of the goods to Customs, bond or private warehouses or to lighters or other port vessels, shall terminate the liability of the carrier and, from that moment onward, the goods shall be regarded as having been delivered to the consignees, unless such delivery is effected on the initiative of the carrier and in his own exclusive interest. It is further provided, however that (c) if the carrier retains the effective material custody and control of the goods, he shall not be liable for any damage, injury or loss which they may undergo through acts and/or circumstances set out in Article IV paragraph 2, of the Hague Rules which are, by agreement between the parties, regarded as cases of *force majeure*, and the carrier shall be covered by the limitation in Article IV paragraph 5 of the Hague Rules (the per package or unit limitation of liability), where applicable.

The clause concludes with the statement that if the carrier is compelled to retain the goods in his keeping because the consignee has not fulfilled his obligation to take possession of them, the carrier shall have the option, subject to the right of retention, of either dispatching them to a warehouse or store or allowing them to remain in the place in which they were unloaded at the consignee's risk and expense.

Commercial and economic aspects of the bill of lading

In their deliberations leading to the proposals for a complete revision of the Hague Rules, the Shipping Committee carefully examined the commercial and economic aspects of the bill of lading. The examination of the commercial aspects included the part played by the bill of lading in the course of maritime trade as a document of title to, and a receipt for goods, as well as a memorandum containing either the contract of carriage or its evidence. What required consideration was whether the bill of lading, as formulated at present, satisfied the expectations of the seller, the carrier, the receiver, the banker and the cargo insurer, all of whom depend upon its contents for their respective needs.

Secondly, the Committee raised the matter of the economic aspects of the bill of lading relating in particular to the consequences of a breakdown in the cargo owner-carrier relationship in ocean carriage, it being borne in mind that, as a negotiable document, a bill of lading passes through many hands, the term "cargo-owner" being used to cover all these holders of the bill of lading.

This analysis by the Committee of the functioning of the bill of lading has produced an important insight into the manner in which this document virtually governs international seaborne commerce, with the exception of certain bulk cargoes when the contract of carriage is evidenced by charter-parties. The enquiries show that the bill of lading is a commercial document with a long history, and has meant different things at different times. Beginning as a bailment receipt for goods it has developed into a receipt containing the contract of carriage, and acquired in time a third characteristic as a negotiable document of title, but changing methods of trade led to great shifts in the legal theory underlying the bill of lading.

Incidentally the important element was possession. Who had the possession of the goods when the litigated question arose, the seller or the buyer? This was particularly important at a time when possession at sea was often determined by force, in the age of pirates and privateers. After piracy and privateering had been eliminated, in the 19th century in Europe the legal emphasis began to shift from 'possession' to 'title'. The question then began to be who had title to (or property in) the goods when the crucial incident occurred. Was it the seller, or buyer, or middleman? It became important to determine at what moment title changed. The enquiries show that in the early 19th century some French Court decisions began to stress the importance of documentary title to seaborne goods, and that English decisions expressing the same idea followed. Title and documents thus became more significant than the possession of the goods at sea, and early forms of CIF sales contracts appeared in the late 1880's.

So it was that the bill of lading, insurance policy, invoice etc., together formed a freely transferable unit or set of documents which could be bought or sold, not merely once but repeatedly, while the ship was at sea, representing the goods that were in the ship and protecting the principle risks of their non-arrival or arrival in bad order. A further legal development occurred in about 1900, when the important question was conceived to be not who has the title to the goods, but who has the risks as to the goods and the transaction. The ultimate question when goods were sold and bought overseas on CIF terms thus became one of who was to bear the risk of loss, and possession, or title to the goods, became less important.

These changes in the commercial and legal basis of the bill of lading have made it a flexible document based on general maritime law, and partly on the special clauses introduced by the parties, as controlled to a greater or lesser extent by the various statutes, international conventions and usages together with local procedural systems that come to regulate its provisions in the course of its world-wide currency. Attention was drawn to the fact that the commercial aspects of the bill of lading must, therefore, be examined against this complex background when the commercial role of the bill of lading is evaluated as one of the indispensable documents in financing the movement of commodities and merchandise throughout the world.

An examination of the commercial role of the bill of lading and a reference to clean bills of lading

The commercial aspects of bills of lading within the context of the enquiry by UNCTAD, broadly include its role in the course of trade as a document of title, a receipt for the goods and a memorandum containing either the contract of carriage or its evidence. What required examination was how well or indifferently the bill of lading, as at present constituted, performs these commercial functions. In other words, does it satisfy the needs of the seller, the shipper (if he is a different person from the seller), the carrier, the receiver, the buyer (if he is a different person from the receiver), the banker and the cargo underwriter, all of whom depend upon its contents for their respective needs.

The principal matters of concern included (a) the negotiability of the bill of lading. In this particular connection the enquiries disclosed no major complaints as to negotiability, except in connection with its status as a receipt, its role in documentary sales, in bank letters of credit or as to its status as a document of title. (b) the efficacy of its role in the sale of goods as regards the passage of property and the risk of loss, and within the terms of the shipment, *e.g.* f.o.b., c.i.f. (c) its role in documentary sales, see remarks under (a). (d) its role in bank letters of credit, again refer to remarks under (a). (e) its efficacy as a receipt for the goods (f) its status as a contract of carriage (g) its status as a document of title, see (a) above. The Committee then proceeded to a brief examination of the relationship between the sales contract for the goods and the bill of lading, the buyers' needs, subsequent purchasers, sales contracts, a review of f.o.b. and c.i.f. contracts, customs and usages of merchants rather than of legislation, terms of shipment and economic impacts.

In this connection the Shipping Committee carried out a brief examination into the relationship between the sales contract for the goods and the bill of lading. The buyer, of course, needs the bill of lading in order to receive the goods, and also to be in a position to prosecute any claim against the carrier, or to transfer these rights to subsequent purchasers. Sales contracts contain the terms on which the goods have been sold, *e.g.* on f.o.b. or c.i.f. or other terms, these terms being the products of the customs and usages of merchants rather than of legislation.

The shipment terms serve several functions, (1) they determine the point at which the property in the goods passes from seller to buyer, and consequently which party bears the risk of loss and what remedies are available to either party on breach by the other; (2) they determine what performance by the seller amounts to a tender which will put the buyer, who thereafter refuses to accept delivery, in breach; (3) they are widely used as a means of quoting price. Since the enquiries did not reveal any specific complaints relating to the legal impact of these terms, it was not considered necessary to investigate the subject further.

In consequence of the spread of the practice of financing international trade by documentary letters of credit, the performance of the sales contract by the seller is completed upon presentation of the required documents to the bank. It was pointed out, a carrier who has issued a non-negotiable bill of lading ordinarily fulfills its obligations by delivering the goods to the consignee named in the bill of lading. The carrier who has issued a negotiable bill of lading does so by delivering the goods to the holder of the bill of lading. In the former case it may not be necessary to produce or even be in possession of the bill of lading, while in the latter its production is indispensable.

The Committee took the view that the problems of property transfer between the seller and the buyer have lost most of their former significance. The seller's interest is to be paid as quickly as possible for goods which he has sold. The "clean" bill of lading is the only acceptable supporting documentary proof he can provide that the goods, of the description specified in the contract, have been shipped by the due dates, and in apparent good order and condition. Most modern bills of lading are what are commonly referred to as "order" bills of lading, by which the carrier undertakes to deliver the goods at the port of destination to the named consignee or to his "order". The word "order" gives to the bill of lading its legally and commercially important characteristic of a document of title to the goods therein described.

The authority for conferring this status on bills of lading is contained in national laws, in the U.K. by the Bills of Lading Act. This legal ownership or possession of the goods can be transferred from the named consignee to other persons without the need for any of them to see or have the goods in their physical possession, for at the time of the transfer the goods may be on the high seas.

Ownership or possession of the goods is transferred initially when the named consignee signs the bill of lading and the document may then pass to other parties until the last holder presents it to the carrier as his demand for delivery of the goods at the port of destination. The various endorsees and holders of the bill of lading are entitled legally to rely upon the "tally" and upon the statements of "apparent (good) order and condition" in the bill of lading as being correct, and may hold the carrier liable under the applicable law for the accuracy of these statements. Once having issued the "clean" bill of lading acknowledging the receipt of the goods in apparent good order and condition, the carrier is estopped from attempting to later prove that the goods were not in the apparent good order as acknowledged by the bill of lading.

It was found that, for all practical purposes, "order" bills of lading are usually treated as being fully negotiable, and that the shipper, consignees and all intervening parties holding negotiable order bills of lading wholly depend on them for the evidence of the shipment of the goods.

It was also found that the carrier faces problems raised by the provisions in the sales contracts when the shipper requests a clean bill of lading for goods which are obviously not as represented, and that the shipper undertakes in return for the issue of a clean bill of lading to indemnify the master, ship and carrier for making, what is, in fact, an incorrect statement. These indemnities are commonly referred to as "letters of indemnity" and they are, in many countries, including the U.K., considered fraudulent.

When the goods are discharged from the ship in a condition otherwise than in the order described in the bill of lading, the owner of the goods will claim on the ship for the depreciated value of the goods and the shipowner will normally have no alternative but to pay. He will then attempt to recoup his loss from the shipper but, in the U.K. in particular, the Courts might not give effect to the letter of indemnity. However, the real damage has been done by the consignee having been duped into paying for sound goods when unsound goods have been shipped. It should be mentioned that the carrier is not obliged to open packages to determine the soundness of the goods contained therein, but only to describe the outward order and condition of the packages.

Requests for clean bills of lading are of two kinds. The shipper either requires a receipt for a certain number of packages or other cargo units, or he wants an acknowledgement that the goods were received in apparent outward good order and condition, or of course both. It is the shipper's responsibility to deliver to the vessel sufficient cargo in a condition that would entitle him to a bill of lading which is "clean" enough to support his sales or credit terms. Neither the vessel nor the master nor the carrier are ordinarily directly concerned with the terms of the sale, their only obligation under maritime law being to issue to the shipper, on demand, a bill of lading stating the quantity and apparent outward condition of the goods.

The Hague Rules require, in this connection, by Article III paragraph 3 that, after receiving the goods into his charge, the carrier, or the master or agent of the carrier, shall, on demand of the shipper, issue to the shipper a bill of lading showing among other things (a) the leading marks necessary for identification of the goods are the same as furnished in writing by the shipper before the loading of such goods start, provided such marks are stamped or otherwise shown clearly upon the goods if uncovered, or on the cases or coverings in which such goods are contained, in such a manner as should ordinarily remain legible until the end of the voyage; (b) either the number of packages or pieces, or the quantity, or weight, as the case may be, as furnished in writing by the shipper; (c) the apparent order and condition of the goods.

In general, the carrier is responsible to bona fide endorsees and purchasers of the order bill of lading for the truth of the tallies as to quantity and whatever representation is made in the bills of lading as to apparent condition of the goods. When goods are found damaged or lost, the claimant is almost always a purchaser of the goods on terms which include the negotiation of the bill of lading. The law in most countries usually provides that a buyer of goods who acquires an order bill of lading which is endorsed to him or in blank, and for which he has paid value in good faith, obtains superior title to that of the original shipper. The reason is that the bona fide purchaser may rely on the "clean" face of the bill of lading and would not usually be affected or limited in his rights against the carrier by what his shipper knew concerning the goods being short or in bad order.

The carrier who issues a clean bill of lading for goods known to be short in amount or in "unclean" condition must therefore, as explained earlier, settle the claim for shortage or damage at the port of destination, and it would be for him to indemnify himself, if he is able, from the shipper on the basis of the letter of indemnity. But, as also explained earlier, in most countries the courts regard letters of indemnity as fraudulent documents and will not give effect to them.

Some sales contracts provide that statements in bills of lading as to shipment and date will be accepted as being conclusive. The Committee commented that such clauses, which may be unknown to the carrier, make it more important than ever that the bill of lading should be as accurate as the carrier can make it. The material available to the UNCTAD Secretariat suggests that so far as the commercial aspects of bills of lading are concerned, the main problem is that of the status and function of the document as a receipt, for it is this status which frequently affects its negotiability. To begin with, a carrier's obligation to answer for one or more of the basic characteristics of the goods may differ in different countries, and reference is made, in this connection to Article III paragraph 3(b) of the Hague Rules, referred to above.

The carrier may mention either the weight or the quantity or both, and would be liable or excused for discrepancies quite arbitrarily according to different laws in the different countries where disputes may arise. It was found that this situation causes uncertainty in the minds of cargo owners, bankers, underwriters and others who depend upon the bill of lading for reliable information as to the quantity, condition and description of the goods carried.

Likewise, the bill of lading must attest that the shipment corresponds as to the quantity specified in the invoices. Some years ago the Courts ruled that if there is an invoice for a specified quantity and the bill of lading is for either an unknown quantity of goods or a quantity of goods substantially different from that in the invoice, the bill of lading would not be a proper bill of lading which the buyer would be compelled to accept. Unless the bill of lading is skilfully filled in by the shipper and the carrier, to make the description of the goods tally with the goods and the documentary or credit sales requirements, the bill of lading suffers from defects which may impair its negotiability or the transferability of the goods.

It was found that these uncertainties as to the accurate description of the quality and weight, or quantity, of the goods tend to reduce the value of the bill of lading, both as a negotiable document and as an acknowledgement of what goods were in fact shipped. It was not possible to deal with the two topics — negotiability and status of the bill of lading as a receipt — separately, and it would appear that at first it must be agreed what essential characteristics should be specifically acknowledged by the carrier as attaching to the goods received, and he would then be unqualifiedly liable for the goods in the condition in which he received them.

The conclusion was reached by the Committee that consideration should be given to the idea that the carrier should be liable for the weight, subject to customary tolerances, in the case of such shipments, but that it had to be appreciated that if rigid laws were introduced, which unreasonably compelled the carrier to guarantee delivery of the goods by weight, his operating costs would rise because of the time occupied in weighing the goods. The Committee did not recommend, therefore, the introduction of strict liability.

The economic aspects of the bill of lading

The discussion of the economic aspects relates to the consequences of a breakdown in the cargo owner/carrier relationship in ocean carriage and, in this connection it has to be remembered that, as a negotiable document, a bill of lading may pass through several hands. The Committee have, therefore, used the term "cargo owner" to cover all these holders of the bill of lading. It was felt that an examination of the sequence of events that follow when goods subject to ocean carriage are lost or damaged, provided the best way of approaching the economic aspects and what required initial investigation was whether the loss lies where it falls, or is specifically imposed on one of the parties to the contract of ocean carriage. This depends on the way in which the risks of ocean carriage are distributed by the functioning and interpretation of the applicable maritime law. Cargo owners usually make a claim against the carrier for loss or damage, and the claim is either rejected or settled partially or fully on the basis of the distribution of risks and the limitation of liability sanctioned by the present existing law. If the cargo owners cannot agree with the carrier's decision, and they wish to pursue the matter, this may be done either by arbitration or litigation. The Committee comment that the amount of loss suffered by the carrier represents the initial economic impact which may be said to be "sanctioned" or permitted by the working and interpretation of the existing laws. It would not represent the full or real economic impact.

Reference was made in this connection to the position of developing countries, enquiries having shown that the bill of lading fails the test of cost effectiveness. It was also shown that the incidence of the costs of the present regime lies heavily on the cargo owner, and this is true wherever the cargo owner is situated. It remains to be seen whether these factors have any special and undue impact on the developing countries. It was found that, where there is an inequitable incidence of costs, no international transfer of income occurs in cases where both parties are in the same country. Where, however, the parties are in different countries, the inequitable incidence of costs leads to a real income transfer between the two countries. The view was taken that since the developing countries are more important as cargo owners than as carriers, the present system is unfavourable to them and gives rise to a real income transfer from "poor" countries to "rich" ones.

Reference was made to the value of cargo claims arising on imports into developing countries which, it was found, would represent the value of the goods lost or damaged, i.e. monetary loss, plus the loss of the use of the goods until replaced. The effect of the loss of the use of the goods would, in most cases, exceed the effects of a similar loss affecting developed countries. It was found that inventory holdings in developing countries are usually minimal because of shortage of working capital, while many countries are distant from their sources of supply, with the consequence that the time taken to replace lost or damaged goods represents a serious practical and economic problem for them. The enquiries also disclosed that, except in the simplest cases, compensation from carriers and insurers usually takes considerable time. The comment was made that this constrasts with the tradition of the prompt settlement of claims for loss of ships and aircraft in first class insurance markets and, except for the simplest cargo claims, most claims take from six months to a year or more for settlement, with many disputes dragged out for several years. Also the re-ordering of the goods, the cost problems of securing additional foreign exchange before the claim for loss is settled, the transit time of the re-ordered goods, all add up to additional economic waste.

The conclusions on this particular part of the discussion can be stated in the form of four simple propositions: (a) the bill of lading as at present constituted fails the test of cost effectiveness; (b) the incidence of the costs involved is mainly on the cargo owners and only to a limited extent on the carriers; (c) there is a real income transfer from countries which are more important as carriers; and (d) the developing countries as a group are among the losers in the real income transfer. It was found that there was a significant uncompensated loss which, in part, arises from the fact that through both specific provisions and omissions, the Hague Rules provide what appear to be an excessive number of opportunities for the shipowner to legally avoid liability for loss of cargo, and so reject the claim made by the cargo owner. In part also, it was found, that it occurs because of the unit limitation, whereby the liability of the shipowner, even where full responsibility is admitted, is limited to a fixed amount irrespective of the actual value of the goods lost. Two questions were asked, firstly, enquiring as to the level of the economic costs imposed in relation to the commercial function performed (that being the cost effectiveness), and secondly, on whom the cost fell.

Most of the difficulties discussed by the Committee in connection with the economic aspects of bills of lading were found to arise when cargo is lost or damaged and the cargo interests lodge a claim with the carrier for compensation. The UNCTAD secretariat endeavoured to obtain information regarding cargo claims for a recent year, hoping to be able to show the total value of the cargo carried by ocean transport during that particular year and, in relation to this, to show the value of the cargo claims made. The figures would then have indicated the magnitude of the losses suffered by cargo owners as a result of loss, damage or delay to cargo. It was hoped to break down the figure of cargo claims to show what percentage of these were accepted in full by the carriers, what percentage of claims was settled by compromise and what percentage was rejected. Had this specific data been available, not only would a valuable perspective have been given, but the extent to which claims were rejected would have been a first indication of the impact of the exceptions listed under Article IV paragraph 2 of the Hague Rules, which permit carriers to avoid liability for cargo damage in a large number of circumstances. Similarly, the value of claims settled by compromise might have provided some indication of the uncertainty inherent in the functioning of the Hague Rules. It seems that questions were asked of bodies such as the International Chamber of Shipping, and in the questionnaire sent to the shipping lines and insurers by the secretariat. However, it was found that global figures could not be obtained since none of the organisations collected such data. Although a good deal of information was obtained regarding the experience of individual insurers, P. & I. Clubs and shipping lines, this was not sufficient to enable the secretariat to calculate the desired magnitudes. With regard to the settlement of claims, the experience reported by different respondents was so diverse that apparently no meaningful indications could be derived. For example, in some cases, up to three-quarters of the claims made were accepted by the carriers, while in other cases the proportion of claims accepted was as low as 20 percent. As a result of all this, a quantitative perspective which would be in any way useful as a true statement of the position, could not be given.

It was stressed, however, that this lack of sufficient quantitative information in no way prevented economic judgments being made, and examined the matter of the cost effectiveness of the bill of lading which, the secretariat found, resolves itself primarily into the question of where the risk for loss lies, and who bears the costs of insuring against that risk. All of this led to the matter of insurance which cargo owners take out to cover the risks of loss or damage, either, because liability for such risks is not accepted by carriers, or because the risks are uncertainly allocated between the parties concerned, or by not being specified. Ideally, as the secretariat commented, cargo owners should not need to insure against the risk of loss or damage to their goods which is covered by the liabilities falling upon the carrier under the contract of carriage, with particular reference to the Hague Rules. These risks and liabilities are spelt out in Article III of the Rules which provide, amongst other things, that apart from the carrier's obligation to make the ship seaworthy, he is required, subject to the provisions of Article IV, to properly and carefully, load, handle, stow, carry, keep, care for and discharge the goods carried. It was found that the apportionment and definition of risks and liabilities were not at all clearly demarcated in the Hague Rules, and that the position was still further complicated by the uncertainties concerning such matters as burden of proof and procedure. In the result the Committee took the view that it frequently happens that cargo owners have no alternative but to over-insure, lest they be exposed to the incident of risk for which carriers might not compensate them, even though the carrier might be legally liable to do so under the provisions of the Rules.

The extent of the insurance cover is a matter of individual preference on the part of the cargo owner, and he may purchase the maximum possible cover, namely an all risks policy, in which event, as UNCTAD comment, he will almost certainly be over insured, since such cover would include liabilities for which the carrier would ordinarily be responsible. However, in the alternative, the cargo owner may elect to insure under a limited form of policy, for example against total loss of cargo only, in which case, in the event of less than total loss, he would be under insured. In the ordinary way, among the risks covered by the insurance premium will be included those for which the cargo owner's contract of carriage places the liability on the carrier. The Committee comment that the additional insurance by the cargo owner includes insurance against risks for which the carriers are already responsible, and that in this way insurance policies overlap, since both carrier and cargo owner are insuring against the same risks. An illustration was given as to the manner in which ambiguity in the definition of risks can lead to this overlapping of insurance, taking as an example, the risk of perils of the sea, in respect of which the carrier is immune from liability for cargo loss or damage, by reason of the provisions of the Hague Rules, and against which the cargo owner can insure. Overlapping insurance can arise, in this way: the immunities under the Rules can be construed in one sense . . . "as a list of possible causes for loss or damage to cargo for which the carrier cannot be blamed. As such, the catalogue of exceptions has of course no legal significance — there are obviously a number of other causes which might be relied upon by a carrier to exculpate himself". This means, said the Committee, that until a cargo owner accepts a statement by the carrier that a peril of the sea caused the loss or damage to cargo, and that the loss is therefore unrecompensable, or it is so decided by arbitration or litigation, the words of the immunity clause have no operative legal force of their own but are uncertain in effect.

The comment was also made that the cargo owner has to continue to insure against "perils of the sea" even though there may be circumstances in which the carrier would be liable to him for loss so caused. The view was taken that if cargo owners could be certain of being covered against some risks by the carrier under the bill of lading, and if they could be assured that they could recover the full value of their claims, there would be no need to pay premiums to underwriters to cover the same risks.

It was thought that the present uncertainty as to where the risk of cargo loss or damage lies could be reduced by clearly demarcating the respective risks of the parties, but that the uncertainty could only be eliminated by shifting all of the risks of sea carriage either to the carrier or the cargo owner. It was thought that, if the risks were redistributed so that the carrier bore a greater responsibility for cargo loss or damage under the terms of the bill of lading, c.i.f. rates would rise, but that this rise would be exactly matched by a fall in the insurance costs borne by the cargo owner. In the same way, if all the risks were shifted towards the cargo owner, c.i.f. rates would fall but insurance costs would rise. It was also thought that, if the P. & I. Clubs became concerned over the volume of claims that would have to be met, and increased the contributions from their members very sharply, shipowners would then increase their freight rates to cover the extra P. & I. insurance. On the matter of economic costs, the view was taken that these would not rise, since the extra cost to the cargo owner by reason of the higher freight would be exactly matched by an extra gain to the carrier, and that there would be a changed incidence of cost, but no actual change in costs. It was decided that action to shift all risks towards the carrier would not increase the overall costs of covering these risks, and that, therefore, the economic cost of the present regime is excessive, the excess being exactly indicated by the extent of the double insurance which arises because of uncertainty.

Another economic cost referred to was that arising out of the delay in the settlement of claims. In this connection the comment was made that if there is no uncertainty as to who bears the risks, then, when the fact of loss or damage has once been proved, there is no reason why cargo claims should not be settled immediately. On the other hand, in the situation of uncertainty, the settlement of claims is frequently very protracted. On the question of the incidence of costs in relation to insurance, it was found that it is the cargo owner who must take and pay for the extra insurance, and that he cannot shift the incidence on to the carrier and hence has to bear this burden. It was also found that the economic burden of delays in settlement fell entirely on the cargo owner, and that, in fact, it was to the carrier's advantage to delay the settlement of claims, and that where carriers determine the venue of arbitration, the costs of attending fall more heavily on the cargo owner than on the carrier. Reference was also made to the unit limitation of liability which the carrier enjoys under the Hague Rules. It was found, particularly in relation to the developing countries, that the bill of lading failed the test of cost effectiveness and that the incidence of the costs of the present regime lies heavily on the cargo owner. Also, that where there is an inequitable incidence of costs, no international transfer of income occurs in cases where both parties are in the same country. On the other hand, where the parties are in different countries, the inequitable incidence of costs leads to a real income transfer between the two countries. UNCTAD made the comment that, since the developing countries are more important as cargo owners than as carriers, the present system is unfavourable to them and gives rise to a real income transfer from poor countries to rich ones. It should be noted, in this connection, that there is exactly the same real income transfer from non-shipowning developed countries.

Payments for exports are usually made against the production of clean bills of lading after shipment, and any cargo claims would be raised against the carrier at destination by importers. It was pointed out that it is the importers who are affected by the present position, and with respect to the exports of developing countries, that so long as the importers are *in* developed countries, any loss would fall on them, so that, insofar as their exports are concerned, the present legal position regarding bills of lading appears to have relatively little direct economic impact on exports "from" developing countries. The value of cargo claims arising on imports into developing countries would represent the value of the goods lost or damaged, plus the loss of the use of the goods until replaced. The effect of the loss of the use of the goods would, in most cases, exceed the effects of a similar loss affecting developed countries and, in many cases, the time taken to replace lost or damaged goods represents a serious practical and economic problem for the developing countries.

The conclusions of UNCTAD on this matter of the economic aspects of the bill of lading were (a) the bill of lading as at present constituted fails the test of cost effectiveness: (b) the incidence of the costs involved is mainly on the cargo owners and only to a limited extent on the carriers: (c) there is a real income transfer from countries which are more important as cargo owners than as carriers to those which are important as carriers: (d) the developing countries as a group are among the losers in the real income transfer.

SECTION II

The review of the Hague Rules by the United Nations Conference on Trade and Development.

In response to the Working Group's wishes, the United Nations Conference on Trade and Development prepared a report which, amongst other things, was directed to the clarification of the needs and aspirations of shipowners and cargo owners as to their expectations from the contract of ocean carriage and, wherever possible emphasis was laid on the special needs of the developing countries.

Two principal issues required examination — namely, when goods are lost or damaged in the course of ocean carriage, was it always known in which cases the carrier has to pay and in which the loss remains where it falls, i.e. on the bill of lading holder. Secondly, there was the question as to what conditions of sea carriage are most consonant with public policy and economic needs. This second issue could perhaps be broken down into several sub-questions — namely, should the carrier or the cargo owner bear all of the risk of cargo loss or damage, or should the risk be apportioned between them, and if so how? How fair is the present apportionment of the risk of loss or damage to goods carried by sea? Is the legal protection given to affected interests in contracts of carriage consonant with what these interests expect today? Are the existing laws, with special reference to The Hague Rules, so framed that they tend to prejudice the interests of the developing countries? And to what extent can the existing balance of liabilities and immunites under The Hague Rules be changed without causing detrimental economic distortions.

Before reference is made to the proposed changes in The Hague Rules, it is necessary to outline briefly the thinking behind the United Nations Committee in their review of the Rules.

To put the issues in realistic terms, the view was taken that ocean carriers sell a service — transportation — for a reward or price, which is the freight. In calculating the freight for the carriage of the goods, ocean carriers must be assumed to have considered the allocation of liability and the apportionment of risk for their loss as between themselves and the owners of the goods.

Relevant factors to be considered by shipowners, when calculating freight rates, are hull insurance and protection and indemnity insurance. Although the problems posed by introducing insurance into the relationship between carriers and cargo owners remain classic in their simplicity, they have proved complex and obdurate of solution.

Duplicated costs

The question arises: Upon whom do the risks of loss or damage to goods from default, accident or negligence, fall — the carriers or upon the cargo owners? If they fall upon the cargo owners, then they will undoubtedly have covered the loss by their insurance on the goods. If, on the other hand, they fall upon the carrier, unless the carrier has chosen to act as his own insurer, then the owners will be protected by their P. & I. Association. The price of the risk is broadly measured by the premium, and if the carrier takes the risk, the price would, in the ordinary course of events, be included in the freight. The freight would then not only be the carrier's reward for actually transporting the goods, but would ordinarily also contain a premium of insurance to cover the risks of carriage undertaken by the carrier.

It follows, therefore, that if the "premium" content in the freight overlaps partially or wholly with a cargo insurance premium paid by the cargo owner, so that each covers to some extent the same risk, there will be a double payment for insurance by the cargo-owner. In other words the cargo-owner may be paying a freight which includes the right to claim compensation from the carrier in respect of loss caused by certain risks, and paying also a cargo insurance premium which gives the right to claim compensation from the cargo insurers in respect of loss attributable to the same risks. On this matter the Secretariat took the view that theoretically, the liability of the carrier and cargo underwriter ought to be successive and not co-extensive and, where this is not so, economic waste is caused.

Procedural clarification

In the report by the UNCTAD Secretariat, the historical development of the status of the ocean carrier and the cargo-owner was examined to see how the present apportionment of their risks and liabilities arose and practical processes involved in cargo claims settlement procedures was also examined so as to clarify what happens in the day-to-day handling of claims of cargo-owners and carriers against each other. The view being that unless these processes were clearly understood, the interests involved on the one side would not understand the difficulties of the other or the legal disciplines to which willingly or unwillingly, they are subject.

What was required was to identify those provisions of The Hague Rules which, through their impact on the distribution of the risks of ocean carriage, as expressed in modern bills of lading, produced an apportionment of equities between the carrier and the cargo-owner that might be considered to be inequitable or unfair. Clearly in order to do this, information had to be collected from as many interested sources as possible.

Simultaneously, the question had to be considered as to what extent national legislation incorporating The Hague Rules, or alternatively, going beyond, or setting aside, certain provisions of the Rules, affected the position. It was also necessary to examine the Rules in their entirety and in detail in order to determine precisely which parts of the Rules were responsible for the difficulties discovered as a result of the inquiries made.

Balancing needs

Lastly, the report of the UNCTAD Secretariat took into account the "needs of economic development in particular in the developing countries" and, from an examination of the replies to the UNCTAD questionnaire it did not appear that the expressed grievances of cargo interests in developing countries were materially different from those in developed countries. However, the economic impact of the existing laws and practices were, in the opinion of the UNCTAD Secretariat, obviously greater on developing than on developed countries. The reason being that, apart from purely economic reasons, the developing countries are predominantly ship-using and cargo-owning countries and hence more markedly affected by the working of international maritime laws and practices which have retained a ship-owner orientation.

The Secretariat commented that there does not appear to be any way in which developing countries alone could be assisted in this field through international legislation. Laws may be revised internationally to reimpose greater liability on carriers so that goods appertaining to developing countries might secure greater protection whilst in transit, but such changes would equally benefit cargo interests from developed countries. However, the developing countries have been mainly responsible for the proposed amendments to The Hague Rules which, when they become international law, will have the effect of placing the ship-owner in the position of being the virtual insurer of the goods carried.

ARTICLES IN THE HAGUE RULES FOUND TO GIVE RISE TO UNCERTAINTY

The principal Articles in the Hague Rules were examined by UNCTAD with particular reference to those Articles and Rules which, as the result of the UNCTAD questionnaire, were found to have caused uncertainty and difficulty in their operation and interpretation. In this connection particular reference was made to Article III rule (2), which provides that: "Subject to the provisions of Article IV, the carrier shall properly and carefully load, handle, stow, carry, keep, care for and discharge the goods carried." Article IV provides a long list of the rights and immunities of the carrier outlining the circumstances in which the carrier may escape liability.

Liability loophole

Considered alone Article III, rule (2), imposes very stringent obligations upon the carrier. But the UNCTAD Committee reached the conclusion that the duties specified in Article III, rule (2), have tended to become obscured by the exceptions available to the carrier by the limitation of his liability and by the rules relating to the burden of proof and other procedural provisions. As a result Article III, rule (2), has not proved to be such an important instrument for protecting cargo-owners as it might appear to be.

The reference to limitation of liability is contained in Article IV, rule (5), which provides that neither the carrier nor the ship shall in any event be or become liable for any loss or damage to or in connection with goods in an amount exceeding £100 per package or unit or the equivalent sum in other currency, unless the nature and value of such goods have been declared by the shipper before shipment and inserted in the bill of lading. This declaration, if embodied in the bill of lading, shall be *prima facie* evidence, but shall not be binding or conclusive on the carrier. By agreement between the carrier, master or agent of the carrier and the shipper another maximum amount than that mentioned in this rule may be fixed, provided that such maximum shall not be less than the figure named above. Finally Article IV, rule (5), provides that neither the carrier nor the ship shall be responsible in any event for loss or damage to or in connection with goods if the nature and value thereof has been knowingly mistated by the shipper in the bill of lading.

This limit of liability was raised, by the terms of the Gold Clause Agreement between shipowners and insurers, to £200, so avoiding a conflict on the provisions of the Hague Rules that the monetary unit was to be taken of gold value. By the Brussels Protocol of 1968 the limit is raised to 10,000 Poincaré Francs and is included in the Amended Carriage of Goods by Sea Act, 1971.

The Committee took the view that it would lead to a more equitable balance between carriers and cargo owners if Article III, rule (2), were restated more forcefully, declaring that carriers must comply with the requirements of the rule before they could claim the benefit of any exemptions granted to them under the Hague Rules. This, however, is not intended to suggest a sequence of proof in litigation, which is a matter of procedural law. Instead it was suggested that (as a matter of substantive law) compliance with the duties specified in Article III, rule (2), should be in every case a prerequisite to the carrier escaping liability under any other provision.

Moreover, the Committee was of the opinion that, in cases of loss or damage, it would appear to be more equitable if the carrier was initially presumed to be in breach of his duties under Article III, rule (2), and so required to prove that he had in fact "properly and carefully" loaded, handled, etc., the cargo. The comment was made that the carrier normally has access to information concerning the cause of loss or damage.

It is perhaps desirable to pause here to consider in a little more detail the exceptions contained in Article IV, which the carrier presently enjoys. It is now suggested that some exceptions should not be open to the carrier except upon proof that the carrier had in fact complied with the provisions of Article III, rule (2), that the carrier shall properly and carefully, load, handle, stow, carry, keep, care for and discharge the goods carried.

Carrier's protection

Article IV of the Hague Rules provides, in the first place, that neither the carrier nor the ship shall be liable for loss or damage arising or resulting from unseaworthiness unless caused by want of due diligence on the part of the carrier to make the ship seaworthy. Also that the carrier will secure that the ship is properly manned, equipped, supplied and to make the holds, refrigerating and cool chambers and all other parts of the ship in which goods are carried fit and safe for their reception, carriage and preservation in accordance with the provisions of Article III rule (1). Thereafter are a long list of exemptions from liability, including, loss or damage arising or resulting from the act, neglect or default of the master, mariner, pilot or the servants of the carrier in the navigation or in the management of the ship. This exception was under particular scrutiny by the Committee. Another exception is in respect of cargo loss or damage caused by fire, perils, dangers and accidents of the sea or other navigable waters, wastage in bulk, insufficiency of packing or insufficiency or inadequacy of marks, latent defects not discoverable by due diligence, etc.

THE HAGUE RULES INDIVIDUALLY EXAMINED

Article I — Definitions

Article I of The Hague Rules contains certain definitions. The first definition contained in Article I (a) is the word "Carrier" and is defined: "'Carrier' includes the owner or the charterer who enters into a contract of carriage with a shipper." This definition, in the opinion of the UNCTAD Committee raised two points for consideration: (a) whether any person other than the owner or the charterer can be a carrier, for example a shipping and forwarding agent; and (b) who is liable as "carrier" when vessels are chartered.

On the first point the committee appointed by United Nations Conference on Trade and Development to review The Hague Rules and make recommendations, said that the word "includes" suggests that the designation of owners was not exhaustive, and that others might be considered carriers. In order to remove any doubt on the matter said the Committee, the definition of "Carrier" might be clarified to confirm that "Carrier" includes the owners, the charterer or any other person who enters into a contract of carriage with a shipper.

With regard to the second point the Committee touched upon a very sore point with cargo interests in that when a shipowner charters a vessel and issues his own bill of lading, cargo interests in the final agonies of the situation in which they are claiming for the recovery of cargo loss or damage, sue the party who issued the bill of lading only to later find that they have sued the wrong person as that person was not the owner of the vessel and, therefore, by a demise clause in the bill of lading their action for recovery was void.

The Committee, on the issue as to who is liable as a carrier, commented that suit could be brought against a charterer whenever there is a demise charter or whenever the charterer contracts in his own name with the shipper and issues a bill of lading. But there was uncertainty where a vessel is time-chartered or voyage-chartered and a bill of lading is issued with the name of the charterers heading the document which contains a so-called "demise" and "identity of carrier" or "agency" clause, and which is signed by the master of the vessel.

Most modern bills of lading contain "demise" clauses to the effect that if the ship is not owned by, or chartered by "demise" to, the shipping company or line by which the bill of lading is issued, the bill of lading shall take effect as a contract with the shipowner or demise charterer and not with the charterer who had dealt directly with the shipper. A demise charter is generally recognised as a charter whereby the charterer becomes the owner of the ship during the currency of the charter, and the master and crew become his servants for all interests and purposes.

A typical demise clause may read to the effect that if the ocean vessel is not owned by or chartered by demise to the company or line by whom the bill of lading is issued the bill of lading shall take effect only as a contract of carriage with the owner or demise charterer as the case may be as principal made through the agency of the said company or line who act solely as agents and shall be under no personal liability whatsoever in respect thereof. It may be further provided that agents signing the bill of lading on behalf of the company or line have only limited authority at common law of a vessel's master signing a bill of lading.

The practice of inserting demise clauses in bills of lading is said to have arisen originally in order to restrict the contract of carriage to one solely between the shipowners and the bill of lading holder, in cases where the vessel was chartered and the charterers were not allowed to limit their liability under the British Merchant Shipping Act but, this has now largely disappeared. The UNCTAD Committee continued by stating that injustice has often been caused to the shipper or consignee when the courts in some countries have held that the shipper or consignee cannot sue the owner of the ship because he is not considered to be the "carrier", and the charterers have been permitted to evade liability because they were not considered to be the "carriers" either.

Cargo-owners expecting a shipping line to carry their goods found instead that, by the use of demise clauses, the bill of lading terms allow the line to substitute a new carrier. They find that the line has not agreed to carry their goods at all, but merely to find a suitable carrier. In the result shipping lines using bills of lading on their own forms and with their own headings, escape liability against shippers or consignees who have no reasonable means of believing other than that the shipping line is the real carrier of the goods.

UNCTAD took the view that the conflict and uncertainty surrounding the effect of the "demise" clause could be relieved if, in addition to expanding the definition of the word "carrier" as outlined above, the Rules were further amended to put beyond doubt the invalidity of such a clause. In any case, as mentioned above, the original reason for the clause has now largely disappeared because of changes in the law relating to limitation of liability.

In this connection it should be mentioned that under the International Convention relating to the Limitation of Liability of Owners of Sea-going Ships, October, 1957, the benefit of limitation of liability now extends to the charterer. However, the limitation of liability of more practical importance in relation to The Hague Rules is the limitation of liability on a per package or unit basis, which will be discussed later.

One cause for dissatisfaction among shippers under many agreements governed by the Hague Rules is the "small print." But "small print" is not necessarily small, just perhaps a little obscure, giving meaning to terms used in the contract which are not exactly what they might appear to immediately mean. Other definitions from Article 1 of the Hague Rules are now examined.

Article I(b) deals with the definition of the words "Contract of Carriage." This rule provides: "'Contract of Carriage' applies only to contracts of carriage covered by a bill of lading or any similar document of title, in so far as such document relates to the carriage of goods by sea, including any bill of lading or any similar document as aforesaid issued under or pursuant to a charter-party from the moment at which such a bill of lading or similar document of title regulates the relations between a carrier and a holder of the same."

The view of the Committee was that if it should be decided to extend the Rules to the period when the goods are in the custody of the carrier before loading or after discharge, the phrase "in so far as such document relates to the carriage of goods by sea" would have to be amended.

Article I(c) defines the word "Goods" and provides, that: "'Goods' includes goods, wares, merchandises, and articles of every kind whatsoever, except live animals and cargo which by the contract of carriage is stated as being carried on deck and is so carried." The UNCTAD Committee commented that deck cargo and live animals, not coming within the present definition of "goods," carriers may contract out of liability for damage to or loss of such cargoes by means of exemption clauses. Furthermore since large quantities of cargo are carried on deck, carriers derive considerable advantages from the narrow scope of this definition.

The Committee made two further very pointed comments — namely, that the exports of many developing countries must necessarily be stowed on deck, for example timber, etc., and live stock. Also the large increase in the carriage of containers on deck emphasises the importance of the Rules relative to deck cargo. In this connection UNCTAD are presumably referring to the carriage of containers on the deck of conventional cargo ships and bulk carriers, and not to the carriage of containers on the decks of the purpose-built container vessel.

The recommendation of the Committee in this connection, was that in order to avoid the present conflicts among the laws of different countries and also to do justice to cargo owners, deck cargo and live animals should be included in the definition of "goods" so that the Rules would apply to them as to other cargo.

Article I(d) of the Rules deals with the definition of the "Ship". It provides, that: " 'Ship' means any vessel used for the carriage of goods by sea." The UNCTAD Committee said that this raised the question as to whether the Rules applied to barges or lighters when used for loading or discharging vessels, and that if barges or lighters are not to be considered "ships," within the meaning of Article I(d), then the Hague Rules may not apply during the time when goods are on board such barges or lighters. In the view of the Committee it was desirable that the Rules should apply to lightering operations when the carrier owns or operates the barges or lighters as part of his contract of carriage and the definition of "ship" could be amended to include such craft. The comments on the provisions of Article I(e) should be considered also in relation to these proposals.

Article I(e) defines the words "Carriage of Goods" and provides, that: " 'Carriage of Goods' covers the period from the time when the goods are loaded to the time when they are discharged from the ship". This brings into consideration the provisions of Article VII of the Rules. Article VII provides, that: "Nothing herein contained shall prevent a carrier or a shipper from entering into any agreement, stipulation, condition, reservation or exemption as to the responsibility and liability of the carrier or the ship for the loss or damage to or in connection with the custody and care and handling of goods prior to the loading on and subsequent to the discharge from the ship on which the goods are carried by sea."

Questions raised

In the context of the words "from the time when goods are loaded on to the time when they are discharged from the ship" in Article I(e) and the provisions of Article VII that the parties may enter into any agreement regarding the carrier's responsibility for goods "prior to . . . loading on, and subsequent to . . . discharge", the UNCTAD Committee said that certain questions raised had caused uncertainty. In the first place the question arose as to when loading began and discharge ceased. Secondly the question arose as to what was the legal position before loading and after discharge.

The Committee, following upon their enquiries formed the opinion that the common practice has been to apply the Rules from ship's tackle to tackle — namely, from the moment that the ship's tackle is hooked on to the cargo at the port of loading until the moment when the cargo is laid down and the hook of the tackle is released at the discharging port. This does not cause difficulties when proper cargo tallies can be taken at ship's side, but this is seldom possible.

However, as the Committee pointed out, many difficulties are caused by the fact that a port depository frequently takes charge of the goods before loading and after discharge. Therefore, the moment of the responsibility of the carrier has, in the opinion of the Committee, been held to apply from the moment that the cargo crosses the ship's rail. But in several cases the tackle to tackle rule has been held to apply when the carrier has undertaken to load and discharge and shore tackle is used.

The conclusion was reached that when goods are being loaded from or into lighters, loading is considered in some countries to commence when the goods are loaded into the tackle and discharge not to cease until the process of unloading all goods into a lighter has been completed.

In the United Kingdom the position, with regard to the liability of the carrier in respect of loading, was extensively discussed in the case of "Pyrene Company, Ltd v. Scindia Steam Navigation Co. Ltd" The case came before Mr. Justice Delvin and is reported in *Lloyd's Law Reports*, 1954, Vol. 1, 321. In construing Article I(b) and (e) in conjunction with Article II of the Rules, the Court held that the operation of the Rules was determined by the limits of the contract of carriage of goods by sea and not by any limits of time. The Court said that the reference to "when the goods are loaded on" in Article I(e) was not intended to do more than identify the first operation in the series which constituted the carriage of goods by sea and that by the contract of carriage the shipowners undertook the whole of the operation of loading: and their rights and immunities extended to the whole of that period, including that part of the operation before the goods had crossed the ship's rail.

The case concerned damage to a fire tender being lifted on to the vessel by the ship's tackle but before it was across the ship's rail, it was dropped and damaged. The situation in relation to discharge was dealt with in the early days of the Hague Rules in the case of "Goodwin Ferreira and Co. Ltd v. Lamport and Holt, Ltd" (34 — *Lloyd's Law Reports* — 192) in which it was held that in the case of goods already discharged into lighter the carriers' liability for such goods did not terminate until the lighter load was complete and the lighter ready to depart for the shore. The American case of "Hoegh Lines *v.* Green Truck Sales, Inc." (*American Maritime Cases*, 1962, 431), followed the same reasoning.

The UNCTAD Committee said that there were so many different methods of cargo handling that it was difficult to generalise on this subject. For example, in the case of loading and discharging through a chute or pipe it would seem that discharge is complete at the last flange supplied by the ship. As mentioned above, Article VII of the Rules allows freedom of contract in respect of the period before loading and after discharging. The UNCTAD Committee commented that unless debarred from doing so by domestic law, the carrier could insert wide exemption clauses to contract out of his duty as a bailee while goods are in his custody during the above mentioned period.

An example was quoted of a typical clause in liner bills of lading. It provided that neither the carrier nor the vessel shall be liable for any loss, detention or damage to the goods howsoever caused while in the custody of the carrier prior to loading on or subsequent to discharge from the ship even though such loss, detention or damage be caused by the negligence of the carrier as warehousemen or otherwise howsoever, and the goods prior to loading or subsequent to discharge are at the sole risk of the owner of the goods.

In this connection the Courts have held valid a clause to the effect that when goods are awaiting removal after discharge, or are carried at through rates or consigned from or to a place beyond the port of discharge the shipowner is not liable for damage thereto or loss thereof, notwithstanding any negligent or wrongful act or default of any person whatsoever in his employ.

It will be recalled that prior to the introduction of the Hague Rules the United States had, many years before, introduced their own legislation in the form of the Harter Act. That Act provides, amongst other things, that it shall not be lawful for the manager, agent, master or owner of any vessel to insert in any bill of lading any clause whereby it, he, or they shall be relieved from liability for loss or damage arising from negligence, fault, or failure in proper loading, stowage, custody, care or proper delivery.

Since, when the United States introduced their Carriage of Goods by Sea Act incorporating the Hague Rules the Harter Act was not repealed, this rule still maintains with regard to the period before the actual loading of the vessel and after the discharge of the goods from the vessel, continuing until the carrier has made a proper delivery. This duty following upon the discharge of the goods until proper delivery, has had the effect of making the carrier responsible in certain circumstances, for the safety and protection of the goods whilst lying on the quay. In other words until the carrier has effected delivery into the hands of the parties entitled to the goods under the bill of lading the carrier is responsible for their care and safety.

The Committee took the view that Article I(e) was badly defined and the coverage should be extended.

The questions where loading commences and discharge ceases are central to an understanding of the law of ocean carriage. UNCTAD made the comment that uncertainties have focussed attention on what has been called "the before and after problem," namely, who remains responsible for the care of the goods, and to what extent, "before" loading and after "discharge." It is understood that after the loading and before discharge the goods would be in the care of the ocean carrier.

Carrier's interest

The carrier is primarily interested in carrying cargo from point A to B and if he uses his own tackle, he does not ordinarily object to accepting responsibility from the point at which he picks up the item of cargo at port A until he releases it at port B. As UNCTAD say, this is a "tackle to tackle" situation. Some fine distinctions are sometimes drawn, for example, the proposition that the carrier's responsibilities are restricted to the period "from ship's rail to ship's rail" but these do not have much practical importance today. If shore gear is used the carrier normally prefers to restrict his responsibility to the period elapsed from the time when the item of cargo was loaded into the ship and his servants or agents began to handle it, until the time when his servants or agents placed the item of cargo in a position to be lifted out of the vessel by the shore gear at the port of destination.

In most situations, particularly in the liner trades, the carrier includes in his freight rate the cost of loading and discharging the goods whether shore or ship's gear is used. The carrier is the person to whom the cargo-owner would look for compensation should the goods be lost or damaged after the cargo-owner had handed over the goods for shipment. However, as the Committee point out, the transfer of the goods from the cargo-owner to the carrier seldom takes place directly between the two of them, this being the source of most of the confusion.

The goods must often be handed over to an authority designated by local laws at the port of shipment as competent to accept, store and load the goods into the carrying vessel. The goods are usually consigned to the order of the carrier or his agents in loading documents while they are in the custody of the warehouse which usually has its own terms of bailment and stipulates its own clauses disclaiming liability.

In this connection it has to be remembered that the extent to which such bailees as port authorities, warehouses, customs agents, wharfingers, etc., are permitted to escape liability is often governed by the local law instead of the maritime law. In some countries the bailee of goods is permitted to contract out of all liability; in others he can escape some liability to shift the burden of proof but in other countries he is not permitted to limit his responsibilities. There is a similar position at the port of destination where the goods are usually delivered to a designated warehouse, which then in turn delivers the goods to the receiver. The carrier has virtually no control over the security of the goods once they are within the custody of the warehouses at the ports of shipment and discharge. Having regard to all this the UNCTAD Committee took the view that the position was clear that, on the basis of the law as expressed in the Hague Rules, the carrier can justifiably claim that he should have no responsibility for the goods before loading and after discharge and that he is entitled to disclaim liability for such periods. Similarly, the cargo-owner would appear to have a legitimate grievance in that he cannot, on the basis of existing laws and practices, pin point responsibility for loss or damage to the goods after having consigned or received them as directed by the carrier.

The Committee took the view that this impasse arises from the fact that the words "loading" and "discharge" as used in the Hague Rules, simply do not fit the widely varying procedures followed in different ports. In the opinion of the Committee the problem could be solved in either of two ways. First, the Rules could be amended to make it clear that the carrier is liable from the moment the goods are delivered in accordance with his instructions to the competent depository at the port of shipment until they are delivered to the cargo-owner at the port of destination. In the view of the committee, if this were to be the solution adopted, the carriers would work out cross-indemnity arrangements with the depositories at the two ports — namely, loading and discharge, which should not concern the cargo-owner. Alternatively the Committee recommended that the Rules be clarified in such a way that "loading" and "discharge" would be defined to mean the handling of the goods from shore or ship's tackle to shore or ship's tackle whenever the carrier is responsible for loading or discharging the goods. When the carrier is not responsible for the loading and discharge of the goods, his liability should be restricted to the time from which he gives a receipt for the goods until he re-delivers them to the competent person entrusted with the discharge of the goods.

So far as the risk of loss before loading and after discharge is concerned, the Committee recommended that this should remain with the cargo-owner. But, when the cargo-owner is compelled to use shore bailees then the law in all countries should uniformly prevent such bailees from limiting their duty of care or contracting out of liability for the full value of the goods.

Article II — Risks

This Article in the Hague Rules does not appear to have called for any particular comment on the part of the Committee.

Article III — Responsibilities and liabilities

Paragraph 1
This Rule provides that the carrier shall be bound, before and at the beginning of the voyage, to exercise due diligence to (a) make the ship seaworthy (b) properly man, equip and supply the ship (c) make the holds, refrigerating and cool chambers, and all other parts of the vessel in which the goods are carried, fit and safe for their reception carriage and preservation.

In connection with this particular provision, the Shipping Committee comments that if a ship sails in an unseaworthy condition, which means that the ship must be cargo worthy as well as regards her hull and manning etc., and such unseaworthiness causes loss or damage to goods, the carrier can avoid liability. He does this by proving that he had exercised due diligence before and at the beginning of the voyage to make the ship seaworthy.

It must be mentioned here that Article IV of the Rules exempts the carrier from liability in respect of cargo loss or damage arising out of latent defects not discoverable by the exercise of due diligence. The Committee make the point that the vessel may be sometimes found unseaworthy because of some latent defect not discoverable by due diligence, and that in such cases the cargo owners, suffering the damage, fail in their claims for compensation against the carriers. However, judicial decisions in various countries have made it more difficult for the carrier to prove the exercise of due diligence, because this duty has been ruled by the Courts to be a personal obligation that cannot be delegated.

Muncaster Castle ruling

The relevant ruling in the United Kingdom on this issue was that of the House of Lords in the case of the *Muncaster Castle*, in which case the ship had been placed by her owners in the hands of reputable ship repairers for special survey and repairs. The damage to the cargo in this case was the result of the negligence of an employee in the repair yard who, after the inspection of the storm valves, insufficiently, and unevenly, hardened up the securing nuts. In heavy weather the nuts worked loose, so allowing water to enter the hold of the vessel and damage the cargo. The House of Lords ruled that the carrier had not discharged the burden of proving that he had exercised due diligence to make the ship seaworthy, since a carrier was not safeguarded by the fact that the negligence in repairing the ship was that of an independent contractor. The obligation imposed on the carrier in the work of repair was one of due diligence by whomsoever the work might be done, even when the work delegated to the independent contractor called for technical and special knowledge or experience, and negligence was not apparent to the shipowner.

This ruling profoundly shook shipowning interests, particularly the Protection and Indemnity Clubs, and eventually led to the proposal in 1963 that the Rules should be amended. However, the move to relieve the carriers of liability for unseaworthiness provided that they had exercised due diligence to appoint ship repairers of repute eventually failed for lack of support at the Stockholm Conference. In the background of this there was the thought that, for practical reasons, it would be preferable for the shipowners to also bear the responsibilities for the negligence of independent contractors appointed by the shipowners. The reason for this was that it would be difficult or impossible for the owners of the cargo to sue the shipyard with which he had no earlier connection. The Committee took the view that the rule established by the *Muncaster Castle* decision that the carrier is liable for unseaworthiness caused by the negligence of his employees or independent contractors, was fair because the carriers retain their right to claim indemnity from their independent contractors. Since this ruling, shipowners have frequently asserted that they are no better off than they were under common law which imposed upon them the absolute duty to provide a seaworthy vessel. However, it has to be mentioned that, under this rule to which the shipowners were subject prior to the modified rule in the Hague Rules, the shipowner could exempt himself from all consequences of cargo loss or damage caused by unseaworthiness by exemption clauses in the contract of carriage evidenced by the bill of lading. The Committee take the view that the carrier must be liable for cargo loss or damage arising out of unseaworthiness even when caused by the negligence of an independent contractor.

Definition of voyage

It was also clear that the interpretation of the words "before and at the beginning of the voyage" in Article III(1) has created difficulties and has caused injustice. In many countries the term "voyage" has been construed to mean the bill of lading voyage, and the common law doctrine, whereby the carrier is under a duty to provide a seaworthy ship at the commencement of each stage of the voyage, does not apply. The recommendation is that the duty of the shipowner or carrier under Article III(1) is to be reimposed at each port of call of the vessel.

By way of example, if the carrier has exercised due diligence to make the ship seaworthy at port "A", the cargo loaded at that port, which is damaged by reason of the failure of the vessel to exercise due diligence prior to leaving port "B", the next port of call, would have no redress against the shipowner. Under this new recommendation the shipowner or carrier would be liable for the damage to the cargo loaded at port A as well as port B.

Paragraph 2

This Rule provides that "subject to the provisions of Article IV, the carrier shall properly and carefully load, handle, stow, carry, keep, care for and discharge the goods carried." It should be noted that when the United States gave effect to the Rules by the passing of their Carriage of Goods by Sea Act, the words "subject to the provisions of Article IV" were omitted. Article IV has reference to the rights and immunities of the carrier containing a list of exceptions relieving the carrier from liability for cargo loss or damage in certain circumstances.

In some countries there has been some uncertainty in the interpretation of the words "properly and carefully". In the United Kingdom the Courts have said that "properly" has a meaning slightly different to "carefully", and means that in addition to taking care the carrier must adopt a system which is sound in the light of all the knowledge which he has or ought to have about the nature of the goods to be carried. The meaning of the word "properly" has been described as tantamount to efficiency. Among the list of exceptions in Article IV is that of "Peril of the Sea" and the strength of Article III(2) is illustrated by a ruling of the Courts of this country that, whilst a vessel encountered the conditions of weather that the master had never experienced in which the vessel rolled violently in steep seas and a heavy cross swell, the shipowner was still liable for damage to cargo due to a breakdown in the stowage on the ground that the stowage was faulty. The Committee took the view that if the full weight of such decisions interpreting the words "properly and carefully" could be incorporated in an Amendment to the Rules, it would greatly assist shippers. This, it was felt, was particularly important as regards the safe carriage of products which require special attention in handling and stowage, for example ventilation.

In the deliberations on this subject it was thought that the question of burden of proof also arose in regard to Article III(2) and that the main issue was whether the effect of the provisions was to place an absolute duty on the carrier to fulfil the requirements of the Rule, or if this duty was to be lessened by the immunities granted under Article IV paragraph 2. In other words, the immunities should not be treated as excuses for failure to perform correctly the stipulated operations, but as being incidents basically unrelated to this overall duty to care for the cargo. The comment of the Committee was that they existed to cover the events where the carrier is not in breach of his duties and where it would be unfair to place responsibility for cargo loss or damage upon the carrier.

Paragraph 6

This Rule also gave the Committee some concern. This provides that unless notice and the nature of loss or damage be given in writing to the carrier or his agent at the port of discharge before or at the time of the removal of the goods into the custody of the person entitled to delivery thereof under the contract of carriage, or, if the loss or damage be not apparent, within three days, such removal shall be prima facie evidence of delivery of the goods as described in the bill of lading. The notice in writing need not be given if the state of the goods at the time of their receipt has been the subject of a joint survey or inspection. The interpretation of this part of the Rule has not given rise to undue difficulties, it being recognised that if the goods are not discharged in the same apparent good order and condition as when shipped, the carrier has the burden of proving that such loss or damage is not his liability. The Committee had no criticism to make of this section of the Rule but criticised that part of the Rule which provides that in any event the carrier and the ship shall be discharged from all liability in respect of loss or damage unless suit is brought within one year of the delivery of the goods or the date when the goods should have been delivered.

The Committee comment that the Rules require that "in any event" suit must be brought "within one year after the delivery or the date when the goods should have been delivered", and that this provision has given rise to a number of questions (a) what constitutes "delivery" in order to start the one-year period running (b) does "brought within one year" mean brought *anywhere* within one year, or brought before a particular court within that time (c) does the word "suit" include arbitration (d) what is the significance of the phrase "in any event" (e) may the parties extend the time limit by agreement. In this connection the view was taken that the limitation period begins to run upon "delivery" or "when the goods should have been delivered," and that the use of the word "delivery" instead of "discharge" appears to be intentional, because "discharge" is used elsewhere in the Rules. Also, that "delivery" ordinarily would mean the moment when the consignee receives the goods from the party competent to deliver them, but that some courts have held that the limitation period begins to run before that time.

The United States Courts have ruled that the time limit begins to run from the time that the discharge was completed "whether it be by complete transfer, possession and control of the goods to the consignee, or by constructive delivery to the consignee's duly authorised agent." The Australian Courts have ruled that delivery is made either when the goods were landed on the wharf and freed from the ship's tackle or, at the latest, when the goods were placed in a depository's premises and became immediately available to the consignee. The Committee reached the conclusion that it was desirable that Article III(6) should be amended to confirm that "delivery" means the moment when the consignee receives, or should receive, the goods.

The feeling was that it was also uncertain whether a suit in one country stopped the running of the one year period in other countries. In at least one English law case it has been held that a suit was barred because it was not brought in England within one year, although it had been initiated previously in another country. In that case, the bill of lading provided for exclusive English jurisdiction but in fact suit was first brought in the United States. This ruling of the Court was much criticised. In the opinion of the Committee, if the object of the time limit is to make cargo owners give prompt notice of claims to carriers, this could be accomplished suitably by permitting commencement of an action in any jurisdiction having a reasonable close connection with the contract of carriage.

The question also arose as to whether arbitration proceedings were to be considered "suits" for the purposes of the one-year time limitation. The Committee said that, if so, the result could be harsh for consignees when the bill of lading has been issued under a charter-party containing an arbitration clause. In such cases, the charter-party is usually incorporated into the bill of lading by reference, and the consignee does not know of its contents. The consignee may begin legal proceedings within one year, only to find out later that he is without a remedy because he did not nominate an arbitrator within the period provided by the charter-party. UNCTAD said that to avoid this result, the word "suit" should be amended to exclude arbitration proceedings.

Another point which required clarification was whether, if "suit" was taken to exclude arbitration, and parties in fact submit to arbitration, this means that they have waived the requirement that suit must be brought within one year. In this connection reference is made to remarks of R. P. Colinvaux that if the judge was right in his judgment in the case of *The Salaverry*, the result could not possibly comply with the requirement that suit should be brought within one year in *every* case in which the parties had submitted to arbitration. It was pointed out that it would be no use the claimant issuing a writ within one year because those proceedings would not be before the arbitrator. Nor could a waiver be inferred of a liability on the carrier which must necessarily be discharged if the dispute is determined according to the submission by arbitration. The Committee referred to the comment of Colinvaux that the astonishing result — that the claimant in an arbitration must inevitably lose *in limine* — follows remorsely from this judgment which, it was submitted, could not be sustained.

There was also a conflict among the Common Law Countries as to the effect of the words "in any event". Under English law, an unjustifiable deviation nullifies the contract of carriage, and The Hague Rules cease to apply. In such circumstances the six year common law time bar would apply. However, in contrast, in the United States the one year time limit continues to apply even in cases of unjustifiable deviation, because of the words "in any event". UNCTAD took the view that this conflict could be resolved by an amendment to the Rules clarifying whether the one-year time limit applies when the contract of carriage is nullified.

50

Time extension

In the day to day settlement of claims for cargo loss or damage it is a common practice for the cargo interests to ask for an extension of time which is usually granted. It seems that under the laws of most maritime nations such an extension is valid, in that Article V of the Rules provides that a carrier shall be at liberty to surrender in whole or in part all or any of his rights and immunities, or to increase any of his responsibilities and liabilities under the Rules, provided such surrender or increase shall be embodied in the bill of lading issued to the shipper. However, there has been doubt as to whether Article V applies to an agreement extending the time limits. The Committee have followed the reasoning at the time of the Brussels Protocol of 1968 with reference to The Hague Rules, in which it is stated that the one year time limit period may be extended if the parties so agree, even if they do so after the cause of action has arisen.

It should be mentioned here that under the provisions of the Gold Clause Agreement between British cargo and shipowning interests, it is provided that the shipowners will, upon the request of any party representing the cargo (whether made before or after the expiry of the one-year limitation period) extend the time for bringing "suit" for a further 12 months unless (a) notice of the claim with the best available particulars has not been given within the period of 12 months or (b) there has been undue delay on the part of consignees, receivers or underwriters in obtaining the relevant information and formulating the claim.

Article IV — Rights and immunities

Article IV of the Hague Rules concerning the rights and immunities of the carrier is extremely important because it contains a catalogue of exemptions from liability in respect of cargo loss or damage from which the carrier may benefit.

Paragraph 1
This Rule provides that neither the carrier nor the ship shall be liable for loss or damage arising or resulting from unseaworthiness unless caused by the want of due diligence to make the ship seaworthy, properly manned, equipped and supplied, and to make the holds, refrigerating and cool chambers and all other parts of the ship in which goods are carried, fit and safe for their reception, carriage and preservation in accordance with the provisions of paragraph 1 of Article III.

Paragraph 2
This Rule enumerates a catalogue of circumstances in a list (a) to (q) in which cargo loss or damage may occur where the carrier may claim immunity from responsibility. In the following analysis of Article IV paragraph 2, the UNCTAD Committee considered the following points (a) the use of several individual exceptions (b) the burden of proof (c)

the position of servants and agents in relation to the exceptions. The Committee took the view that several of the exceptions were redundant, for they were all included within the broader exception of "perils of the sea", or under the catch-all exception of Article IV paragraph 2(q). This provides that neither the carrier nor the ship shall be responsible for loss or damage arising or resulting from "any other cause arising without the actual fault or privity of the carrier, or without the fault or neglect of the agents or servants of the carrier. The burden of proof shall be on the person claiming the benefit of this exception to show that neither the actual fault or privity of the carrier nor fault or neglect of the agents or servants of the carrier contributed to the loss or damage."

Examples of the exceptions referred to are "act of God", "act of war", "act of public enemies", "arrest or restraint of princes, rulers or people, or seizure under legal process", "quarantine restrictions", "riots and civil commotions", "saving or attempting to save life or property at sea". The exception of "insufficiency or inadequacy of marks" was not considered by the committee as no serious problems in this regard were raised. Article IV paragraph 2(a) received a great deal of criticism. This exception provides that neither the carrier nor the ship shall be responsible for loss or damage arising or resulting from, act, neglect, or default of the master, mariner, pilot or the servants of the carrier in the navigation or in the management of the ship, and, as the Committee commented, this exception is probably the most important in the "catalogue". It has been severely criticised by cargo interests, and some Courts have interpreted the exception so broadly that carriers have escaped liability even for defective stowage of goods resulting from a technical fault of the Master of the vessel which impaired the ship's stability. The master's action has been interpreted as a fault in the navigation and management of the ship, and not a fault in the care and custody of the cargo.

There has also been much uncertainty over the distinction between management of ships and management of cargo. In the case of *Gosse Millard Ltd* v. *Canadian Government Merchant Marine*, which reached the House of Lords, the Court expressed the distinction in the following manner. If the cause of the damage is solely, or even primarily a neglect to take care of the cargo, the ship is liable, but if the cause of the damage is neglect to take reasonable care of the ship, or some part of it, the ship is relieved from liability. If the negligence is not negligence toward the ship, but only negligent failure to use the apparatus of the ship for the protection of the cargo, the ship is not so relieved.

The Committee comment that in most borderline cases the test has been "was there want of care of the cargo or was there want of care *indirectly* affecting the cargo". If it is the former then the carrier is liable because he has breached Article III paragraph 2, but if it is the latter then the carrier would not be liable under Article IV paragraph 2(a). If the loss or damage arises from both unseaworthiness and management of vessel, the carrier remains responsible unless he can separate the losses, in other words show how much of the damage was due to unseaworthiness and how much to neglect in the management of the vessel.

The trend of cases may be summarised in the following manner: an error in the navigation of the ship or in her management is an error fundamentally affecting the ship. This might be defined as an erroneous act or omission, the original purpose of which was primarily directed towards the ship, her safety and well being, or towards the venture generally. An error in the care of the cargo is an erroneous act or omission directed principally towards the cargo. UNCTAD comment that the carrier is frequently exempted from liability if both ship and cargo have been affected by the same error, even when bad seamanship has been equated with errors in navigation and management. It also seems that carriers have escaped liability for damage to cargo resulting from many ordinary acts of seamanship, such as berthing a ship, and damage or delay caused by bunkering may in some circumstances be brought within the exception of "management of ship".

The initial views of the shipping committee on the need for an amendment of the Rule have already been stated, but the committee at the same time said that each case had to be treated on its individual merits. They stated that the Rule causes uncertainty and considerable confusion in attempting to form any conclusions to guide carriers and cargo owners as to exactly where the line is drawn between what does and does not constitute an error in the navigation or management of the ship within the meaning of the exception. Its existence is considered to be an anachronism by cargo interests in most countries, and either one or both parts of the exception might with profit be removed or redefined more narrowly.

There are in fact two precedents that might be followed in considering the elimination of this exception, the committee points out. Firstly, the fact that one leading maritime power has dispensed with it in its domestic sea trades, and secondly, the International Convention for the Unification of certain Rules of Law relating to the transport of luggage or passengers by sea, imposes liability on the carrier for loss or damage due to the fault or neglect of the carrier or his servants or agents acting within the scope of their employments. The recommendation of the Committee is that, as stated above, either one or both parts of this particular rule be removed or redefined more narrowly.

Proceeding now to Article IV Rule 2(b) which provides that neither the carrier nor the ship shall be responsible for loss or damage arising or resulting from fire, unless caused by the actual fault or privity of the carrier. In this connection the Committee commented that in some countries fault and privity of the carrier is taken to mean the fault of the carrier himself and not merely his employee or agent. In the view of the Committee the principal questions seemed to be (a) should this exception be retained, despite the fact that carriers are expected to install up-to-date communications, fire protection and extinguishing equipment (b) if the exception is retained, is it possible to coordinate its operation with that of the "Fire Statutes" existing in some countries so that uncertainty arising from overlapping may be avoided (c) should it be clarified in the Rules that the carrier must show how the fire was caused? If the cause could not be established then perhaps the carrier should remain liable.

Reference should perhaps be made here to the case of the vessel which caught fire whilst in port, involving the question of relationship between fire and unseaworthiness. The case concerned was that of *Maxine Footwear* v. *Canadian Government Merchant Marine*. The vessel was lying at Halifax, Nova Scotia, and during the loading of the cargo it was found that certain waste pipes were frozen and, in the course of applying heat to the pipes, fire broke out. The master was eventually forced to order the scuttling of the ship, which resulted in the destruction of the cargo. When the case came before the Privy Council it was held that from the time that the ship caught fire she was unseaworthy, and it was that unseaworthiness which caused the damage to the cargo. The negligence of the shipowner's servants caused the fire, which was, said the Court, in fact a failure to exercise due diligence to make the ship seaworthy. In that case the carrier was denied the benefit of Article IV rule 2(b) providing the shipowner with exemption from liability.

Article IV rule 2(c) provides that neither the carrier nor the ship shall be responsible for loss or damage arising or resulting from "Perils, dangers and accidents of the sea or other navigable waters". This provision is perhaps the defence most frequently raised by carriers, and it is usually contended that the provision covers accidents resulting from the impact of waves or other dangers inherent in navigation, such as violent storms, fog, sandbanks, collisions and stationary or moving objects encountered by the vessel. The Committee comments that every vessel must be sufficiently strongly built and prepared to withstand such dangers. However, if a carrier can prove (the burden being upon the carrier to bring himself within the terms of the exception) that the damage or loss suffered by the ship or cargo was caused by maritime hazards beyond his control, he can escape liability for the cargo loss or damage suffered. The committee took the view that the definition of "perils of the sea" is, therefore, crucial because more fact than law is involved. In some jurisdictions the clause has been very strictly interpreted, in the sense that the peril must have been "something so catastrophic as to triumph over those safeguards by which skilful and viligant seamen usually bring ship and cargo into port safely". It is also well established that the weather encountered must be of a nature that could not reasonably have been anticipated, having regard to the nature of the voyage and the time of the year undertaken.

In some countries the Courts have taken a more lenient view of the exception. For example it has been held that to constitute a peril of the sea the accident need not be of an extraordinary nature or arise from an irresistible force, but that it is sufficient for the cause of the damage to goods by sea to be by the violent action of the wind and waves, when such damage cannot be attributed to someone's negligence. The view of the Committee was that the exception be abolished or perhaps amended in accordance with the stricter judicial interpretation.

Article IV paragraph 2(i) of The Hague Rules provides that neither the carrier nor the ship shall be responsible for loss or damage arising or resulting from "Act or omission of the shipper or the owner of the goods, his agent or representative." As a result of their enquiries and deliberations on this provision, the shipping committee of the United Nations Conference on Trade and Development concluded that although no serious difficulties were raised by this exception, because carriers pleading its benefit had sometimes succeeded in escaping liability on the ground that shippers had misdescribed goods when offering them for shipment, even though the misdescription had no connection with the cause of the loss or damage to cargo, the exception required further definition.

Article IV paragraph 2(j) grants the carrier immunity from liability for cargo loss or damage arising or resulting from "strikes, lockouts, stoppages or restraint of labour from whatever cause, whether partial or general." This exception is of paramount importance to carriers and, amongst other things, has enabled them, in the event of labour disturbances at the port of discharge, to divert the vessel to a convenient port and there discharge the goods. This can be undertaken without any further liability to the ship or shipowner, or responsibility for the safekeeping of the goods or their eventual delivery to the port of discharge when the strike has ceased. On occasions, goods have been delivered to a port of another country, for example, goods bound for London being discharged in Rotterdam or Hamburg.

As the Committee pointed out, this strike exception is used frequently and forms a source of recurring complaint by cargo interests. Another complaint was that the exception was frequently raised in connection with Article IV paragraph 4 which provides immunity for the carrier from liability for cargo loss or damage arising out of any deviation in saving or attempting to save life or property at sea, or arising out of any reasonable deviation. As mentioned above, the carrier may decide to change his ports of call either to avoid a strike-bound port or to sail from one to discharge the goods at another port. If the carrier can prove the reasonableness of the deviation then the Courts of most countries confirm that he is within the exception and is not in breach of his obligation to the cargo not to deviate from the contract voyage. There is then said to be no "deviation" only a "change of voyage."

The situation is well illustrated by the case of "G. H. Renton & Co. Ltd v. Palmyra Trading Corporation," which eventually reached the House of Lords.

Briefly the facts were that the steamship *Caspiana* loaded a cargo of timber in Canada for London (in the case of three bills of lading) and Hull (in the case of one bill of lading). At the time the vessel was due to discharge at London and Hull these ports were strikebound, and the cargo was unloaded at Hamburg. The original freight was then paid by the cargo owners, as well as the storage costs of the cargo at Hamburg and the costs of eventually forwarding the goods to London and Hull.

The bills of lading were governed by The Hague Rules as incorporated in the Canadian Water Carriage of Goods Act, and provided by clause 14(c) that should it appear that epidemics . . . labour trouble, labour obstructions, strikes, lockouts (any of which on board or on shore), or difficulties in loading or discharging are likely to prevent the vessel from leaving the port of loading, reaching or entering the port of discharge or their discharging in the usual manner or leaving again, (all of which safely and without delay) the master may discharge the cargo at the port of loading or any other safe and convenient port. Clause 14(f) of the bill of lading provided that the discharge of any cargo under the provisions of the clause should be deemed due fulfilment of the contract. It also provided that, in connection with the exercise of any liberty under this clause, if any extra expenses are incurred, they shall be paid by the merchant in addition to the freight, together with the return of the freight if any and a reasonable compensation for any extra services rendered to the goods.

Hamburg was admittedly a "convenient port" for the shipowners but the cargo owners claimed damages on the ground that the shipowners failed to deliver the goods at the port of delivery, causing the vessel to deviate to Hamburg, and failed to forward the goods from Hamburg to the ports of delivery. It was contended by the cargo owners that (1) under common law, that paragraphs (c) and (f) of clause 14 should be disregarded, as they were in conflict with the express promise to deliver at London or Hull and in fact defeated the main object and intent of the contract. Secondly it was submitted that the provision of Article III paragraph 2 of The Hague Rules that "the carrier shall properly and carefully ... carry ... and discharge the goods" involved an obligation to discharge at the proper ports. And clause permitting the shipowners or carriers to deliver elsewhere or any clause allowing deviation in terms wider than Article IV paragraph 4, were avoided by Article III paragraph 8 according to the cargo owners. This provides that any clause covenant or agreement in a contract of carriage relieving the carrier or the ship from liability for loss or damage to or in connection with goods arising from negligence, fault or failure in the duties and obligations provided in Article IV, or lessening such liability otherwise than as provided in the Rules, shall be null and void and of no effect.

Thirdly it was submitted that clause 14(c) and (f), if construed literally, would permit a shipowner to discharge at the port of loading and claim full freight, which, it was argued, would be repugnant to the Rules.

The Committee drew particular attention to this case and the ruling of the House of Lords and it is now proposed to outline the opinion of the House of Lords on this problem. In particular, apart from the effect of this Article in the Hague Rules, there were two clauses in the bill of lading purporting to give the master the right to discharge at another safe and convenient port (clause 14(c)) and that such discharge was to be deemed to be due fulfilment of the contract, (clause 14(f)).

The ruling of the House of Lords, was that clause 14(c) should not be regarded as a liability to deviate but rather as providing an agreed substituted method for the performance of the contract of carriage in circumstances particularly envisaged. In proceeding to Hamburg, which was a convenient port, the ship was acting in accordance with the contract of carriage and by clause 14(f), this was to be regarded as performance of the contract of carriage. It was also held that the words in Article III paragraph 2 that "the carrier shall properly and carefully . . . carry . . . and discharge the goods carried" did not define the scope of the contract service, but merely required that the carrier must perform the duties of carriage in a proper and careful manner. In addition, it was left to the parties to determine the port of discharge, and that by the terms of the bills of lading Hamburg was such a port. Further, it was held, Clause 14(c) and (f) were not concerned with deviation, as cargo interests had argued, but provided substituted ways of performing the contract in certain events.

This position gave rise to concern on the part of the Committee, and their enquiries established that disagreements usually arise between carriers and cargo owners regarding the time carriers take to assess the situation, and about the merits of that assessment. It seems that cargo owners usually consider that carriers should not decide as quickly as they do that a situation is serious enough to warrant sailing the ship to another port or to discharge the goods in an unsuitable place at the risk and expense of the cargo owners. The trend of most Court decisions in cases concerning both strikes and deviations, is that carriers, in attempting to bring themselves within the exception of strikes and reasonable deviation, should ensure that the actions they take are made in the interest of all the parties concerned. They should also take into account the surrounding circumstances, the terms of the contract, the benefits to be derived, and the increase of risks that may be occasioned by the proposed action. The Committee took the view that the position must be clarified.

Amongst other things, reference was made to the complaints of cargo owners that when a strike causes goods to be discharged or abandoned at a different port from that mentioned in the bill of lading, they must bear the risk and expense of forwarding the goods to their destination. This is the result of Court decisions allowing carriers to discharge goods when a strike has forced them to deviate. UNCTAD took the view that what needs to be clarified is that the carrier, although authorised to deviate from the itinerary in certain circumstances, must continue to comply with his duties under Article III paragraph 2, regarding care towards goods while carrying them to an alternative port.

Moreover, the Committee pointed out that there seemed to be some doubts as to what is expected from the carrier after discharging the goods at the alternative port of discharge. One authority on this subject states that the master shall take all required measures to preserve and forward the goods that he has discharged. However, the Hague Rules are completely silent on this matter and the Committee recommend that they be clarified on this point.

It is now proposed to pass to the deliberations of the UNCTAD Committee on Article IV paragraph 2(m), which has important reference to the carriers' immunity in respect of cargo loss or damage due to inherent vice. The full provision in the Rule is that neither the carrier nor the ship shall be responsible for loss or damage arising or resulting from "wastage in bulk or weight or any other loss or damage arising from inherent defect, quality or vice of the goods". This exception is very important to the carrier. The Committee noted, in connection with this exception, that in recent years it has been much used by carriers through their P. & I. Associations, the latter going to considerable trouble and expense by using biochemists to show that damage to goods had arisen through their inherent vice and not through any fault of the carrier. The Rule is applied frequently to the deterioration of perishable goods when these changes are the results of ordinary processes going on in the goods themselves. The Committee draw attention to the fact that the exception particularly affects loss or damage occurring in major exports of developing countries, such as perishables. It is mentioned that sometimes insufficiency of packing will contribute to the inherent vice of the cargo, but UNCTAD point out that both the burden and method of proving inherent vice are somewhat uncertain. They recommended clarification by the amendment of the Rule, on the lines that the loss or damage must be shown to be due to the inherent quality or vice of the goods. It must be further shown that the carriers have taken all reasonable measures in the care of the cargo.

Many disputes arise over the interpretation of this Rule because cargo owners often fail to recognise that it is natural for some products, principally those shipped in bulk, to suffer a small deterioration during carriage which is not the carrier's fault. The Committee took the view that it might avoid unnecessary waste of time and money if the Rule mentioned such customary tolerances as a specific illustration of "inherent vice", for which the carrier is excused from liability. They also recommend that the extent to which carriers should be charged with a knowledge of the nature and stowage requirements of the cargo should be clarified.

Article IV — Paragraph 2(n) of the Rules exempts the carrier from liability in respect of loss or damage arising or resulting from insufficiency of packing. Normal or customary packing in a trade, which invariably prevents all but the most minor damage under normal conditions of care and carriage, is generally considered to be sufficient packing, but, at the same time some damage may be expected even where normal packing is used. The Committee point out that packing capable of preventing even the most minor damage is not practicable or expected in the case of the carriage of some commodities, just as care by carriers in avoiding minor damage is not practicable or expected in some cases. The Committee took the view that the needs of carriers and cargo owners must therefore be assessed according to some rule of reasonableness to determine the degree of packing required, the care to be taken, and the minor damage to be expected.

Reference is made to a ruling of the American Courts that to stow the goods as the consignees insisted was required would impose a loss on the ship; to case them, a loss upon the shipper. Moreover, it is as legitimate an answer for the ship to make to the shipper, that if he delivers the goods knowing that the customary stowage may damage them, he cannot insist that the stowage is bad, as it is for the shipper to make to the ship that if the vessel accepts the goods uncased, it is bad stowage not to limit the tiers. The Court went on to say that in the carriage of goods the trade must always come to some accommodation between ideal perfection of stowage and entire disregard of the safety of the goods. When it has done so, that becomes the standard for that type of goods.

The Committee took good note of this ruling and then went on to refer to the frequent practice of carriers to inset in their bills of lading clauses such as "without responsibility for the possible deterioration of cargo insufficiently packed" or "unpacked crate, no responsibility for breaking." Both of these clauses have been held valid in some jurisdictions, although only the former was said to be within the scope of Article IV paragraph 2(n).

The view taken by the Committee was that the status of these "insufficiency of packing" clauses was uncertain, and that it was not clear what effects the different types of clauses had. It was also uncertain whether they validly exonerate carriers, affect the burden of proof, or are invalid by virtue of Article III paragraph 8. This provides that any clause, covenant or agreement in a contract of carriage relieving the carrier or the ship from liability for loss or damage to or in connection with goods arising from negligence, fault or failure in the duties and obligations provided in the Article, or lessening such liability otherwise than as provided in the Rules, shall be null and void and of no effect.

Court decisions, it was felt, were often confusing, particularly when they attempted to distinguish between notations on bills of lading which are said to be valid as notes of insufficiency of packing, but invalid as "non responsibility" clauses. Furthermore, although the exceptions of inherent vice and insufficiency of packing are broadly similar, the burden of proof is different. In the case of insufficient packing the carrier often has difficulty in contradicting his clean bill of lading, but this is not usually so in the case of inherent vice.

In this connection, reference is made to a ruling in the English Courts (*Silver* v. *Ocean Steamship Co.*) which concerned a consignment of eggs packed in large rectangular metal cases with sharp edges and which were liable to damage each other. On arrival at the destination, a large number of cases were found to be in a defective condition by reason of large gashes in some and smaller perforations in others. When delivering judgment in the Court of Appeal in connection with the cargo owner's claim on the shipowners, it was held (1) that since the shipowners had given bills of lading stating that the goods were shipped in apparent good order and condition, they were estopped from proving damage prior to shipment (2) that the gash damage prior to shipment would have been ascertainable by reasonable examination of the shipment, and accordingly the shipowners were estopped from relying on gash damage prior to shipment (3) that the shipowners were not entitled to rely on the insufficiency of the packages which was apparent on shipment. This case illustrates the point made by UNCTAD on the matter of onus of proof and clean bills of lading relative to the exception "insufficiency of packing".

Carriers often use the exception "insufficiency of packing" when the damage or loss is attributable to wear and tear of stowage or strains and stresses incident to transportation. The Committee thought that this might be considered reasonable, but for the fact that carriers also frequently attempt to use the exception improperly in order to excuse themselves from liability where goods have been pilfered. Considerable confusion has been caused in many trades by carriers' attempts to use the exception in respect of goods packed in cartons, second hand bags, or sacks etc., and in order to forestall this exception the cargo owner must use diligence to pack his cargo adequately either because he knows that the goods are likely to suffer damage or because it has become customary in the trade to wrap this type of cargo, and he should also take into account the nature of the voyage and the means of loading and unloading in the ports.

It seems that most of the cargo owner's problems arise from the uncertain effects of the qualifications of alleged insufficiency of packing which carriers inset in their bills of lading, and over burden of proof. The view taken is that clarification is necessary with regard to burden of proof and the exact status of notations in regard to packing as inserted in bills of lading. Further, it seems necessary to clarify that the carrier would not benefit from the use of the exception unless he shows that the loss or damage arose solely out of the insufficiency of packing, and did not arise out of, and was not in part attributable to, any fault, failure or neglect on the part of the carrier, his agents or servants.

Article IV paragraph 2(p) provides that neither the carrier nor the ship shall be responsible for loss or damage arising or resulting from latent defects not discoverable by due diligence, and this rule, the UNCTAD Committee state, must be considered in relation to Article III paragraph 1 and Article IV paragraph 1. The first mentioned provides that the carrier shall be bound before and at the beginning of the voyage, to exercise due diligence to (a) make the ship seaworthy (b) properly man, equip, and supply the ship (c) make the holds, refrigerating and cool chambers, and all other parts of the ship in which goods are carried, fit and safe for their reception, carriage and preservation. Article IV paragraph 1 provides that neither the carrier nor the ship shall be liable for loss or damage arising or resulting from unseaworthiness unless caused by want of due diligence on the part of the carrier to make the ship seaworthy, and to secure that the ship is properly manned, equipped and supplied, and to make the holds, refrigerating and cool chambers and all other parts of the ship in which goods are carried fit and safe for their reception, carriage and preservation in accordance with the provisions of paragraph 1 of Article III. It should be mentioned that whenever loss or damage has resulted from unseaworthiness, the burden of proving exercise of due diligence is on the carrier or other person claiming exemption under Article IV paragraph 1.

Latent defect

The point is made in relation to Article IV paragraph 2(p) that it would appear that the degree of diligence required in its exception is the same as that required under the two above mentioned Rules, except that because there is no mention of "before and at the commencement of the voyage" in the latent defects exception, due diligence must be exercised on every occasion when inspection should reasonably be made.

A latent defect is usually a defect in construction, or in manufacture. In a ruling in the American Courts it was held that a true latent defect is a flaw in the metal and a defect that could not be discovered by any known or customary test, and that it is not the result of gradual deterioration. Some guidance on what is, and what is not, a latent defect was given by Mr. Justice Porter some years ago when delivering judgment over the question of liability for cargo damage caused by leaky rivets. He commented that the defects were latent since, in spite of careful examination of the vessel by responsible persons, the defect was not discovered. The shipowners having exercised due diligence to make the ship seaworthy were therefore not liable in respect of the cargo damage resulting from those latent defects. His Lordship agreed first of all that "latent defect" does not mean latent to the eye, but to the senses — i.e., it may be hammer tested, or there may be other tests. The only question is whether "latent" means that you have to use every possible method to discover its existence, or whether the use of reasonable methods applies. His Lordship took the view that it meant an examination which a reasonably careful man, skilled in that area, would make.

A definition usually relied upon in Common Law countries is that a latent defect is a defect which could not be discovered by a person of competent skill and using ordinary care. A representative definition in Civil Law countries is a defect which an attentive examination does not discern. However, difficulties over burden of proof make the exception one of the less understood of the exceptions contained in Article IV. As the Committee comment, in most legal systems the carrier must first prove that a latent defect caused the loss, and then, as in other exceptions, he must prove that he exercised due diligence to make the vessel seaworthy before and at the commencement of the voyage, and that the defect was not discoverable by reasonable diligence or an attentive examination.

Restrictive interpretations of the exception by the Courts usually assist the cargo claimant, but not always. Claim settlements are sometimes delayed for long periods while the carrier attempts to prove the existence of latent defects, due diligence etc. The exception, originating as it does in some undetectable flaw in the construction or material of the carrying vessel, concerns the responsibility of the carrier so basically and touches that of the cargo owner so remotely, that, in the opinion of the UNCTAD Committee, it might be discarded more easily than others. Latent defect is not mentioned as a specific excepted peril in the national legislation of many States and the Committee recommended the dropping of the exception or altering the burden of proof to make it easier for the cargo owner to secure compensation for loss.

The last of the exceptions contained in Article IV paragraph 2, — (q), any other cause — provides that neither the carrier nor the ship shall be responsible for loss or damage arising or resulting from any other cause without the actual fault or privity of the carrier, or without the fault or neglect of the agents or servants of the carrier. The burden of proof shall be on the person claiming the benefit of this exception to show that neither the actual fault or privity of the carrier nor the fault or neglect of the agents or servants of the carrier contributed to the loss or damage.

Article IV paragraph 2(q) has been referred to as a "catch all" exception and questions have been raised as to what the words "any other cause" were intended to cover. There seems to be no doubt that the intention of the framers of the Rules was to protect the carrier from responsibility for loss or damage, of whatever nature not already specifically covered by the Rules, unless arising with the fault or privity of the carrier or with the fault or neglect of the agents or servants of the carrier. However, the exception is not so widely used as its language might suggest, for the reason that carriers tend to use the exceptions in Articles IV paragraphs (a) to (p) whenever possible. This is because in their use the cargo owner has the burden of proving default or negligence on the part of the carrier, whereas in order to benefit from the "catch all" exception, the burden is on the carrier to show that neither his own default or privity nor the neglect by the agents or servants of the carrier contributed to the damage. Despite this comment, it is generally accepted that, for example, in the case of a plea of "perils of the sea" in defence of a cargo owner's claim for damage to his goods, the carrier must prove that the damage did in fact arise out of a peril of the sea and was not contributed to, for example, by faulty stowage.

The other reason given for the general failure on the part of the carrier to use the exception contained in Article IV paragraph 2(q) is that because of the large number of exceptions listed in this paragraph there are, in practice, very few "other causes".

However, the important thing here is the burden of proof and one or two leading legal decisions at this point might be examined.

The first case referred to is that of *Pendle and Rivett* v. *Ellerman Lines* which concerned the question of the shipowner's liability for the loss in two cases of wool and silk piece goods. The bill of lading stated "weight unknown", but prior to its receipt the shippers had received a mate's receipt which omitted these words. On the arrival at the port of discharge one of the cases was found to be empty. The Court found that (1) having regard to the unqualified statement in the mate's receipt, the shipowners must be taken to have received the cases of the weight specified (2) that having regard to the inexplicable conflict of evidence as to when the case became empty, the shipowners must be held to have failed to shift the burden of proof upon them by Article IV.

In the case of *Hourani* v. *Harrison*, which concerned the theft of goods by stevedores who were engaged by the ship's agents to discharge the cargo, it was held by the Court that (1) the stevedore's men were the agents of the shipowners to effect the discharge of cargo and (2) that the stealing of the cargo was not an act in the management of the ship, and, therefore, the shipowners were not protected by Article IV. It was also held that the word "or" in the words "or without" in Article IV paragraph 2(q) should be used conjunctively and not disjunctively. Therefore, the shipowners had to prove that both they themselves and their servants or agents were free from blame, and that this they had failed to do because the stevedores were their servants or agents.

The Committee went on to comment that the case law which bears on the question of whether the carrier must show how the loss occurred has been described as "vague and apparently faulty, in particular because virtually all the information, if available at all, is available to the carrier alone. To exempt a carrier from liability when the cause of the loss is unknown is to make it beneficial for carriers not to discover the cause."

In their examination of Article IV paragraph 2, the Committee took the view that these exemptions have not been extended to the carrier's servants or agents in those countries where there is a fundamental legal principle that only a party to a contract can take the benefit of its terms. Servants and agents can be sued in such jurisdictions for negligence, and their liability is broader than that of the carrier, but this facility is usually of dubious value to cargo owners.

The deliberations of UNCTAD disclose that carriers often insert clauses into their bills of lading extending the exceptions contained in Article IV paragraph (2) to their servants or agents. However, both the Courts in the U.K. and the U.S. have confirmed that (1) subject to clear and express intent being declared in the bill of lading that the exemptions and limitations of liability conferred upon the carrier shall extend to the benefit of the carrier's agents or servants, and (2) subject to it being made clear in unambiguous language that the carrier is contracting also for the benefit of his agents or servants, including independent contractors, the stevedores may have the benefit of the limitations of liability that the carrier enjoys. The value of the clauses in the bill of lading extending to the carrier's agents or servants the exemptions contained in Article IV paragraph (2) has not been tested conclusively.

Referring back to the "catch all" Rule of Article IV paragraph (2)q the shipping Committee refer to the case of the *Leesh River Tea Co. Ltd v. British India Steam Navigation Company*, which concerned the damage to goods by seawater owing to the stevedores, employed by the carrier, stealing a brass storm valve cover during the unloading and loading of the ship at Port Sudan. In that case, the Court of Appeal held unanimously that the removal of the plate was in no way incidental to the process of the discharge and loading of the vessel, and that the act of the thief was that of a stranger who was performing no duty at all for the carrier. Since the stevedore was, with regard to the theft of the storm valve cover, acting outside the scope of his employment and the theft could not have been prevented by any reasonable diligence by the shipowners, the Court ruled that the carrier was entitled to the benefit of the "catch all" exception. It seems that the Committee did not propose to make any special recommendations to this rule except to draw attention to the fact that it has to be borne in mind that the effect of the rule has not been conclusively tested.

Paragraph 4

Under this Rule, any deviation in saving or attempting to save life or property at sea, or any reasonable deviation shall not be deemed to be an infringement or breach of the Rules, or of the contract of carriage, and the carrier shall not be liable for any loss or damage resulting therefrom. When the United States brought the Rules into force there was added to this Rule the words "Provided, however, that if the deviation is for the purpose of unloading cargo or passengers it shall 'prima facie' be regarded as unreasonable." There is, therefore, that difference between the American version of the Rules and the Rule itself as introduced into the Statute Books of other maritime nations.

It is perhaps apt to mention here the case of *Foscolo, Mango & Co. v. Stag Line* (The *Ixia*) which concerned a claim of cargo interests for the loss of their cargo when the vessel foundered off the Cornish Coast after having landed two passengers in the form of engineers who had embarked upon the vessel with a view to testing the operation of superheating apparatus on board the ship. The master of the vessel decided to land the two men at St. Ives Bay and this was done, which involved a departure from the usual route the vessel would have taken. On leaving St. Ives the master, instead of at once getting on to what would have been his course if he had not deviated, proceeded to coast round the Cornish cliffs at a distance of about 1½ miles with the result that the *Ixia* stranded on the coast and both ship and cargo were lost.

The bill of lading was subject to the provisions of the Carriage of Goods by Sea Act, which gives effect to the Rules, but the bill of lading also contained a clause providing that the vessel was at liberty to call at ports in any order for bunkering or other purposes or to make trial trips, etc. The cargo interests claimed that the shipowners were liable for the loss of the cargo, on the grounds that the owners were in breach of the Rules because of an "unreasonable" deviation.

The case reached the Court of Appeal where it was held that there was a deviation from the agreed route, and that the deviation into St. Ives was not excused by the clause in the bill of lading giving liberty to the carrier to "call at any ports in any order, for bunkering or other purposes." It was also held that the common law principles of deviation were not affected by the Carriage of Goods by Sea Act, and that the deviation was not "reasonable" within the meaning of Article IV paragraph 4 of the Hague Rules. The inference is therefore, that although when the Carriage of Goods by Sea Act was introduced, the Rule was not amplified as was done in the United States, the law of this country on deviation for the purpose of landing or embarking passengers falls into line with the American viewpoint.

In the event that the carrier should claim that a deviation from the agreed route was reasonable then the onus of proof is upon the carrier to show that the deviation was reasonable, deviation being usually defined as a departure from the customary or contractual route, or, as the Committee pointed out, delay whereby the character and incidence of the voyage are altered. Some American Courts have considered the term to include such occurrence as over-carriage, misdelivery, carriage on deck, when not permitted under the contract or by custom etc. There must be a departure from both the customary route and the contractual route if the two are different. The Committee made the point that the Rules neither define deviation as such, nor do they indicate the consequences of an unreasonable deviation, the Rules merely proving that any deviation for the purpose of saving or attempting to save life or property or any reasonable deviation is not to be considered a breach of contract. This uncertainty was found to be the subject of complaint by cargo interests.

Attention was drawn to one authority which states that the true test seems to be what departure from the contract voyage might a prudent person controlling the voyage at the time make and maintain, having in mind all the relevant circumstances existing at the time, including the terms of the contract and the interest of all the parties concerned, but without obligation to consider the interests of anyone as conclusive. The Committee's enquiries also showed that the burden of proof is a second source of uncertainty in cases of deviation, it usually being held that, because the carrier has greater access to the facts, he has the burden of proving the contractual route, and that the loss took place whilst the vessel was on that route. The burden would then be on the cargo claimant to prove the deviation or the unreasonable change in the route.

In connection with these problems, enquiries showed that the bill of lading normally states only the ports of loading and discharge, if it mentions a specific route or other ports of call, this would in effect be the agreed route, and the real geographical route would probably only be found from a study of (a) the customary routes taken by the shipping line in the past (b) the notices and advertisements before the voyage (c) the booking note and (d) the bill of lading itself.

Referring to one authority on this subject, the burden of proof in questions of deviation does not sit squarely on the shoulders of either party. Rather, deviation appears to be one of those legal questions in which each party is obliged to, and, to protect its interests, should do everything that he can make proof of his own contentions. If, however, a rule of burden of proof exists as to deviation, it is probably that the carrier must prove the geographic route of the contract and that the loss took place on the route. The deviation must then be proven by the cargo claimant, and the reasonableness of the deviation must, at that point, be proven by the carrier, and the Committee made a special reference to this.

Continuing upon the uncertainties regarding the interpretation and effect of the important exemption from liability for the carrier contained in Article IV — paragraph 4 (Deviation), reference is made to the comment regarding Common Law systems, where unjustified deviation is considered to have the effect of nullifying the contract of carriage. This has the consequences that liabilities are then based upon, not the Hague Rules, but on Common Law principles, and it is not altogether certain whether all or only some of the Rules are thus affected.

In the opinion of the Committee these problems might be clarified and simplified if deviations were presumed to be unjustified, and if carriers were held liable for all risk and expense of bringing the goods to the port of destination, unless they could prove that compelling conditions for the benefit of both ship and cargo forced them to deviate. The effect of such an alteration in the Hague Rules can be seen, in particular, with reference to deviations arising out of strikes or labour disturbances at the named port of destination. It was also suggested that the provision in the

United States that any deviation for the purpose of loading or unloading cargo or passengers must be considered unreasonable.

Paragraph 5

Under the provisions of Article IV paragraph 5 (Limitation of Liability) neither the carrier nor the ship becomes, in any event, liable for cargo loss or damage to or in connection with goods in an amount exceeding £100 per package or unit (or the equivalent of that sum in other currency) unless the nature and value of such goods have been declared by the shipper before shipment and inserted in the bill of lading. Such a declaration if embodied in the bill of lading constitutes 'prima facie' evidence of the value and is not binding or conclusive on the carrier. By agreement between the carrier, master or agent of the carrier and the shipper another maximum amount may be fixed, provided that such maximum shall not be less than the £100 per package or unit limitation. It is provided also in this Article that neither the carrier nor the ship shall be responsible if the nature or value of the goods has been knowingly mis-stated by the shipper in the bill of lading.

This limitation was laid down over 50 years ago and in this present day and age the amount of the limitation bears no relation to the actual damage suffered by the cargo owner. In 1950 shipowning interests recognised this and in association with cargo interests an agreement was drawn up between British shipowners and marine insurers known as the Gold Clause Agreement. Under this it was provided, amongst other things, that the shipowner's liability under the Rules (whether contested or not) in respect of any such claim shall be limited to £200 sterling per package or unit of cargo, unless the nature and value of the cargo has been declared by the shipper before loading and inserted in the bill of lading. The term "Gold Clause" has its origin in the fact that in Article IX of the Rules it is provided that the monetary units mentioned in the Rules are to be taken as gold value. There is only one monetary unit mentioned in the Rules, namely that referred to above and it was to avoid litigation to decide the effect of Article IX that the agreement was drawn up.

Further, it has to be remembered that the Carriage of Goods by Sea Act 1971 incorporates the amendments made to the Hague Rules of 1924 by the Brussels Convention of 1968, which provides, amongst other things, that the limitation of the shipowner's liability shall be based on weight (kilo) as an alternative to package or unit. The Act lays down that the limit of liability per package or unit is raised from £100 to Poincare francs 10,000 (at that time representing £276) and the limit of liability per kilo is Poincare francs 30 (at that time £842 per ton).

The Shipping Committee comment, in relation to the £100 limitation, that it no longer has any relation to the actual damage sustained by the cargo owner, and point out that limitations of liability have evolved historically in different forms from the sixteenth century statutes in Western Europe, designed initially to encourage investment in shipping.

They were enunciated in their present form in the Rules to impose a mandatory minimum liability on carriers to prevent them from limiting their liability to ridiculously low amounts on the plea that they wished to exempt themselves from liability on packages containing goods of an unanticipated high value. At the 1921 Hague Conference when the Rules were first framed, it was stressed by shipowning representatives that carriers should be protected against excessive and quite unanticipated cargo claims. The view that the right of limitation was available only in respect of high value packages was eventually rejected at the final conference where the Hague Rules were agreed. Article IV paragraph 5 was adopted to invalidate bills of lading clauses that had come to limit carriers' liabilities to almost nominal charges.

The word "unit" was subsequently added to extend the limitation of liability to goods not shipped in packages and Article IV(5) was made to apply irrespective of the nature and the value of the cargo. UNCTAD comment that it was this feature of the Rule that in course of time was considered likely to be decidedly awkward and arbitary in its application, frequently leading to results which, in the concrete case, are felt unjustified or unreasonable. It is pointed out that the limitation of liability is composed of two elements (a) the stipulated amount (b) the quantitative unit of the goods by which to calculate the carrier's maximum liability. UNCTAD comment that the first element raises the straight forward question of whether the present limitation is too low, and should be raised. Also that the proper basis for calculation raises more complex questions, because the terms "package" or "unit" have not been interpreted uniformly. One reason is that the Carriage of Goods by Sea Acts of several countries depart significantly from the Convention in their provisions on limitation of liability. For example the United States version of the Rules states that their limitation of liability of $500 applies to packages or in the case of goods not shipped in packages, per customary freight unit. This has led to a great deal of litigation in the United States between cargo interests and shipowners and the Committee drew attention to two particular instances.

In the first case a tractor, weighing some 43,000 lbs, was shipped without skids but with the superstructure partly encased with wooden planking. It was delivered in a damaged condition and the carrier attempted to limit his liability to $500, contending that the tractor was a "package". However, the Court held that the carrier's liability for damage could only be limited to $500 per measurement ton on which basis the freight was computed, and, since the tractor weighed 34.6 measurement tons, the resulting figure was $17,300.

Another case referred to concerned the loss of ten locomotives and tenders which were uncrated and, therefore, could not be defined as packages. In that case, the United States Court of Appeals held that, since the freight rate was calculated $10,000 per unit of locomotive and tender, the carrier's liability was limited to $500 per unit of locomotive and tender, or $5,000 in all. This case, UNCTAD comments, illustrates the immense benefit to carriers of Article IV paragraph 5 of the Hague Rules. However, in other maritime nations views on the per package limitation differ — for example, the Polish Maritime Code uses the expression "one package of cargo or any other unit of cargo as by custom used in trade". The Czechoslovak Maritime Law states "per package or customary freight unit of cargo."

The enquiries of the Committee revealed a second reason for difficulty in calculating the limitation of liability, namely that the terms "package" and "unit" are not sufficiently precise to fit various shipping practices. Difficulties have arisen, for example, in attempting to determine how much packing or covering is required to establish that the goods constitute a package. The French "colis" and the Scandinavian "kollo" do not appear to fit precisely within this definition of "package", as they would include goods shipped in a wrapping or container that might not be appropriately called a package. The law cases of the United States seem to support the view that a package, under the Rules, need not be completely covered, wrapped or packed. On occasions authorities have referred to the word "unit" as flagrantly ambiguous, and UNCTAD refer to the fact that it may refer to the physical shipping unit — for example, an unboxed car or unboxed machinery, a bale, barrel, sack etc., *i.e.* a unit of cargo, or it may mean the unit on the basis of which the freight is calculated, i.e. the freight unit. UNCTAD have found that because the amount of freight is usually based on the weight or volume of the cargo, even for cargo consisting of shipping units, the total amount of the damage recoverable will vary according to whether liability is limited on the basis of shipping units (packages) or freight units. Usually calculations based upon freight units will cause the limitation to be larger than those based upon shipping units.

The Committee also found that there is some doubt as to whether the carrier's liability for bulk cargoes is subject to the limitation, and the prevailing view seems to be that the Rule applies to all types of cargo. However, said the Committee, it should be clarified in future amendments to the Rules whether to apply to bulk cargoes the freighting unit, *i.e.* weight or volume, or the weight or volume unit in which the goods are described in the bill of lading. Anomalous decisions have also arisen in cases where the freight was quoted as a lumpsum for one shipping unit or a consignment consisting of several shipping units. Also problems arise with regard to containers and pallets, which were not even contemplated at the time when the Hague Rules were drafted. However, once again, in this connection, one has to refer to the Brussels Protocol of 1968, and the Carriage of Goods by Sea Act, 1971, which deal with this problem.

The 1971 Act, giving effect to the Protocol, provides that where a container, pallet or similar article of transport is used to consolidate goods, the question as to whether the limitation is based on a "package" or "unit" or on weight is to be decided by referring to the bill of lading itself. If the packages or units are enumerated in the bill of lading as being packed in the container then the unit basis is to be adopted. Otherwise the container itself will be the basis and, since it will almost certainly weigh more than 333 kilos, the weight basis will apply, as explained above. As the position now stands, there is nothing in the Rules which deals with the problem of the application of the limitation of liability to containers and pallets. Also there has been a dearth of law cases in this country to decide the extent to which the carrier may limit his liability under the Rules regarding goods which have been containerised or palletised, and for guidance on this problem reference has to be made to the cases which have come before the United States for a ruling. However, the position is still obscure.

In this connection reference is made to one or two cases before the United States Courts. In one case, 54 cartons each containing 40 television tuners were strapped to 9 separate pallets, and the question before the Court was whether the number of packages was 9 or 54. It was held that because each pallet constituted an integrated unit, capable of, and intended for, handling, there were only 9 packages and that the carrier could limit his liability to $500 per pallet, this being the carrier's liability per package or freight unit under the provisions of the United States Carriage of Goods by Sea Act, which incorporates the Hague Rules. It has to be mentioned here that the Court, when reaching this decision, was heavily influenced by the fact that all the shipping documents, invoices, bills of lading etc., referred to 9 packages and that the shipper could have obtained full coverage simply by declaring the value of the goods in the bill of lading. A distinction must, however, be made between containers that contain goods all destined to one consignee and containers, commonly referred to as groupage containers, which contain goods shipped by more than one shipper for more than one consignee and in connection with which separate bills of lading have been issued for the individual shipments. In this situation the container obviously cannot constitute a single package.

As stated above, the limitation of liability under the Rules applies unless the nature and value of the goods have been declared by the shipper before shipment and inserted in the bill of lading. However, this apparent option to the shipper to secure a more complete protection has had little practical effect. Enquiries show that shippers have rarely declared cargo values in bills of lading, and this reluctance stems from the fact that to declare the value of the goods would undoubtedly attract additional ad valorem rates of freight and could lay the consignees open to paying additional taxes at destination. As far as the carriers are concerned, they have stated that the *ad-valorem* charge protects them against declarations of excessive value by cargo owners, and that as the ad valorem freight rate is usually a high percentage, cargo owners generally find it cheaper to obtain their own insurance rather than declare the value. In the result, cargo owners rarely declare the value of the goods to avoid the limitation of liability and, consequently, the limitation upon the carrier's liability normally applies.

It was also noted that there is uncertainty as to the type of losses to which the unit of limitation of liability applies. The prevailing view appears to be that direct as well as indirect damage is subject to limitation. However, in some cases it would seem that the carrier's liability for loss because of wrongful delivery to a person not empowered by the bill of lading to take delivery, is not a liability according to this article of the Rules. Also it would seem that the liability of the carrier is not limited for misrepresentations in the bill of lading, if it can be proved that no loss or damage has occurred whilst the goods were in the custody of the carrier.

Meanwhile they refer to another matter which their enquiries reveal needs clarification, namely the words "in any event" contained in Article IV paragraph 5. It is felt unjust that the carrier should be protected by this limitation of liability irrespective of the nature of the breach or of the faults which caused the loss or damage. Enquiries showed that in some countries the carrier can apparently take advantage of the limitation when he is in breach of Article III paragraph 1, (which refers to the duty of the carrier to provide a seaworthy ship), and Article III paragraph 2 (which refers to the duty of the carrier to properly and carefully load, stow etc., the cargo carried), even if the act or omission of the carrier is done recklessly or with intent to cause damage.

In other countries the proposition seems to be that the carrier cannot rely upon the limitation of liability when the damage is imputable to serious faults by the carrier. In the Brussels Protocol of 1968, which has been continuously referred to in this book, the amendments to the Rules state that "neither the carrier nor the ship shall be entitled to the limitation of liability if the damage resulted from an act or omission of the carrier done with intent to cause damage or recklessly and with knowledge that damage would probably result."

UNCTAD and the Brussels Protocol of 1968

Reference was made to the Brussels Protocol of 1968, when there was international agreement on proposed amendments to the Rules in certain respects, one of which concerned the limitation of liability in relation to the carriage of goods in containers.

It was recognised that in the amendments contained in the Brussels Protocol of 1968, the new Article IV paragraph 5, with which we are presently concerned, considerably improves the position of cargo owners with respect to limitation of liability. Not only does it raise the limit of liability but it also makes a special rule for containers and other similar articles for transport. The new rule raises the limitation to 10,000 Francs Poincare per package or unit or Poincare francs 30 per kilo, whichever is the higher, the first limit being intended to apply to light valuable cargo while the second limit is intended to apply to heavy cargo. Although the weight unit limitation appears to have improved matters for cargo owners, the figure is considerably below those in other international transport conventions and UNCTAD recommended that the limit of liability in Article IV paragraph 5 of the Rules should be amended so as to be more in line with those conventions. The new Article IV paragraph 5 of the Brussels Protocol of 1968, further states that where a container, pallet or similar article of transport is used to consolidate goods, the number of packages or units enumerated in the bill of lading as packed in such article of transport shall be deemed to be the number of packages or units for calculating the limitation of liability.

This amendment clearly improves the position of cargo owners. For example, if 100 boxes of cargo, valued at £60,000 and weighing 10 tons, are stowed in one container and the container is lost overboard during sea transit, and the 100 boxes have been enumerated in the bill of lading, the limit of liability would be 100 × Poincare francs 10,000. If the boxes have not been enumerated in the bill of lading, so that the container becomes the package or unit, the cargo owner can still take the benefit of the weight limit so that the limit will be 10 × 30 Poincare francs × 1,000.

However, whilst the provisions of the Brussels Protocol of 1968 have been borne in mind, it might well be that the amendments to the Rules agreed at that time may never become effective, even though in the United Kingdom the Carriage of Goods by Sea Act of 1971, giving effect to the Protocol has received Royal assent. The reason for this is that it is laid down in the Protocol that it shall come into force three months after the date of the deposit of 10 instruments of ratification or accession, of which at least five shall have been deposited by states that have a tonnage equal or superior to one million gross tons.

It was felt that the existing Article IV paragraph 5 is unsatisfactory and in need of considerable modification, even though the amendments to the Rules contained in the Brussels Protocol of 1968 have made some improvements. It was submitted that carriers would not be able to secure competitive P. and I. insurance rates if limitation rules were relaxed in favour of cargo owners, but this submission was found to be hardly tenable.

Article V — Surrender of rights and immunities and increase of responsibilities and liabilities

This Rule provides that a carrier shall be at liberty to surrender in whole or in part all or any of his rights and immunities, or to increase any of his responsibilities and liabilities under the Rules, provided such surrender or increase shall be embodied in the bill of lading issued to the shipper. Article V also provides that the provisions of the Rules shall not be applicable to charter-parties, but if bills of lading are issued in the case of a ship under a charter party they shall comply with the terms of the Rules. It is also provided that nothing in the Rules shall be held to prevent the insertion in a bill of lading of any lawful provision regarding general average.

The Committee referred to the difficulties encountered by charterers, shippers, carriers and receivers in identifying their liabilities when the charter-party terms are incorporated into bills of lading. Since the Committee made a special study of this and have dealt with the situation in their review and recommendations covering bill of lading clauses not specifically covered by the Rules (but none the less having relation thereto) it is proposed to deal with their proposals with regard to Article V as a special matter later in Section IV.

Article VI — Special conditions

Under Article VI — Special Conditions — it is provided that, notwithstanding the provisions of the previous Articles, a carrier, master or agent of the carrier, and a shipper shall, in regard to any particular goods, be at liberty to enter into any agreement in any terms as to the responsibility and liability of the carrier for such goods. Also with regard to the rights and immunities of the carrier in respect of such goods, or his obligation as to seaworthiness, so far as this stipulation is not contrary to public policy, or the care or diligence of his servants or agents in regard to the loading, handling, stowage, carriage, custody, care and discharge of the goods carried by sea, provided that in this case no bill of lading has been or shall be issued and that the terms agreed shall be embodied in a receipt which shall be a non-negotiable document.

The Committee thought that the phrase "ordinary commercial shipment made in the ordinary course of trade" was rather vague and might be clarified by amendment.

Conclusions on the need for revision of the Hague Rules.

The terms of reference of the UNCTAD Working Group on International Shipping Legislation drew attention to UNCITRAL's programme of reviewing shipping legislation — with a particular provision for the Working Group to make recommendations on legislative changes. The Working Group primarily concerned itself with the manifold aspect of bills of lading legislation and (1) considered existing rules and practices, with their adverse effects on cargo interests; and (2) concluded that some practices contained ambiguities in the application of law or contract terms, resulting in avoidable cost to international trade, while also imposing inequitable liability on the cargo-owner, as compared with the carrier. Being aware that the cargo-owner's liability is particularly onerous in developing countries and that it has been resolved by the UN General Assembly that UNCTAD and

UNCITRAL work with closer co-operation a number of recommendations were drawn-up.

It was considered that the rules and practices concerning bills of lading, including those contained in the International Convention for the Unification of certain Rules of Law relating to Bills of Lading (The Hague Rules of 1924) and in the Protocol to amend The Hague Rules (The Brussels Protocol of 1968†) should be revised and amplified. If appropriate, a new international convention may be prepared for adoption under the auspices of the United Nations. (†The Brussels Protocol of 1968 is contained in the amended Carriage of Goods by Sea Act in the United Kingdom).

The view was taken that a revision and amplification should mainly aim at the removal of such uncertainties and ambiguities as exist.

Also to be sought was an equitable distribution of responsibilities and liabilities and a balanced allocation of risks between the cargo-owner and the carrier, with appropriate provisions concerning the burden of proof. In particular the following areas, should be considered for revision and amplification: (a) responsibility for cargo for the entire period it is in charge or control of the carrier or his agents (which may have the effect of making the carrier responsible from warehouse to warehouse); (b) the scheme of responsibilities and liabilities, and rights and immunities, incorporated in Article III and IV of The Hague Rules and their interaction. Particular emphasis was put on the elimination of what is considered unjustified exceptions to the carrier's liability — deviation, seaworthiness and unit limitation of liability.

Also reviewed was the revision of the Rules in respect of: (c) burden of proof; (d) jurisdiction; (e) responsibilities for deck cargoes, live animals and transhipment; (f) extension of the period of limitation; (g) definitions under Article I of the Rules; and (h) the elimination of invalid clauses in bills of lading.

The Working Group on International Shipping Legislation recommended that, in the spirit of co-operation between UNCITRAL and UNCTAD, enjoined by the above resolutions of the General Assembly, UNCITRAL be invited to undertake such revision and amplification of the Rules, as appropriate and to prepare the necessary draft texts.

The bill of lading, its function and purpose was discussed at length. Many criticisms of the carriers' attitude to cargo-owners, particularly in the case of cargo loss or damage, were made. The replies received to an UNCTAD questionnaire showed that the cargo-owner, when faced with substantive procedural complications arising out of bill of lading terms and conditions, often stops pursuing a claim for cargo loss or damage against the carrier and, either, absorbs the loss or claims against his insurers. In the ordinary course of events, of course, the cargo-owner will recover his loss from the insurer and then the insurer will pursue the claim against the carrier. Many of the respondents complained that, in consequence of the lengthy procedure in establishing a claim against the carrier with its acknowledged further result of blurring the cogency of evidence or lightening its weight, claims often become time-barred.

The Working Committee of UNCTAD commented that it was readily apparent that in order to establish his case the cargo-owner faces the hurdle of procedural laws of the country in which he prosecuted his claim. A further comment, amongst many others, was that a prime difficulty faces the cargo-owner over the burden of proof to establish his claim against the carrier, which burden rests initially upon the cargo-owner.

Evidence before the Working Committee of UNCTAD on the need for revising The Hague Rules, beyond the 1968 Brussels Protocol when amendments to the Rules were agreed, came from several sources. In the first place there was the response to UNCTAD enquiries. Secondly, from a study of standard texts and periodicals, and, thirdly, there was the result of the analysis of the commercial and economic aspects and consequences of the present position, and of the analysis of The Hague Rules themselves.

It seems that the main ground for concern was the uncertainty in the application of laws, (namely, difficulties in establishing where and how the loss or damage to the goods occurred, burden of proof, allocation of responsibility for loss or damage to cargo). This uncertainty was the subject of complaints both by carrier and cargo interests. Then there was the matter of the continued retention in bills of lading of exoneration clauses of doubtful validity and the existence of restrictive exemption and time limitations clauses under which cargo is deposited with warehouses and port authorities. Furthermore, there are the exemptions in The Hague Rules which are peculiar to ocean carriage, in cases where the liability for cargo loss or damage should be logically borne by the ocean carrier. Included are those which excuse the carrier from liability in respect of negligence of his servants or agents in the navigation or management of the vessel and in respect of perils of the sea, etc. The view was taken that uncertainties were caused by the interpretation of terms used in The Hague Rules, such as "reasonable deviation," "due diligence," "properly and carefully," "in any event," "subject to," etc.

Reference was made to the ambiguities surrounding the seaworthiness of vessels for the carriage of goods, and the unit of limitation of liability (a sore point for cargo interests) was questioned and also jurisdiction and arbitration clauses.

Special cargoes

The point was made of the insufficient legal protection for cargoes with special characteristics that require special stowage, adequate ventilation, etc., and cargoes requiring deck shipment. Additionally called into question were clauses which permit carriers to divert vessels, and to tranship or land goods short of or beyond the port of destination specified in the bill of lading, at the risk and expense of cargo-owners, and clauses which apparently entitle carriers to deliver goods into the custody of shore custodians on terms which make it almost impossible to obtain settlements of cargo claims from either the carrier or the warehouse.

Comment was made that there was a significant uncompensated loss in respect of cargo loss or damage, and the view was taken that in part this arose from the fact that through both specific provisions and omissions, the Hague Rules provided what appear to be an excessive number of opportunities for the shipowner to avoid, legally, liability for loss of cargo and so to reject the claim made by the cargo owner. It was also felt that, in part, it occurs because the unit limitation, whereby the liability of the shipowner, even where full responsibility is admitted, is limited to a fixed amount irrespective of the actual value of the goods lost or damaged.

Overlapping insurance

An important matter dealt with concerns the question of overlapping insurance, so stressed by the developing nations, and accepted by UNCTAD. For the purposes of the present it will suffice to say that there was discussed and considered the extent to which "overlapping" or "double insurance" is effected by cargo-owners, who may be forced, because of uncertainty in the apportionment of the risks and burden of proof, to insure risks which in fact are borne by carriers.

The next point of examination by the Committee was how this uncompensated loss and the extent of double insurance would be affected if the risks of ocean carriage were redistributed by a change in the laws, bearing in mind also the effect of any consequential changes in the freight and insurance rates. It was concluded that there was no reason to expect that if risks were so redistributed as to eliminate uncertainty and, hence the need for double insurance, there would be any overall increase in the combined cost of freight and insurance, as was often feared. In fact the view was taken that there should be reduction of the overall costs borne by cargo interests, and that further, the elimination of uncertainty which would follow a change should reduce the frequency of recourse to arbitration and litigation, and so reduce expenses in that respect.

In considering the Hague Rules in relation to the needs of the present trading situation, the UNCTAD Secretariat said that the following criteria may be adopted: (a) balancing of equities between carriers and cargo interests; (b) commercial efficacy; (c) economic considerations; (d) clarification of the law and practices, particularly as to allocation of liability for cargo loss or damage; (e) removal of anachronisms.

Based upon this criteria the opinion was formed that the operation of certain parts of The Hague Rules was unsatisfactory and that there were strong grounds for revising the Rules for the establishment of a new international convention.

Damages

After it has been established that the carrier is liable for cargo loss or damage under the Hague Rules, the question then arises as to the method to be adopted in calculating the amount of the damages that the carrier must pay. This matter is not specifically mentioned in the Hague Rules but was introduced later in the amendments to the Rules as set out in the Brussels Protocol of 1968. Article 2 of the 1968 amendments provides that the total amount recoverable shall be calculated by reference to the value of such goods at the place and time at which they were discharged from the ship in accordance with the contract, or should have been so discharged. It is also provided that the value of the goods shall be fixed according to the commodity exchange price, or, if there be no such price, according to the current market price, or by reference to the normal value of goods of the same kind and quality. The rule of thumb method has been to establish the amount of the damages by taking the sound market value less the damaged market value but in practice the cargo and shipowning interests agree, in the day to day business of settling these matters, to accept the c.i.f. value.

The shipping committee of the United Nations Conference on Trade and Development commented that the effect of the new Rule in the 1968 amendments, was to codify the principles which have been generally accepted over the years but, in the opinion of the committee, the difficulty of establishing the market value of the goods would still remain. The committee recommended the adjustment of the damages based on the c.i.f. value plus a percentage for profit, or upon invoice value plus freight, insurance and a percentage for profit. It was felt that this would lead to greater certainty in the matter and would avoid protracted litigation between parties.

Delay in delivery

Another omission from the Hague Rules which the Committee dealt with in their recommendations with regard to the amendment of the Rules was that of loss suffered because of delay in the delivery of the goods. Their investigations showed that in some countries the words "loss or damage" in the Rules include damage caused by delay, so that cargo owners can claim damages for delay caused by the fault of the carrier. In a leading American case it was held that the words "loss or damage" covered loss by delay without physical damage to cargo. One of the most important cases in the U.K. was that of the *Ardennes*, which concerned a shipment of mandarines. It was alleged that there was an oral promise by the ship's agent that the vessel would proceed direct to London from the loading port and a "received for shipment" bill of lading was issued containing the usual liberties to ship by any vessel etc. The vessel was ordered by her owners to proceed first to Antwerp, with the result that the vessel arrived late in London resulting in the receivers of the cargo having to pay increased import duty and suffering loss of market. The Court ruled that the cargo owners were entitled, as damages, to an amount represented by the increase in the import duty, plus an amount calculated on the estimated market value had the ship proceeded to London direct.

It is common to see clauses in liner bills of lading either excluding or limiting liability for delay, but such clauses would appear to be invalid by the application of Article III paragraph 8 of the Rules. This provides that any clause, covenant or agreement in a contract of carriage relieving the carrier or the ship from liability for loss or damage to, or in connection with, goods arising from negligence, fault or failure in the duties and obligations provided in Article III, or lessening such liability otherwise than as provided in the Rules, shall be null and void and of no effect.

The deliberations of the Committee showed that in practice cargo interests find considerable difficulty in obtaining compensation for loss suffered by delay, because such losses are difficult to prove and to quantify. The Rules are quite silent on this matter and Courts have generally held that a carrier is liable for loss or damage arising from delay caused by his fault as legally defined. However, losses due to delay are often difficult to establish precisely and carriers are frequently successful in denying liability for cargo or damage so caused. It was felt that the considerable uncertainty on this point should be removed, and recommend the amendment of the Rules to confirm that delay is included within the concept of "loss or damage", so that carriers would be liable for delay arising through their fault or negligence.

Delay in relation to seaworthiness and strikes

Illustrative of the importance of the matter of liability for delay, attention was drawn to two well known cases that came before the English Courts, namely the case of *G. H. Renton & Co. Ltd v. Palmyra Trading Corporation*, when the House of Lords was dealing with delays and deviations and liabilities of the carrier in relation to strikes. The other case which also reached the House of Lords, being that of *Anglo-Saxon Petroleum Company Ltd v. Adamastos Shipping Company Ltd* which arose out of unseaworthiness causing delay.

The first case concerned the deviation of the vessel because the ports of London and Hull were strike bound, and goods destined for these ports were discharged at Hamburg. The cargo owners claimed damages from the shipowners, it being alleged that the latter had failed to deliver the goods at the port of delivery and had caused the vessel to deviate and carry the goods to Hamburg where they were discharged. They had also failed to forward the goods from Hamburg to the ports of delivery. These proceedings were, of course, bound up with the Hague Rules exemption in respect of loss or damage caused by strikes, and also the exemption from liability in respect of loss or damage resulting from a reasonable deviation.

With regard to the second case referred to above, this involved a dispute arising out of a voyage charter and delays on the voyages with unseaworthiness, being involved. However, for the purposes of the present, it was held in the House of Lords that there was nothing in Article IV of the Rules which governs the rights and immunities of the carrier, which expressly limited loss or damage to physical loss or damage to the goods.

A summary of proposals for the amendment of the Hague Rules

Seaworthiness

In many countries the interpretation of the phrase "before and at the beginning of the voyage" contained in Article III paragraph 1 of The Hague Rules have, in the views of the UNCTAD Shipping Committee, led to an unreasonable result, and the term "voyage" is interpreted as a single bill of lading voyage, regardless of the number of stops the ship may make at ports along the way. For example, a carrier whose ship takes on cargo at ports A, B, and C, and then sinks because the vessel was unseaworthy on leaving the port C, becomes liable only to the cargo owners who shipped from port C, and not to those who shipped from ports A and B, provided that the vessel was seaworthy when it left those ports. The Committee reached the conclusion that the Rule would be more simple and reasonable if it were amended to require the carrier to exercise due diligence to provide a seaworthy vessel upon leaving every port of call, and throughout the voyage, and to make the carrier liable for all cargo damage, regardless of where loaded, if the carrier should fail to comply with the Rules.

There is uncertainty over the interaction between the carrier's duty towards the cargo expressed in Article III paragraph 2 and the exemptions from liability contained in Article III paragraph 2 and the exemptions from liability contained in Article IV paragraph 2, this uncertainty being complicated by the statement in Article III paragraph 2 that it is subject to the provisions of Article IV. It was felt that this problem would be relieved if Article III paragraph 2 were amended to state clearly that the carrier must comply with its requirements in order to escape liability, and that these requirements are not affected by Article IV paragraph 2.

Commencement of proceedings

The Committee dealing with this subject had much to say in regard to the one year limitation period contained in the Rules and noted that it is not clear whether the one year limitation period for the commencement of proceedings begins to run from the delivery of the goods or from the date of the discharge of the goods. If the Rules were amended to apply to the entire period during which the goods are in the carrier's custody, then the time limitation period would begin to run from "delivery" and, in the opinion of the Committee, the uncertainty would then be resolved. On the other hand, in the event that the Rules are not amended in this way then, the Committee observe, it would still be useful to amend Article III paragraph 6 to clarify that "delivery" means the moment when the consignee received, or should receive, the goods. In this particular connection the Committee recommend that Article III paragraph 6 should be amended further to state that it would be sufficient for proceedings to be brought in any jurisdiction having reasonably close connection with the contract of carriage, such as the country of shipment or of destination. In addition, the cargo interests should not be restricted to bring the proceedings in a particular jurisdiction as the carrier commonly requires in the present day conditions of the bill of lading.

In this same connection there is some question as to whether the word "suit" in Article III paragraph 6 includes arbitration proceedings. The Committee took the view that to include arbitration proceedings could be unfair to consignees when the bill of lading has been issued under a charter-party, and recommend that the Rule be amended to exclude arbitration proceedings from the word "suit". In some jurisdictions the one year period of limitation for proceedings ceases to apply when the contract of carriage has been nullified by an unjustifiable deviation from the contemplated voyage, and in other countries it continues to apply because of the words "in any event". The clarification of "in any event" was called for.

Navigation

Dealing with the provisions of Article IV paragraph 2(a) which exempts the carrier from liability in respect of cargo loss or damage caused by "negligence in the navigation or the management of the ship", the Committee summarised their detailed views on this by stating that this is an anachronism, which today causes great confusion and much litigation over what is "management of ship" as opposed to care of the cargo, allowing carriers to escape liability for the negligence of their servants in a large number of cases. Hence their recommendations for the abolishment of the exception.

Fire

On the issue of the carrier's exemption from liability for cargo loss or damage caused by fire, contained in Article IV paragraph 2(b), this was thought to raise three problems which might be resolved by amendments to the Rules as detailed earlier. In the first place the view was taken that the exception could be eliminated, or at least limited severely, in view of the fact that modern ships are required by law to carry extensive fire protection equipment, and can maintain radio contact with shore authorities or other vessels at sea. Secondly there was the question as to whether the Rules should be amended to prevent local fire statutes in various countries from granting to the carrier a wider immunity in case of fire than he would enjoy under the Rules. Thirdly there was the question as to whether any amendment to the Rules should make it clear that the burden is upon the carrier to show how the fire was caused, and to bring himself within the exception. In the case that the carrier could not prove the cause of the fire then it was felt that he should remain liable for the cargo or damage.

Perils of the sea

In the case of the exception from liability in the case of cargo loss or damage caused by perils of the sea, which exception is contained in Article IV paragraph 2(c), it was felt that the exception was in vague terms and subject to widely varying interpretations. They concluded that it perhaps becomes an anachronism for similar reasons as those for the exception in respect of negligent navigation.

Shipper's act or omission

The exception contained in Article IV paragraph 2(i) which grants the carrier exemption from liability in respect of cargo loss or damage caused by an "act of omission of the shipper," which the Committee thought should be defined more precisely, in order to prevent carriers from disclaiming liability on this ground when there has merely been a misdescription of the goods or some other trivial lapse on the part of the shippers, quite unconnected with the cause of loss or damage to cargo.

Demise clauses

In summarising their views on the need for the revision of the Hague Rules, the Committee stated that their first concern was Article 1(a) of the Rules regarding the definition of "carrier". This raised two uncertainties (a) whether persons, such as shipping and forwarding agents who issue bills of lading, might be considered "carriers" for the purpose of the operation of the Rules, and (b) whether the shipowner or the charterer is liable as "carrier" when a ship has been chartered and the bill of lading contains a "demise clause". It was thought that the first question could be resolved by amending the definition of "carrier". Since charterers can limit their liability in the same way as shipowners, the demise clause has become a confusing anachronism and the Rules should be amended to the extent that "demise clauses" are invalid.

Contract of carriage

Article 1(b) contains the phrase "in so far as such document relates to the carriage of goods by sea" and the Committee felt that the Rules should be extended to cover the period when the goods are in the carrier's custody before loading and after discharge.

Deck cargoes

The definition of "goods" in Article 1(c) excludes deck cargo and live animals, so that the Rules do not apply to those items. In the opinion of the Committee there is no justification for maintaining this exclusion, in that if it were abolished carriers would still be protected adequately by the exceptions in the Rules and the limitation of liability. Moreover a large number of containers are now carried on deck and it appears reasonable that the same principles should apply to containers carried on deck as to those carried below deck. Therefore, the definition of "Goods" should be amended to include all goods whether carried on deck or not, including live animals.

Definition of ship

The Committee raise an important matter with regard to Article 1(d) namely the definition of "ship", in that it is doubtful whether the definition includes barges and lighters which are used to load and discharge vessels. In their opinion the Rules should apply to lightering operations in cases where the carrier owns or operates the barges or lighters as part of his contract of carriage, and the Rules should be amended so that the definition of "ship" includes such craft.

Period of application of Rules

Problems also arose over the definition of the period of carriage during which the Hague Rules are to apply, which is defined as " . . . from the time . . . goods are loaded on" until "they are discharged from the ship." The definition raises two problems: firstly, that the Rules do not apply to periods when the goods may be in the carrier's custody before loading and after discharge, and that during those periods the carrier may contract out of liability to the extent allowed by local law. Secondly, the terms "before loading" and "after discharge" are not sufficiently precise to define the moment at which the Rules begin and cease to apply.

In the opinion of the Committee there was no justification for allowing carriers to escape liability for loss or damage to goods in their possession before and after the "carriage of goods" period, and that both of these problems would be resolved if the Rules were amended to apply to the entire period while the goods are under the control or custody of the carrier. On the other hand, if the period during which the Rules apply was not extended, then the terms "loading" and "discharge" should be so clarified as to mean the handling of goods from shore or ship's tackle in the port of loading or ship's tackle at discharge.

If this alternative were to be adopted it would still be difficult for cargo owners to recover for loss or damage caused where the goods are in the custody of shore bailees, and the need would exist to uniformly prevent shore bailees from limiting their duty of care, or contracting out of liability. In this connection reference should be made to the recommendations of the Committee that the Rules should apply to the entire period during which the goods are in the control or custody of the carrier, his agents or servants.

Non negotiable receipts

The Hague Rules, by reason of the provisions of Article VI, do not apply to "non-negotiable receipts" provided that certain conditions are fulfilled, one of those conditions being that the carriage must not be an "ordinary commercial shipment made in the ordinary course of trade". It should also be mentioned that the Rules are not applicable to charter-parties, but nevertheless apply to bills of lading issued pursuant to a charter-party. As pointed out earlier, serious difficulties are often encountered by charterers, shippers, carriers and receivers in identifying their liabilities when the terms of the charter-party are incorporated into bills of lading. It was recommended that both of these matters should be clarified by amendments to the Rules.

Measure of damages

At the present time the measure of damages to which a cargo owner is entitled in the event of loss or damage to his goods, depends upon the market value or the normal value which is often difficult to establish and has led to litigation to decide the question in the individual cases concerned. The Committee took the view that this uncertainty would be removed by the adoption of more precise standards of measurement, such as the c.i.f. value plus a percentage for profit, or invoice value plus freight, insurance and a percentage for profit.

Strikes

On the exception in respect of loss or damage arising from strikes contained in Article IV paragraph 2(j), the Committee commented that carriers too readily take advantage of the exception in order to justify route deviations in situations which are not in fact sufficiently serious to warrant them. The Committee decided that the Rules should be amended to provide guide lines for determining in what cases a strike is sufficiently serious to justify a deviation from the itinerary, and to ensure that the interest of all parties is considered in making this determination.

Inherent Vice

The burden and method of proving inherent vice of the goods referred to in Article IV paragraph 2(m) of the Rules should, in the opinion of the Committee, be clarified by amendment and the Rules should mention specifically customary tolerances as an "inherent vice" by reason of which the carrier is excused from liability.

Insufficiency of packing

The question of liability for loss or damage arising out of "insufficiency of packing" is dealt with in Article IV paragraph 2(n) and the Committee took the view that it was not clear in what circumstances carriers could claim exemption from this cause. In addition, it was not clear precisely what type of notation in the bill of lading is effective for claiming this exception. These points, the Committee said, must be clarified by amendments.

Latent defects

With regard to the exception in respect of losses arising out of "latent defects", contained in Article IV paragraph 2(p) the Committee took the view that this exception should be eliminated so that it could be claimed, if at all, only under Article IV paragraph 2(q), the "catch all" exception.

Act of God — Act of War — etc.

There are a number of other exceptions contained in Article IV paragraph 2, which the Committee did not deal with in detail and therefore, have not been discussed in detail earlier. These exceptions are contained in paragraphs 2(d), (e), (f), (g), (h), (k), (l), (o). Paragraph 2(d) provides that neither the carrier nor the ship shall be responsible for cargo loss or damage arising out of Act of God. (e) Provides similarly for Act of War. (f) Public enemies. (g) Arrest or restraint of princes, rulers, or people, or seizure under legal process. (h) Quarantine restrictions. (k) Riots and civil commotions. (1) Saving or attempting to save life or property at sea, and (o) Insufficiency or inadequacy of marks. UNCTAD recommend that all these exceptions be eliminated since the circumstances to which they refer can again be covered by 2(q), the "catch all" exception.

Problem of interaction between Article III(2) and Article IV(2)

It will have been noted that there is a problem of interaction between the provisions in Article III paragraph (2) regarding the carrier's duties and the catalogue of exceptions contained in Article IV paragraph 2. This has not been satisfactorily resolved, so that it is often uncertain what each party must prove in order to prevail. This uncertainty, the Committee recommended, should be removed through appropriate amendments to clarify the matter of the burden of proof. It was reasonable, the Committee said, that the carrier should be required to prove both his compliance with the provisions of Article III paragraph 2, and his exemption under one of the provisions of Article IV paragraph 2.

Deviation

The Hague Rules neither define "deviation", as expressed in Article IV paragraph 4, nor do they state the consequences of an unreasonable deviation. In the result, the whole subject is clouded with uncertainty and it is extremely difficult for cargo owners to prove that an "unreasonable deviation" caused their loss. In summarising their detailed views already discussed in earlier sections in this book, the Committee took the view that there are at least two ways in which the problem could be clarified and simplied, namely, (a) the Rules to be amended to state that a deviation is to be presumed to be unjustified unless the carrier proves that the compelling conditions forced him to deviate for the benefit of the ship and the cargo, and (b) clauses similar to those found in the United States Carriage of Goods by Sea Act, discussed earlier in this book, might be added to Article IV. See also notes under Delay in delivery.

Limitation of liability

In summarising their views on the provisions of Article IV paragraph 5, which limits the carrier's liability to 100 pounds sterling per package or unit, the Committee commented that the phrase "per package or unit" has caused considerable uncertainty, principally because (a) there are significant departures from the Rules in the Carriage of Goods by Sea Acts of many countries, (b) because it is not clear whether "unit" should mean a unit of goods or the weight of volume unit by which freight is calculated, (c) the term "package or unit" does not always fit the wide variety of forms in which goods may be shipped, and in some cases the number of packages may differ from the number of units and (d) it is not clear whether a "container" or "pallet" constitutes a single "package".

It was felt that these difficulties would be relieved somewhat if the Rules were amended to define the terms "package" and "unit" more precisely. In making this recommendation the Committee added that merely to increase the limitation amount is not sufficient to resolve the problems and remove the uncertainties, all of which have been dealt with earlier.

SECTION III

THE HAMBURG RULES

As passed by the Final Act of the United Nations Conference on the Carriage of Goods by Sea, at Hamburg 6–31 March 1978

In this section the Hamburg Rules are discussed Article by Article. At the same time opportunity has been taken to afford an Article-by-Article comparison with the Hague Rules illustrating the amendments thereto, and reasons therefore.

PART I. GENERAL PROVISIONS

Article 1 — Definitions

In this Convention:

1. "Carrier" means any person by whom or in whose name a contract of carriage of goods by sea has been concluded with a shipper.

2. "Actual carrier" means any person to whom the performance of the carriage of the goods, or of part of the carriage, has been entrusted by the carrier, and includes any other person to whom such performance has been entrusted.

3. "Shipper" means any person by whom or in whose name or on whose behalf a contract of carriage of goods by sea has been concluded with a carrier, or any person by whom or in whose name or on whose behalf the goods are actually delivered to the carrier in relation to the contract of carriage by sea.

4. "Consignee" means the person entitled to take delivery of the goods.

5. "Goods" includes live animals; where the goods are consolidated in a container, pallet or similar article of transport or where they are packed, "goods" includes such articles of transport or packaging if supplied by the shipper.

6. "Contract of carriage by sea" means any contract whereby the carrier undertakes against payment of freight to carry goods by sea from one port to another; however, a contract which involves carriage by sea and also carriage by some other means is deemed to be a contract of carriage by sea for the purposes of this Convention only in so far as it relates to the carriage by sea.

7. "Bill of lading" means a document which evidences a contract of carriage by sea and the taking over or loading of the goods by the carrier, and by which the carrier undertakes to deliver the goods against surrender of the document. A provision in the document that the goods are to be delivered to the order of a named person, or to order, or to bearer, constitutes such an undertaking.

8. *"Writing" includes,* inter alia, *telegram and telex.*

Article 1 of the Hague Rules, which contains the definitions, provides that a "carrier" includes the owner or the charterer who enters into a contract of carriage with a shipper. This is amended in Article 1 paragraph 1 of the Hamburg Rules to read "carrier" meaning any person by whom, or in whose name, a contract of carriage of goods by sea has been concluded with a shipper. Underlying this alteration is the fact that, the definition raises two points for consideration: (1) Whether any person other than the owner or the charterer can be a carrier and (2) Who is liable as "carrier" when vessels are chartered? The word "includes" in the Hague Rules definition does suggest that others may be considered carriers. On the second point, there is presently considerable uncertainty where a vessel is time or voyage chartered and a bill of lading is issued with the name of the charterers heading the document. This bill of lading will, generally speaking, contain a demise clause, providing that if the ship is not owned or chartered by demise to the company or line by whom the bill of lading is issued, the bill of lading takes effect only as a contract with the owner or demise charterer, as the case may be, as principal made through the agency of the said company or line who act as agents only and shall be under no responsibility whatsoever in respect thereof.

Much injustice has sometimes been caused to cargo interests when a court has held that a cargo owner cannot sue the owner of a ship because he is not considered to be the "carrier", and the charterers have been permitted to avoid liability because they were not to be considered the "carrier" either. By the use of these demise clauses, the line is allowed to substitute a new carrier, and cargo interests find that the line has not agreed to carry their goods at all, but merely to find a suitable carrier. In the result, shipping lines using bills of lading on their own forms and headings, though the vessel is not owned by them, escape liability against cargo interests, and when perhaps they have brought proceedings against the parties who issued the bill of lading, in order to protect the one year time bar, it is found too late that the action has been brought against the wrong parties and the claim against the proper parties, the owners of the ship, is now time-barred. As will be seen from the drafting of the new Convention clause, the cargo interests may now be protected against such situations by the definition "carrier" as defined in Article I of the Hamburg Rules.

Article 1 paragraph 2 of the new Convention introduces a new and additional definition "Actual carrier", which, in the light of the provisions of Article 10, would seem to make the position even more clear. Article 10 captioned "Liability of the carrier and actual carrier" provides in paragraph 1 that "Where the performance of the carriage or part thereof has been entrusted to an actual carrier, whether or not in pursuance of a liberty under the contract of carriage by sea to do so, the carrier nevertheless remains responsible for the entire carriage according to the provisions of this Convention. The carrier is responsible, in relation to the carriage performed by the actual carrier, for the acts and omissions of the actual carrier and of his servants and agents acting within the scope of their employment".

Article 1 paragraph 3 is a new and additional provision which has no counter part in the Hague Rules.

Article 1 paragraph 4 is also a new additional definition.

Article 1 paragraph 5 defines "Goods", which drastically amends its counterpart in the Hague Rules, at the same time including provisions relative to the modern containerised method of transportation of goods.

In the Hague Rules, as they presently stand, the definition of goods is contained in Article 1 (c) which states that the term "goods" includes goods, wares, merchandises, and articles of every kind whatsoever, except live animals and cargo carried on deck. Behind this alteration was the conviction that there was no justification for the definition "goods" as presently defined in the Hague Rules, and the thought that, if the definition were abolished, carriers would still be protected adequately by the exceptions and the limitation of liability. Furthermore, in the new concept of container carriage, a large number of containers are now carried on deck, and it seems reasonable that the same principles should apply to containers carried on deck as to those carried below.

Article 1 paragraph 6 of the Hamburg Rules defines "Contract of carriage by sea" revising completely the definition "Contract of carriage" contained in the Hague Rules as they presently exist namely "Contract of carriage" applies only to contracts of carriage covered by a bill of lading or any similar document of title in so far as such document relates to the carriage of goods by sea, including any bill of lading or any similar document as aforesaid issued under or pursuant to a charter-party from the moment at which such bill of lading or similar document of title regulates the relations between a carrier and a holder of same.

In the Hamburg Rules paragraph 6 of Article 1 defines "Contract of Carriage by sea" and reads — means any contract whereby the carrier undertakes against payment of freight to carry goods by sea from one port to another; however, a contract which involves carriage by sea and also carriage by some other means is deemed to be a contract of carriage by sea for the purposes of this Convention only in so far as it relates to the carriage by sea.

The Hague Rules make the Rules obligatory only when bills of lading are issued, but the Hamburg Rules, by this definition, would seem to apply to any contract whereby the carrier undertakes against payment of freight to carry goods from one port to another.

Article 1 paragraph 7 of the Hamburg Rules defines "Bill of Lading" whereas the Hague Rules contain no such definition.

Although in the Hague Rules there is no definition of "Bill of lading", "Contract of Carriage" is defined as applying only to contracts of carriage covered by bill of lading or any similar document of title, in so far as such document relates to the carriage of goods by sea, including any bill of lading or similar document issued under or pursuant to a charter-party from the moment at which such bill of lading or similar document of title, regulates the relations between a carrier and a holder of the same.

With regard to bills of lading issued pursuant to charter-parties, the position is covered in Article 2 of the Hamburg Rules.

The definition of "Bill of lading" in the Hamburg Rules seems to recognise the principal purpose of that document in enabling the owner of the goods to which it relates, to dispose of them rapidly upon the arrival of the vessel at the port of discharge.

Finally, there is contained in Article 1 (7) a new definition, "Writing", which includes, "inter alia, telegram and telex." The inclusion of this definition has no doubt been necessary in the light of modern day communications. For example, Article III paragraph 6 of the Rules as they presently exist, provides that unless notice of loss and the general nature of such loss or damage be given "in writing" to the carrier or his agent at the port of discharge. . . ."

Two other definitions contained in the Hague Rules in their present form have also been dropped, namely "Ship" and "Carriage of Goods". With regard to the former, the Committee felt that this definition, which covers "any vessel used for the carriage of goods by sea", raised the question as to whether the Rules applied to barges or lighters when used for loading or discharging vessels. The view was taken that if barges or lighters are not to be considered "ships", within the meaning of the definition, then the Hague Rules may not apply during the time when goods are on board such barges or lighters. In this connection, reference is made to the definition "Carriage of Goods", which is presently defined in the Hague Rules as covering the period from the time that the goods are loaded to the time when they are discharged from the ship, which might have the effect of further limiting the application of the Rules. It was also felt that the Rules should apply to lightering operations when the carrier owns or operates barges or lighters.

A number of factors contributed to the decision to delete the present definition of "Carriage of Goods", including the question of when loading starts and discharge ceases, and the question of the legal position before loading and after discharge. The Committee had in mind the effect of Article VII of the Hague Rules, which provides that nothing in the Rules "shall prevent a carrier or a shipper from entering into any agreement, stipulation, condition, reservation or exemption as to the responsibility and liability of the carrier or the ship for the loss of or damage to or in connection with the custody and care and handling of goods prior to the loading and subsequent to the discharge from the ship on which the goods are carried by sea."

The committee took the view that this Rule allowed freedom of contract in respect of the period before loading and after discharge, and that, unless debarred from doing so by domestic law, the carrier could insert wide exception clauses in the bill of lading to contract out his duty as a bailee while goods are in his custody during these periods. The question of where loading commences and discharge ceases is central to an understanding of the law of ocean carriage, and these uncertainties, the Committee felt, focused attention on what has been called the "before and after problem," i.e. who remains responsible, and to what extent, for the care of the cargo before loading and after discharge, it being understood that after loading and before discharge, the goods would be in the care of the ocean carrier.

The fact is that the words "loading" and "discharge" do not fit the widely varying procedures followed in different ports and with different goods, and it was these considerations that led, in part, to the dropping of the definition "Carriage of Goods".

However, the Hamburg Rules do deal with this problem of loading and discharge and the question of the carrier's liability before loading and after discharge, but in a different way which will become clear when looking at other Articles in the Hamburg Rules.

Article 2 — Scope of application

1. The provisions of this Convention are applicable to all contracts of carriage by sea between two different States, if:

(a) the port of loading as provided for in the contract of carriage by sea is located in a Contracting State, or

(b) the port of discharge as provided for in the contract of carriage by sea is located in a Contracting State, or

(c) one of the optional ports of discharge provided for in the contract of carriage by sea is the actual port of discharge and such port is located in a Contracting State, or

(d) the bill of lading or other document evidencing the contract of carriage by sea is issued in a Contracting State, or

(e) the bill of lading or other document evidencing the contract of carriage by sea provides that the provisions of this Convention or the legislation of any State giving effect to them are to govern the contract.

2. The provisions of this Convention are applicable without regard to the nationality of the ship, the carrier, the actual carrier, the shipper, the consignee or any other interested person.

3. The provisions of this Convention are not applicable to charter-parties. However, where a bill of lading is issued pursuant to a charter-party, the provisions of the Convention apply to such a bill of lading if it governs the relation between the carrier and the holder of the bill of lading, not being the charterer.

4. If a contract provides for future carriage of goods in a series of shipments during an agreed period, the provisions of this Convention apply to each shipment. However, where a shipment is made under a charter-party, the provisions of paragraph 3 of this article apply.

Article 2 of the Hamburg Rules covers the scope of application. This new rule has the effect of cancelling out Article II of the Hague Rules which is captioned "Risks" and provides in its terms that, subject to the provisions of Article VI, under every contract of carriage of goods by sea (the "contract of carriage" being defined in Article I(b) (which has been amended in the Hamburg Rules) the carrier, in relation to the loading, handling, stowage, carriage, custody, care and discharge of such goods, shall be subject to the responsibilities, and entitled to the rights and immunities contained in the Rules. Article VI gives the carrier liberty to contract in any terms as regards "particular" goods, provided that no bill of lading is issued and the terms agreed are embodied in a non-negotiable receipt. The Article does not, however, apply to ordinary shipments made in the ordinary course of trade, but only to shipments where the character or condition of the goods to be carried, or the circumstances, terms and conditions under which the carriage is to be performed, are such as to reasonably justify a special agreement.

After the Hague Rules were finally agreed at the Brussels Convention in 1924, they were immediately given the effect of law in the United Kingdom by the passing of the Carriage of Goods by Sea Act, 1924, which came into effect on the 1st January, 1925. Similar legislation in the British Empire, as it then was, quickly followed, but outside the Empire nations, Belgium was the only country to take early action giving effect to the Rules which became operative in 1929. The United States, for example, did not give legal effect to the Rules until 1936. This was because the Brussels Conference did not make the Rules mandatory, and it was left to the nations themselves to decide when and if the Rules were to have the force of law. In Article 2 paragraph 1 of the Hamburg Rules it seems that, when the Hamburg Rules are finally given effect, they will be given mandatory effect between the Contracting States by reason of the provisions of this Article, subject to the provisions of Article 1(a), (b), (c), (d), (e). One other point that should be mentioned here is the fact that, whereas the original Hague Rules were, by the provisions of the Carriage of Goods by Sea Act, made applicable only to bills of lading covering outward shipments from the U.K., certain other countries, including Belgium and the United States, made the Rules applicable to bills of lading both in respect of shipments to and from those countries, the effect of which has been clearly made evident over the years. Under the provisions of Article 2, paragraph 1, of the Hamburg Rules the Rules are applicable "to all contracts of carriage between two ports in two different States", subject to 1(a), (b), (c), (d), (e). However, it would seem that the present Hague Rules will apply until such time as the non-Contracting States voluntarily adopt the Rules, that is when the bill of lading is not issued in a contracting State. This may present a problem when a claim for cargo loss or damage is made at a port of discharge not within a contracting State.

Article 2 paragraph 2 of the Hamburg Rules states that the provisions of the Convention are applicable without regard to the nationality of the ship, the carrier, the actual carrier, the shipper, the consignee or any other interested persons. Paragraph 3 of this Article provides that the provisions of the Convention shall not be applicable to charter-parties. However where a bill of lading is issued pursuant to a charter-party, the provisions of the Convention will apply to such bill of lading if it governs the relations between the carrier and the holder of the bill of lading, not being the charter. In the Hague Rules the provision with regard to charter-parties was contained in the definition "Contract of Carriage" which, the definition states, applies only to contracts of carriage covered by a bill of lading or any similar document of title, in so far as such document relates to the carriage of goods by sea, including any bill of lading or any similar document as aforesaid issued under or pursuant to a charter-party, from the moment at which such bill of lading or similar document of title regulates the relations between a carrier and a holder of same. This amended Rule in the Hamburg Rules should be read in conjunction with Article 1 paragraphs (1) and (2) of the Hamburg Rules which define "Carrier" and "Actual Carrier", the reason for which will be illustrated when dealing with other new provisions in the Rules later.

Paragraph 4 of Article 2 has no counterpart in the Hague Rules and would seem to have in mind a contract for the carriage of goods by sea from port A to port B with transhipment into other vessels at some port or ports en route.

Article 3 — Interpretation of the Convention

In the interpretation and application of the provisions of this Convention regard shall be had to its international character and to the need to promote uniformity.

It is difficult to see the manner in which this Article can be made to operate since different nations will no doubt need to apply the Rules having regard to the interpretation of the Rules in the light of their own legal precedents.

PART II. LIABILITY OF THE CARRIER

Article 4 — Period of responsibility

1. The responsibility of the carrier for the goods under this Convention covers the period during which the carrier is in charge of the goods at the port of loading, during the carriage and at the port of discharge.

2. For the purpose of paragraph 1 of this article, the carrier is deemed to be in charge of the goods.

(a) from the time he has taken over the goods from:
  (i) the shipper, or a person acting on his behalf; or
  (ii) an authority or other third party to whom, pursuant to law or regulations applicable at the port of loading, the goods must be handed over for shipment;

(b) until the time he has delivered the goods:
  (i) by handing over the goods to the consignee; or
  (ii) in cases where the consignee does not receive the goods from the carrier, by placing them at the disposal of the consignee in accordance with the contract or with the law or with the usage of the particular trade, applicable at the port of discharge; or
  (iii) by handing over the goods to an authority or other third party to whom, pursuant to law or regulations applicable at the port of discharge, the goods must be handed over.

3. In paragraphs 1 and 2 of this article, reference to the carrier or to the consignee means, in addition to the carrier or the consignee, the servants or agents, respectively of the carrier or the consignee.

The period of responsibility in the Hague rules was shortly stated, in Article 1 (e), as covering the period of time from the time when the goods are loaded on, to the time when they are discharged from the ship. However, in this context, it has to be remembered that Article III paragraph 2 of the Hague rules provides, amongst other things, that the carrier shall properly and carefully load the goods carried, which covers the actual loading of the goods.

The Shipping Committee of the United Nations Conference on Trade and Development found that the definition in Article 1(e) raised two particular problems, the first being that the Rules did not apply to periods when the goods may be in the carrier's custody before loading and after discharge, and that during those periods the carrier may contract out of liability to the extent allowed by local laws. The second was that the terms "before loading" and "after discharge" were not sufficiently precise to define the moments at which the rules begin and cease to apply.

The Committee took the view that there appeared to be no sufficient justification for allowing carriers to escape liability for loss or damage to goods in their possession before and after the "carriage of goods" period. The recommendation was that both of these problems could be resolved if the rules were amended to apply during the entire period that the goods are under the control or custody of the carrier. The Committee felt that if the period during which the Rules apply was not extended, then it might be clarified that the terms "loading" and "discharge" mean the handling of the goods from shore or ship's tackle in the port of discharge, all cases in which the carrier is responsible for loading and discharging the goods.

It was thought that if this alternative were to be adopted, it would still be difficult for cargo owners to recover for loss or damage caused when the goods were in the custody of shore bailees. Therefore, the conclusion was reached that the need would exist to prevent uniformly shore bailees from limiting their duty of care, or of contracting out of liability for the full value of the goods.

In this connection, it must also be remembered that Article 7 of the Hague Rules provides that the parties may enter into any agreement regarding the carrier's responsibility for the goods "prior to the loading on, and subsequent to the discharge" from the ship.

In this context, uncertainty has been caused as to when loading begins and discharge ceases, and the legal position before loading and after discharge.

Common practice has been to apply the rules from ship's tackle to tackle, that is from the moment when the ship's tackle is hooked on to cargo at the ports of loading, until the moment when the cargo is laid down and the hook of the tackle released at the discharge port, but even to this day the position as to when the carrier's liability begins and ceases, particularly if lighterage is concerned, is by no means clear. When shore tackle is used, the present rules have been traditionally held to apply, in some countries, from the moment when cargo crosses the ship's rail, but the laws of the more important maritime nations mostly recognise that the responsibility for the actual operation of loading is that of the carrier, and similarly the responsibility of the carrier continues until the goods have been properly discharged. When goods are being loaded from or into lighters, loading is considered, in some countries, to commence when the goods are hooked into the tackle, and that discharge does not cease until the process of unloading all the goods into the lighter has been completed.

There are so many different methods of cargo handling that it is difficult to generalise on this topic. For example, in the case of loading or discharging through a chute or pipe, does the loading commence when the cargo reaches the ship's end of the chute or pipe and is discharge complete at the last flange of the ship? These are some of the problems that the Committee had before them, prior to their recommendations leading to the new definition of the period of responsibility. As mentioned above, Article 7 of the Hague Rules allows freedom of contract in respect of the period before loading and after discharging, and, unless debarred from so doing by domestic law, the carrier can insert wide exemption clauses to contract out of his duty as bailee while goods are in his custody during these periods. This, however, is not so in the United States, where the Harter Act still governs before loading and after discharge of the goods, nullifying the effect of negligence clauses while the goods are in the carrier's custody up to the time of delivery to the consignee or his agents. All of these considerations have led to the Hamburg amendments in the rules in relation to the "period of responsibility".

In the result, paragraph (1) of Article 4 of the Hamburg Rules provides that the responsibility of the carrier for the goods under this Convention covers the period during which the carrier is in charge of the goods at the port of loading, during the carriage, and at the port of discharge.

The manner in which the Hamburg Rules have extended the period of responsibility of the carrier as defined in the Hague Rules is immediately apparent, in that under the Hague Rules the period is limited to the commencement of the loading of the goods to the completion of the discharging operations, under the Hamburg Rules the responsibility of the carrier for the goods covers the period during which the carrier is in charge of the goods at the port of loading and at the port of discharge, as provided for in paragraph 1 of Article 4. There then follows, in paragraph 2 of this Article the time at which the carrier is deemed to have taken over the goods from the shipper or a person acting on his behalf, or an authority or other third party to whom, pursuant to law or regulations applicable at the port of loading, the goods must be handed over for shipment. Paragraph 2 of Article 4 then goes on to provide for the time at which the carrier is to be deemed to have delivered the goods, by handing over the goods to the consignee, or, in cases where the carrier does not receive the goods from the shipper, by placing them at the disposal of the consignee in accordance with the contract or with the law or with the usage of the particular trade, applicable at the port of discharge, or by handing over the goods to an authority or other third party to whom, pursuant to law or regulations applicable at the port of discharge, the goods must be handed over.

So far as the period prior to the commencement of the voyage is concerned one may anticipate many problems arising out of the provisions of Article 4 because the carrier may, in certain circumstances, have taken over the goods before they even reach the docks for the purpose of loading on board the vessel. For example the carrier may send a container to a shipper's warehouse inland and there take over the goods, or the carrier may take over the goods by collection from the shipper's or packer's warehouse. Although it is doubtful that the

Hamburg Rules were intended to extend the period of the responsibility for the goods to such limits the issue would appear to be wide open for argument and dispute. Problems may also arise in the determination of the point at which the carrier can be deemed to have delivered the goods because, unlike the Hague Rules, where the responsibility of the carrier ceases from the time of the completion of the discharge of the goods at the port of discharge, the Hamburg Rules would appear to have extended the period of responsibility for the goods way beyond that period to the time when the carrier has actually handed over the goods to the consignee, or in cases where the consignee does not himself receive the goods from the carrier, by placing them at the disposal of the consignee in accordance with the contract, or with the law or with the usage of the particular trade, applicable at the port of discharge, or by handing over the goods to an authority or other third party to whom, pursuant to law or regulations applicable at the port of discharge, the goods must be handed over. In the background to extension of the period of the responsibility of the carrier beyond the time of the discharge of the goods from the ship, there was no doubt in mind, amongst many other things, the provisions of the Harter Act, 1893 which places upon the carrier the responsibility for the "proper delivery of the goods", but although the Hamburg Rules have defined "delivery", it may be found very difficult in practice to determine the question as to when the goods have been delivered, in the circumstances of any particular case, within the meaning of Article 4.

Paragraph 3 of Article 4 provides that in paragraphs 1 and 2 of this article, reference to the carrier or to the consignee means, in addition to the carrier or the consignee, the servants or agents, respectively of the carrier or the consignee. The reference to the servants or agents of the carrier brings the Hamburg Rules into line with the Hague Rules and in this connection reference must be made to certain of the test cases brought before the Courts following upon the introduction of the Hague Rules, when the Courts decided that the reference to "servants or agents of the carrier" in the Hague Rules included stevedores and others, and the Hamburg Rules will no doubt be construed in connection with paragraph 3 of Article 4 along the same lines as the precedents laid down by the Courts in the interpretation and construction of the Hague Rules.

Article 5 — Basis of liability

1. The carrier is liable for loss resulting from loss of or damage to the goods, as well as from delay in delivery, if the occurrence which caused the loss, damage or delay took place while the goods were in his charge as defined in article 4, unless the carrier proves that he, his servants or agents took all measures that could reasonably be required to avoid the occurrence and its consequences.

2. Delay in delivery occurs when the goods have not been delivered at the port of discharge provided for in the contract of carriage by sea within the time expressly agreed upon or, in the absence of such agreement, within the time which it would be reasonable to require of a diligent carrier, having regard to the circumstances of the case.

3. The person entitled to make a claim for the loss of goods may treat the goods as lost if they have not been delivered as required by article 4 within 60 consecutive days following the expiry of the time for delivery according to paragraph 2 of this article.

4. (a) The carrier is liable
>   *(i) for loss of or damage to the goods or delay in delivery caused by fire, if the claimant proves that the fire arose from fault or neglect on the part of the carrier, his servants or agents;*
>   *(ii) for such loss, damage or delay in delivery which is proved by the claimant to have resulted from the fault or neglect of the carrier, his servants or agents, in taking all measures that could reasonably be required to put out the fire and avoid or mitigate its consequences.*

>   *(b) In case of fire on board the ship affecting the goods, if the claimant or the carrier so desires, a survey in accordance with shipping practices must be held into the cause and circumstances of the fire, and a copy of the surveyor's report shall be made available on demand to the carrier and the claimant.*

5. With respect to live animals, the carrier is not liable for loss, damage or delay in delivery resulting from any special risks inherent in that kind of carriage. If the carrier proves that he has complied with any special instructions given to him by the shipper respecting the animals and that, in the circumstances of the case, the loss, damage or delay in delivery could be attributed to such risks, it is presumed that the loss, damage or delay in delivery was so caused, unless there is proof that all or a part of the loss, damage or delay in delivery resulted from fault or neglect on the part of the carrier, his servants or agents.

6. The carrier is not liable, except in general average, where loss, damage or delay in delivery resulted from measures to save life or from reasonable measures to save property at sea.

7. Where fault or neglect on the part of the carrier, his servants or agents combines with another cause to produce loss, damage or delay in delivery the carrier is liable only to the extent that the loss, damage or delay in delivery is attributable to such fault or neglect, provided that the carrier proves the amount of the loss, damage or delay in delivery not attributable thereto.

Paragraph 1 of Article 5 provides that the carrier is liable for loss resulting from loss of or damage to the goods, as well as from delay in delivery, if the occurrence which caused the loss, damage or delay took place while the goods were in his charge as defined in Article 4, unless the carrier proves that he, his servants or agents took all measures that could reasonably be required to avoid the occurrence and its consequences. Paragraph 2 of Article 5 provides that delay in delivery occurs when the goods have not been delivered at the port of discharge provided for in the contract of carriage by sea within the time expressly agreed upon or, in the absence of such agreement, within the time which it would be reasonable to require of a diligent carrier, having regard to the circumstances of the case.

These two paragraphs of Article 5 virtually replace Article III paragraphs 1 and 2 of the Hague Rules. Also gone are paragraphs 1 and 2 of Article IV of the Hague Rules, which provide a whole catalogue of exemptions from liability that the carrier presently enjoys. Article III paragraph 1 of the Hague Rules provides that the carrier shall be bound, before and at the beginning of the voyage, to exercise due diligence to make the ship seaworthy, properly man, equip, and supply the ship, and make the holds, refrigerating and cool chambers, and all other parts of the ship in which goods are carried, fit and safe for their reception, carriage and preservation. Paragraph 2 of Article III provides that, subject to the provisions of Article IV, the carrier shall properly and carefully load, handle, stow, carry, keep, care for and discharge the goods carried.

It might appear on the face of it that the carrier has been relieved of certain burdens under the Hamburg Rules, but a careful study of Article 5 paragraph 1 of the Hamburg Rules clearly indicates that this covers cargo loss or damage from whatever cause, and that the carrier will be liable unless he is able to discharge the burden of proof now placed upon him that he, his servants and agents, took all preventive measures reasonably required.

Under the Hague Rules if a ship sails in an unseaworthy condition, which causes loss or damage to goods, the carrier can avoid liability by proving that he exercised due diligence to make the vessel seaworthy before and at the beginning of the voyage, and it may sometimes be found that the vessel was in an unseaworthy state because of some latent defect not discoverable by due diligence. In such a case, the cargo interests would fail in their claim against the carrier. At the present time, the carrier would be liable for cargo loss or damage arising out of the negligence of his employees or independent contractors in making the ship seaworthy. It remains to be seen whether such parties will be deemed to be servants or agents of the carrier, but it is apparent that this must have been contemplated in the drafting of the new Rule. It should also be noted that the requirement of the exercise of due diligence to make the ship seaworthy "before and at the beginning of the voyage", has been dropped, no doubt for the reason that, when the Committee considered this Rule, they found that this provision often caused injustice. In many countries the term "voyage" is, perhaps quite naturally, termed the "bill of lading voyage". In other words, the vessel has left with certain cargo from port A and proceeds to port B where she loads further cargo, but leaves port B without having exercised due diligence to make the vessel seaworthy. In such a case, the owners of the cargo shipped at port A would be unable to recover for damage to cargo arising out of the failure to exercise due diligence at port B.

Article 5 of the Hamburg Rules would give the carrier no benefit of this kind.

With regard to the provision in Article III paragraph 2 of the Hague Rules, namely that the carrier shall properly and carefully load, handle, stow, carry, keep, care for and discharge the goods carried, there have been uncertainties in interpreting the terms "properly and carefully", in that it has been held that "properly" has a different meaning from "carefully". Further, this ruling is made subject to the provisions of Article IV of the present Rules, which lay down numerous exceptions from liability that the carrier may enjoy. When this matter was under consideration by the Committee, it was felt that the intention was to place an absolute duty on the carrier to fulfil the requirement that the carrier "shall properly and carefully load, stow, etc. the goods to be carried", and this duty should not be modified or lessened by the immunities granted to the carrier under the provisions of Article IV. In other words, the immunities should not be treated as excuses for failure to perform correctly the stipulated duties.

This provision in Article 5 of the Hamburg Rules once again takes care of the situation in the interest of the cargo. There is no definition of the carrier's duties in this respect, this having given way to a simple mandatory statement that the carrier shall be liable for loss or damage to the goods, unless he is able to prove that he or his agents or servants took all measures that could reasonably be required to avoid the occurrence and its consequences. On the other hand, it is provided in Article 4 of the Hamburg Rules that the responsibility of the carrier for the goods covers the period during which the carrier is in charge of the goods at the port of loading.

Once again Article 5 paragraph 1 of the Hamburg Rules would seem to take over, in that it is provided that if the occurrence which caused the loss or damage or delay in the cargo took place while the goods were in the carrier's charge, unless he proves that he, "his servants or agents" took all measures that could reasonably be required to avoid the occurrence and its consequences, then the carrier will be liable. Presumably, if the carrier employed other parties to carry out the loading of the vessel, and those parties did not take all measures that could reasonably be required to avoid the loss or damage, then the carrier would be liable.

There is no counterpart of Article 5 paragraph 2 in the Hague Rules, and this new condition provides that "Delay in delivery occurs when the goods have not been delivered at the port of discharge provided for in the contract of carriage by sea within the time expressly agreed upon or, in the absence of such agreement, within the time which it would be reasonable to require of a diligent carrier, having regard to the circumstances of the case.''

Delay in the delivery of the goods can arise out of many causes, such as deviations, strike or labour disturbances at the port of loading or discharge, accidents, perils of the sea etc., and the Hague Rules, carry in Article IV a whole catalogue of exceptions from liability which the carrier enjoys including loss or damage arising out of perils, dangers and accidents of the sea or other navigable waters, strikes or lock-outs or stoppage or restraint of labour from whatever cause, whether partial or general, any deviation in saving or attempting to save life or property at sea, or any reasonable deviation, negligence in the navigation or management of the ship. Presently, the carrier may escape liability for loss arising out of delay if he can show that the loss was caused by one of the excepted perils, but the Committee have scrapped them with the exception of "fire" and deviation, and now the carrier will be liable for loss arising out of delay unless he proves that he, his servants and agents took all measures to avoid the occurrence and its consequences, or the loss arose out of deviation arising out of measures to save life or reasonable measures to save property at sea (see paragraph 6 of Article 5).

The Committee, in reviewing the Rules, considered that the exception "Negligence in the navigation or management of the ship" was probably the most important in the "catalogue" of exceptions, since it exempted the carrier for loss or damage arising or resulting from the act, neglect, or default of the Master, mariner, pilot, or the servants of the carrier in the navigation or management of the ship. The exception has also been criticised by cargo interests because it causes uncertainty and confusion in attempting to form any conclusions as to exactly where the line is drawn between what does, and what does not, constitute an error of navigation and management of the ship. The Committee, in reviewing the Rule, felt that it should be removed, so that, in the event that delay should result from collision caused by the negligence of the carrying vessel, the carrier, under the new rule, would seem to be liable.

The exception in the Hague Rules giving the carrier immunity from liability in respect of loss resulting from "Perils, dangers and accidents of the sea or other navigable waters", also came under much criticism when the Rules were being reviewed, in that it is usually argued that this exemption covers accidents resulting from the impact of waves or other dangers inherent in navigation, such as storms, fog, strandings, collisions, etc. The Committee was of the opinion that the definition of "Perils of the Sea" was crucial because more fact than law is involved. In some jurisdictions, the exception has been strictly interpreted, in the sense that the peril must be one of an extraordinary nature preventing the vessel to be brought safely and timely into port by skilful and viligant mariners. On the other hand, some courts in other countries have taken a more lenient view, and it has been held that to constitute a peril of the sea the accident need not be of an extraordinary nature nor need it arise from an irresistible force. The Committee took the view that the exception could be omitted, and this has been done.

Strikes, labour disturbances and lockouts are, of course, a major cause of delay in the delivery of goods, and when the exception contained in the present Rules was being considered, the Committee took a very serious view of the extent that the carrier could gain immunity from liability for, amongst other things, delay in the delivery of the goods at their final destination. The strike exception is frequently used and has been the source of much complaint by cargo interests, and is often raised when the carrier decides to change his ports of call either to avoid a strike-bound port or to sail from such port to another to discharge the goods. Disagreements usually arise between carriers and cargo owners concerning the time that carriers take to assess the situation arising out of a strike, and the UNCTAD Committee found that cargo interests suffered because of the carriers' early decision that a situation was serious enough to warrant the sailing of a ship to another port, or to discharge the goods in an unsuitable place at the risk and expense of the cargo owners. A further complaint of cargo interests was that when a strike causes goods to be discharged or abandoned at a different port from that mentioned in the bill of lading, the cargo owners must bear the risk and expense of forwarding the goods to their destination. At the time of considering this position of cargo interests, the Committee took the view that the carrier, in making such a deviation, must comply with his duties, under the Rules, to take proper care of the goods, but nothing under the Hague Rules prevents the carrier discharging the goods at the nearest convenient port and there to rid himself as to the responsibility for the care and safe custody of the goods after discharge from his vessel. The exemption in respect of loss, or loss arising out of delay in the delivery of goods due to strikes or labour disturbances, has been of considerable benefit to the carrier, as has been made evident by the many Court decisions in the U.K. and in the United States, but under the provisions of the Hamburg Rules there is no provision for the exemption of the liability of the carrier in respect of loss resulting from delay caused by strikes or labour disturbances etc. Article 5 paragraphs (1) and (2) of the Hamburg Rules seem to make it quite clear that the carrier shall be liable for loss arising out of delay in the delivery of the goods unless the carrier proves that he, his servants and agents took all measures that could reasonably be required to avoid the occurrence and its consequences.

Paragraph 3 of Article 5 of the Hamburg Rules has no counterpart in the Hague Rules. Paragraph 3 of article 5 of the Hamburg Rules provides that the person entitled to make a claim for the loss of goods may treat the goods as lost when they have not been delivered, as required by Article 4, within 60 days following the expiry of the time for delivery according to paragraph 2 of Article 5. The latter, in turn, provides that delay in delivery occurs when the goods have not been delivered at the port of discharge provided for in the contract of carriage within the time expressly agreed upon or, in the absence of such an agreement, within the time which it would be reasonable to require of a diligent carrier, having regard to the circumstances of the case.

Paragraph 4 of Article 5 deals with the liability of the carrier in respect of cargo loss or damage caused by fire. The Hague Rules presently provide in Article IV Paragraph 2(b), that neither the carrier nor the ship shall be responsible for loss or damage arising or resulting from fire unless caused by the actual fault of the carrier. When this provision was under consideration, one of the questions raised was whether, having regard to the fact that modern ships are required by law to carry extensive fire protection equipment and to instal up-to-date equipment, and are already subject to many rules and regulations to prevent fire, the exception should be retained in the Rules at all. On the other hand, the question was asked whether the carrier should show how the fire was caused, and, if the cause could not be established, then perhaps the carrier should remain liable. Article 5 paragraph 4 of the Hamburg Rules does not seem to have been drafted with these thoughts predominantly in mind, for, in the new Rule, the carrier is liable for cargo loss or damage caused by fire, provided the cargo interests prove that the fire arose from fault or neglect on the part of the carrier, his servants or agents. No doubt the first thing that will strike the reader is that the onus of proof has been passed to the cargo claimant, whereas under the old Rule the onus of proof was upon the carrier to show that the fire arose without the fault or privity of the carrier. The onus of proof is a difficult burden to discharge and, throughout the whole of the exceptions contained in the existing Rules, that onus is upon the carrier to bring the loss within the exceptions and, but for this requirement, there would have been countless cases of cargo claimants failing to recover their loss.

Under this new rule in the Hamburg Rules the cargo owner may find that the discharge of this burden of proof a difficult matter in that it will almost always be the case that the information necessary to determine the cause of the fire will be in the hands of the carrier.

Article 5 paragraph 5 of the Hamburg Rules deals with the carriage of live animals, where the Hague Rules has been completely altered. This provision is presently dealt with in Article I paragraph (c) of the Hague Rules which defines "Goods" as including goods, wares, merchandises, and articles of every kind whatsoever, "except live animals . . .", so allowing the carrier to carry on his own terms. It is provided in the Hamburg Rules that, with respect to live animals, the carrier is not liable for loss, damage or delay in delivery resulting from any special risks inherent in that kind of carriage. If the carrier proves that he has complied with any special instructions given to him by the shipper respecting the animals and that, in the circumstances of the case, the loss, damage or delay in delivery could be attributed to such risks, it is presumed that the loss, damage or delay in delivery was so caused unless there is proof that all or a part of the loss, damage or delay in delivery resulted from fault or neglect on the part of the carrier, his servants or agents.

In the Hamburg Rules, there is introduced a new Rule in paragraph 6 relative to deviation but limiting the exception to measures to save life or reasonable measures to save property. The present Rule contained in Article IV paragraph 4 of the Hague Rules has been re-drafted. The Hague Rules provide that any deviation in saving or attempting to save life or property at sea, or any reasonable deviation, shall not be deemed to be an infringement or breach of the Rules or of the contract of carriage, and the carrier shall not be liable for any loss or damage resulting therefrom. The Hague Rules do not define "deviation" as such, and disputes have consequently arisen on many occasions between cargo interests and carriers between cargo interests and carriers as to what is a reasonable deviation. It was found that the burden of proof was a second source of uncertainty in cases of deviation, and that it was usually held that, because the carrier has the greater access to the facts, he has the burden of proving the contractural route and that the loss took place whilst the vessel was on that route, leaving the claimant then to prove the deviation or the unreasonable change in the route. A third uncertainty arose from the fact that, as a result of a deviation, goods were often discharged somewhere other than at the port of destination, and in such cases it is uncertain who must bear the risk and expense of bringing the goods to the port of destination. It was felt by the Committee that these problems might be clarified and simplified if deviations were presumed to be unjustified, and carriers were held liable for all risks and expense of bringing the goods to the destination port, unless they could prove that compelling conditions for the benefit of both ship and cargo forced them to deviate. The new Hamburg Rule in Article 5 paragraph 6 replaces the old Rule by a brief and succinctly stated provision that "The carrier shall not be liable, except in general average, where loss, damage or delay in delivery resulted from measures to save life or from reasonable measures to save property at sea."

Paragraph 7 of Article 5 of the Hamburg Rules provides that where fault or neglect on the part of the carrier, his servants or agents combines with another cause to produce loss, damage or delay in delivery the carrier is liable only to the extent that the loss, damage or delay in delivery is attributable to such fault or neglect, provided the carrier proves the amount of the loss, damage or delay in delivery not attributable thereto.

This paragraph seems to place beyond doubt the liability of the carrier when there may be two or more causes of damage to goods and in respect of which the carrier may be liable only for part of the damage caused.

The Hague Rules do not define the position of the carrier in such a case, but it is generally believed that if, for example, damage to goods has been caused by improper stowage, for which the carrier would be responsible, and also by perils of the sea, for which the carrier would not be responsible, the goods being damaged by these combined causes, then the carrier would be responsible for the total damage unless he can show what proportion of the damage arose out of the cause for which the carrier was not liable under the exceptions from liability contained in the Hague Rules.

This has from time to time, in the day to day business of the adjustment of claims between carriers and cargo interests, given rise to a great deal of dispute, but the new rule laid down in Article 5 paragraph 7 of the Hamburg Rules defines the position of the carrier in such cases.

Article 6 — Limits of liability

1. (a) The liability of the carrier for loss resulting from loss of or damage to goods according to the provisions of article 5 is limited to an amount equivalent to 835 units of account per package or other shipping unit or 2.5 units of account per kilogramme of gross weight of the goods lost or damaged, whichever is the higher.

(b) The liability of the carrier for delay in delivery according to the provisions of article 5 is limited to an amount equivalent to two and a half times the freight payable for the goods delayed, but not exceeding the total freight payable under the contract of carriage of goods by sea.

(c) In no case shall the aggregate liability of the carrier, under both subparagraphs (a) and (b) of this paragraph, exceed the limitation which would be established under subparagraph (a) of this paragraph for total loss of the goods with respect to which such liability was incurred.

2. For the purpose of calculating which amount is the higher in accordance with paragraph 1 (a) of this article, the following rules apply:
(a) Where a container, pallet or similar article of transport is used to consolidate goods, the package or other shipping units enumerated in the bill of lading, if issued, or otherwise in any other document evidencing the contract of carriage by sea, as packed in such article of transport are deemed packages or shipping units. Except as aforesaid the goods in such article of transport are deemed one shipping unit.

(b) In cases where the article of transport itself has been lost or damaged, that article of transport, if not owned or otherwise supplied by the carrier, is considered one separate shipping unit.

3. Unit of account means the unit of account mentioned in article 26.

4. By agreement between the carrier and the shipper, limits of liability exceeding those provided for in paragraph 1 may be fixed.

Article 6 of the Hamburg Rules deals with the limits of liability of the carrier, and completely alters the position of the carrier under the Hague Rules. By Article IV paragraph 5 of the Hague Rules it is provided that neither the carrier nor the ship shall in any event be or become liable for any loss or damage to or in connection with goods in an amount exceeding £100 per package or unit, or the equivalent of that sum in other currency, unless the nature and value of such goods have been declared by the shipper before shipment and inserted in the bill of lading. This declaration if embodied in the bill of lading shall be *prima facie* evidence, but shall not be binding or conclusive on the carrier.

It is also provided in this paragraph that by agreement between the carrier, master or agent of the carrier and the shipper another maximum amount than that mentioned in this paragraph may be fixed, provided that such maximum shall not be less than the figure above named, and neither the carriage nor the ship shall be responsible in any event for loss or damage to or in connection with goods if the nature or value thereof has been knowingly misstated by the shipper in the bill of lading.

In this connection reference must be made to Article IX of the Hague Rules which provides that the monetary units mentioned in the Rules are to be taken to be gold value. The maritime countries, when incorporating the Rules into their own domestic legislation, have not been uniform in the manner in which they gave effect to the Rule. Some countries, including the U.K. adopted the gold clause, but others, including the U.S. deliberately avoided it. This raised a number of difficult problems and in particular that of its effect upon the limit of £100 referred to above. To resolve these problems an agreement was reached between British shipping interests, insurance and cargo interests and such others who wished also to be associated with the agreement, that the carrier's liability should be limited to £200 sterling.

When the Committee examined the position with regard to this Rule, they found that the phrase "per package or unit" caused considerable uncertainty, principally because (a) there are significant departures from the model Rules in the Carriage of Goods by Sea Act Legislation of several countries; (b) it was not clear whether "unit" should mean a unit of goods or the weight or volume unit by which freight is calculated: (c) the term "package or unit" did not always fit into the wide variety of forms in which goods may be shipped, and in some cases the number of packages may differ from the number of units; and (d) it was not clear whether a container or pallet constituted a single "package". (This point has given rise to endless litigation in America.)

The words "in any event" in Article IV paragraph 5 of the existing Rules, outlined above, were questioned, since it had been felt somewhat unjust that the carrier should be protected by this limitation of liability irrespective of the nature of the breach or of the faults which caused the loss or damage. It was found that in some countries the carrier can take advantage of the limitation when he is in breach of the Articles III(1) and (2), which lay down the responsibilities of the carrier. The matter was again considered under the 1968 Protocol with proposed amendments to the Rules, in which it is provided that neither the carrier nor the ship shall be entitled to the limitation of liability if the damage to the goods resulted from an act or ommission of the carrier done with intent to cause damage, or recklessly with knowledge that damage would probably result.

Before proceeding to the new Rule in the Hamburg Rules, to enable the new Rule to be fully appreciated it is desirable to mention briefly the amendments to Article IV paragraph 5, with respect to limitation of liability proposed under the 1968 protocol. Not only did the new Rule, proposed at the time, raise the limit of liability, but it also made a special rule for containers and other similar articles for transport. The 1968 Rule raised the limitation to Francs Poincare per package or unit or 30 francs per kilogram of the gross weight of the goods, whichever be the higher. The first limit was intended to apply to light, valuable cargo while the second was intended to apply to heavy cargo.

This 1968 Rule also provided that where a container, pallet or similar article of transport is used to consolidate goods, the number of packages or units enumerated in the bill of lading, as packed in such article of transport, shall be deemed to be the number of packages or units for calculating the limitation of liability.

Article 6 of the Hamburg Rules will be found to have followed closely on this reasoning and to have completely altered the position of the carrier vis a vis the Hague Rules. Further, Article 6 has been so drafted as to deal also with the problems that have arisen in connection with the application of the Hague Rules limits of liability in the case of goods unitised or palletised or packed in containers for carriage.

Paragraph 1(a) of Article 6 provides that the liability of the carrier for loss resulting from loss of or damage to the goods according to the provisions of Article 5 is limited to an amount equivalent to 835 units of account per package or other shipping unit or 2.5 units of account per kilogramme of gross weight of the goods lost or damaged which ever is the higher. Paragraph 1(b) provides that the liability of the carrier for delay in delivery according to the provisions of Article 5 is limited to an amount equivalent to two and a half times the freight payable for the goods delayed, but not exceeding the total freight payable under the contract of carriage of goods by sea.

The UNCTAD Committee found that because the amount of freight is usually based on the weight or volume of the cargo, even for cargo consisting of shipping units, the total amount of damage recoverable will vary according to whether liability is limited on the basis of the shipping unit (package) or freight unit. The Committee also found that there was doubt as to whether the carrier's liability for bulk cargoes was subject to the limitation. The prevailing view at the time was that the Rule should apply to all types of cargo, but there was the need to clarify the situation as to whether, in the case of bulk cargoes, the Rule should apply to the freighting unit, *i.e.* weight or volume, or the weight or volume unit in which the goods are described in the bill of lading. These considerations, coupled with the problem of the application of the limitation Rule to goods carried in containers, or unitised etc. have led to the introduction of this new Rule, Article 6, in the Hamburg Rules.

Paragraph (c) provides that in no case shall the aggregate liability of the carrier, under both subparagraphs (a) and (b) of this paragraph, exceed the limitation which would be established under sub-paragraph (a) of this paragraph for total loss of the goods with respect to which such liability was incurred.

Paragraph 2 of Article 6 provides that—For the purpose of calculating which amount is the higher in accordance with paragraph 1(a) of this article, the following rules apply:
(a) Where a container, pallet or similar article of transport is used to consolidate goods the package or other shipping units enumerated in the bill of lading, if issued, or otherwise in any other document evidencing the contract of carriage by sea, as packed in such article of transport are deemed packages or shipping units. Except as aforesaid the goods in such article of transport are deemed one shipping unit. (b) In cases where the article of transport itself has been lost or damaged, that article of transport, if not owned or otherwise supplied by the carrier, is considered one separate shipping unit.

Paragraph 3 of Article 6 states — Unit of account means unit of account mentioned in Article 26. Paragraph 4 provides that — By agreement between the carrier and the shipper, limits of liability exceeding those provided for in paragraph 1 may be fixed.

The unit of account referred to is the Special Drawing Rights as defined by the International Monetary fund, with special provisions for states which are not members of the fund.

Article 6 seems to follow on the lines of the international agreement reached at the time of the Brussels Protocol of 1968 and will clear up many uncertainties presently apparent under the existing Rules. When the Committee completed their deliberations on this issue, they found that the phrase "per package or unit" had caused considerable uncertainty, principally because (a) there are significant departures from the model in the Carriage of Goods by Sea Act of several countries: (b) it is not clear whether "unit" should mean a unit of goods or the weight or volume unit by which freight is calculated; (c) the term "package or unit" does not always fit the wide variety of forms in which goods may be shipped, and in some cases the number of packages may differ from the number of units; and (d) it is not clear whether a container or pallet constitutes a single "package".

It was also thought that the terms "package" and "unit" were not sufficiently precise to fit various shipping practices. The word "unit" has been called "flagrantly ambiguous", in that it may refer to a physical shipping unit, for example, an unboxed car or machinery, a bale, a barrel or sack, *i.e.* a unit of cargo, or it may mean the unit of the basis of which freight is calculated, *i.e.* the freight unit. This is a problem that has resulted in much litigation in the United States because the wording in the American Act refers to "freight units" whereas the Rules refer to per "package or unit", omitting the word freight.

Before leaving Article 6 it is as well to draw attention to the fact that limitation of liability under the Hamburg Rules is not available to the carrier in the event that it is proved that the loss damage or delay in delivery resulted from an act or an omission of the carrier done with the intent to cause such loss, damage or delay, or recklessly and with knowledge that such loss, damage or delay would probably result. This is provided for in Article 8 of the Hamburg Rules.

One further point must be mentioned before leaving Article 6, namely that the Article does not contain any similar provision to that contained in Article IV paragraph 5 of the Hague Rules, namely that the declaration of value, if embodied in the bill of lading shall be 'prima facie' evidence, but shall not be binding or conclusive on the carrier.

Article 7 — Application to non-contractural claims

1. The defences and limits of liability provided for in this Convention apply in any action against the carrier in respect of loss or damage to the goods covered by the contrast of carriage by sea, as well as of delay in delivery whether the action is founded in contract, in tort or otherwise.

2. If such an action is brought against a servant or agent of the carrier, such servant or agent, if he proves that he acted within the scope of his employment, is entitled to avail himself of the defences and limits of liability which the carrier is entitled to invoke under this Convention.

3. Except as provided in article 8, the aggregate of the amounts recoverable from the carrier and from any persons referred to in paragraph 2 of this article shall not exceed the limits of liability provided for in this Convention.

This is a completely new article and has no counterpart in the Hague Rules and deals with a question over which there has been much controversy, particularly in the United States, namely whether agents or servants of the carrier can enjoy the benefits of limitation of liability and exemptions from liability contained in the Hague Rules.

In order to understand the underlying intention of Article 7, reference should be made to two legal actions, one in the U.K. and another in the U.S.A., both, coincidentally, running almost concurrently. The U.K. case was finally resolved in the House of Lords and the case in the

U.S.A. was finally decided by the Supreme Court. The issue concerned in both cases was whether the stevedoring contractor was entitled to limit liability for cargo loss or damage arising out of the negligence of the stevedores by seeking the benefit of the terms and conditions of the contract of carriage, evidenced by a bill of lading, between the carrier and the shipper. There is nothing in the Hague Rules, as they presently exist, which covers this situation, but throughout these notes it has to be remembered that the carrier may contract for the benefit of his servants provided that this intention is clearly expressed in the contract of carriage in unambiguous language. Dealing firstly with the English case, *Midland Silicones, Ltd v. Scruttons, Ltd,* the stevedoring contractor was engaged by the owners of the *American Reporter* to discharge their vessels at London and to act as their agents in the delivery of the goods to the consignees. The stevedoring contract expressly provided that stevedores were to be responsible for any damage to goods caused by negligence, but the stevedoring contractor was to have such protection as was afforded by the terms, conditions and exceptions of the bills of lading westbound and eastbound. During the course of the discharge, the stevedores were handling a drum of chemicals which had been stored temporarily, after discharge from the vessel, in a shed. When lowering the drum on to the consignees' vehicle, the stevedores negligently dropped the drum and caused damage to the amount of approximately £600, for which sum this present action was brought against the stevedoring contractor. The latter contended that they were entitled to the protection of the bill of lading conditions, which were governed by the United States Carriage of Goods by Sea Act, and maintained that their liability was limited to $500, being the equivalent in U.S.A. currency of the limitation provision of the Rules.

The bill of lading contained a clause providing that the word "carrier" shall include the ship, her owner, operator and demise charterer, and also any time-charterer or person to the extent bound by the bill of lading, whether acting as carrier or bailee. The question that then arose was whether the word "carrier" in the Rules included the stevedoring contractor. The latter contended that the limitations of liability contained in the bill of lading inured for the benefit of the servants or agents of the carriers, including the stevedoring contractor performing the duties of the carrier. It was submitted that it was an implied term of contract of carriage that such limiting provisions should inure for the benefit of the stevedoring contractor, and that the carrier contracted as agents for the stevedoring contractor as undisclosed principals or stevedores were sub-bailees of the goods, and, as such, stevedores were entitled to the benefit of the limiting provisions of the contract. It was further submitted that there was an implied contract between the cargo owners and the stevedoring contractor that the latter should have the benefit of the limiting provisions in the bill of lading, and that as they were carrying out the carriers' duty under the contract of carriage, they could claim the protection of the limiting provision of that contract upon the theory of vicarious immunity from liability for torts. The House of Lords ruled that the word "carrier" in the bill of lading or in the United States Carriage of Goods by Sea Act did not include stevedoring contractors, that the relation of stevedoring contractor to carriers in this case was that of independent contractors, that the carriers were not contracting as agents for stevedores, and that there was no ground for implying a contract between the cargo owners and the stevedoring contractor.

The case before the U.S. courts concerned a stevedoring contractor who sought to limit his liability to $500 in respect of damage to machinery caused during loading, seeking the benefit of the bill of lading contract between the cargo owners and the shipowner. The Supreme Court ruled that there was nothing in the provisions, legislative history and environment of the Carriage of Goods by Sea Act, or in the limitations of liability provisions in the bill of lading to indicate any intention of Congress of the Act, or of the contracting parties by the bill of lading, to limit the liability of negligent agents of the carrier. The bills of lading in these cases did not contain any provision to the effect that the stevedoring contractors were to have the benefit of the bill of lading or that the shipowner was also contracting on behalf of his agents and servants. It is now clear from subsequent litigation that, had those bills of lading contained a clause, in clear unambiguous terms, stating the intention of the parties to the contract evidenced by the bill of lading that the stevedoring contractors shall have the benefit of that contract, it would have been valid.

Article 7 of the Hamburg Rules is in three parts (1) The defences and limits of liability provided for in this Convention apply in any action against the carrier in respect of loss of or damage to the goods covered by the contract of carriage by sea as well as a delay in delivery, whether the action is founded in contract, in tort or otherwise. (2) If such action is brought against a servant or agent of the carrier, such servant or agent, if he proves that he acted within the scope of his employment is entitled to avail himself of the defences and limits of liability which the carrier is entitled to invoke under this Convention. (3) Except as provided for in Article 8, the aggregate of the amounts recoverable from the carrier and from any persons referred to in paragraph (2) of this Article, shall not exceed the limits of liability provided for in this Convention. It will be seen that Article 7 will enable the stevedoring contractor to so limit his liability.

Article 8 — Loss of right to limit responsibility

1. The carrier is not entitled to the benefit of the limitation of liability provided for in article 6 if it is proved that the loss, damage or delay in delivery resulted from an act or omission of the carrier done with the intent to cause such loss, damage or delay, or recklessly and with knowledge that such loss, damage or delay would probably result.

2. Notwithstanding the provisions of paragraph 2 of article 7, a servant or agent of the carrier is not entitled to the benefit of the limitation of liability provided for in article 6 if it is proved that the loss, damage or delay in delivery resulted from an act or omission of such servant or agent, done with the intent to cause such loss, damage or delay, or recklessly and with knowledge that such loss, damage or delay would probably result.

Before proceeding to examine this Article mention should be made that when the Committee examined Hague Rules with regard to the carrier's right to the limitation of liability, it was found that in some countries, including the United Kingdom, the carrier can take advantage of the limitation when he is in breach of Article III paragraph 1, and Article III paragraph 2 of the Hague Rules. Article III(1) requires that the carrier shall be bound to exercise due diligence to make the ship seaworthy and Article III(2) provides that the carrier shall properly and carefully load, handle, stow, carry, keep, care for and discharge the goods carried. This present right to limit liability obtains even though the act or omission of the carrier is done recklessly or with intent to cause damage. This situation was in fact recognised at the time of the Brussels Protocol of 1968, at which Convention a new rule was agreed which provided that neither the carrier nor the ship shall be entitled to the benefit of the limitation of liability if it is proved that the damage resulted from an act or omission of the carrier done with intent to cause damage, or recklessly and with knowledge that damage would result.

Article 8 has no counterpart in the Hague Rules but the catalogue of exceptions contained in paragraph 2 of Article IV of the Hague Rules concludes by providing that neither the carrier nor the ship shall be responsible for loss or damage arising or resulting from "any other cause arising without the actual fault or privity of the carrier, or without the fault or neglect of the agents or servants of the carrier", the burden of proof being upon the carrier.

The effect of Article 8 (which seemingly should have been captioned Loss of right to limit "liability" instead of "responsibility") confers upon the carrier well defined limits of liability in respect of cargo loss as set out in Article 6, which limits of liability are also available to servants or agents of the carrier as provided for in Article 7, unless it be proved that the loss, damage or delay in delivery resulted from an act or omission of the carrier done with intent to cause the loss, damage or delay in delivery or recklessly and with knowledge that such loss, damage or delay in delivery would probably result. A servant or agent also loses the right to limit liability upon such proof, and emphasis must be laid upon the fact that the burden of proof is upon the claimant, a matter of extreme importance.

Article 9 — Deck cargo

1. The carrier is entitled to carry the goods on deck only if such carriage is in accordance with an agreement with the shipper or with the usage of the particular trade or is required by statutory rules or regulations.

2. If the carrier and the shipper have agreed that the goods shall or may be carried on deck, the carrier must insert in the bill of lading or other document evidencing the contract of carriage by sea a statement to that effect. In the absence of such a statement the carrier has the burden of proving that an agreement for carriage on deck has been entered into; however, the carrier is not entitled to invoke such an agreement against a third party, including a consignee, who has acquired the bill of lading in good faith.

3. Where the goods have been carried on deck contrary to the provisions of paragraph 1 of this article or where the carrier may not under paragraph 2 of this article invoke an agreement for carriage on deck, the carrier, notwithstanding the provisions of paragraph 1 of Article 5, is liable for loss of or damage to the goods, as well as for delay in delivery, resulting solely from the carriage on deck, and the extent of his liability is to be determined in accordance with the provisions of Article 6 or Article 8 of this Convention, as the case may be.

4. Carriage of goods on deck contrary to express agreement for carriage under deck is deemed to be an act or omission of the carrier within the meaning of Article 8.

The Hague Rules contain a reference to deck cargoes in Article I (Definitions) and in defining "Goods" in paragraph (c) it is stated that "Goods" include goods, wares, merchandises, and articles of every kind whatsoever, except live animals and cargo which by the contract of carriage is stated as being carried on deck and is so carried. In Article I of the Hamburg Rules, which deals with "definitions" it is provided that "Goods" includes live animals; where goods are consolidated in a container, pallet or similar article of transport or where they are packed, "goods" includes such article of transport or packaging if supplied by the shipper. Deck cargoes receive no mention in the Hamburg Rules definition and to determine the position of the carrier in regard to such cargoes reference has to be made to Article 9 of the Rules. When the Committee were considering amending the existing definition of "goods", the view was taken that there was no justification for maintaining this exclusion of deck cargoes, in that if it were abolished, carriers would still be protected adequately by the exceptions in the Rules and the limitation of liability. Moreover, a large number of containers are now carried on deck, and the view was taken that the same principles should apply to containers carried on deck as to those carried below deck. Presently, carriers may contract out of all liability for cargo loss or damage when the goods are stated to be carried on deck and are in fact so carried but the exception has been made when containers are carried on the deck of a container purpose-built vessel.

In drafting Article 9 of the Hamburg Rules, there has been a compromise and it is provided in Article 9(1) that the carrier is entitled to carry goods on deck only if such carriage is in agreement with the shipper or with the usage of a particular trade or is required by statutory rules or regulations. Problems may arise here over the interpretation of the words "with the usage of the particular trade", in that there have been many cases in the past when much argument has arisen as to whether or not a particular carriage has come with the meaning of the words. Article 9 paragraph (2) provides that if the carrier and the shipper have agreed that the goods shall or may be carried on deck, the carrier must insert in the bill of lading, or other document evidencing the contract of carriage by sea, a statement to that effect. In the absence of such a statement, the carrier has the burden of proving that an agreement for carriage on deck has been entered into; however, the carrier is not entitled to invoke such an agreement against a third party, including a consignee who has acquired a bill of lading in good faith. Problems may arise here over the modern concept and development of containerised carriage and the carriage of containers in the container purpose-built vessel, and it is surprising that, as regards deck carriage, the Hamburg Rules have not recognised the need for some separate rule relating to such carriage. There is a wide gulf between the shipment of a container on the deck of a conventional dry cargo ship, or on the deck of a bulk carrier, and the loading of a container on the decks of a vessel built for the sole purpose of carrying containers, which may be in the cellular regions below decks or above deck on the specially provided stowage arrangements. In Article 9(2) it is provided that if the carrier and the shipper have agreed that the goods shall or may be carried on deck, the carrier must insert in the bill of lading, or other document evidencing the contract of carriage by sea, a statement to that effect. This presupposes that at some time before the loading of the cargo on board the vessel the shipowner must notify the shipper of the intent to load the cargo on deck and obtain his agreement. Paragraph 2 goes on to provide that, in the absence of such a statement, the carrier has the burden of proving that an agreement for carriage on deck has been entered into, but the carrier is not entitled to invoke such an agreement against a third-party including a consignee who has acquired the bill of lading in good faith. In the case of the conventional dry cargo ship, this rule makes good sense in that it does clarify the position of the shipowner and the cargo interests. Presently, the carriage of goods on the deck of a conventional dry cargo vessel when an under deck bill of lading has been issued constitutes a deviation under the contract of carriage and, generally speaking, the carrier may lose the right to invoke the exceptions and limitations contained in the Hague Rules in the event of the cargo suffering loss or damage. Certain cargoes, by the practice of the trade (such as timber), would not of course come within these comments.

The Hague Rules provide that goods which by the contract of carriage are stated as being carried on deck and are so carried are exempt from the Rules, although a clause in the bill of lading giving the carrier the liberty to carry on deck would not be tantamount to a statement that the goods were so carried. Therefore, while the carrier may so express his right to carry on deck, such carriage would be subject to the provisions of the Rules regarding the carrier's liabilities and responsibilities. The Hamburg Rule places upon the carrier the burden of proving, in the event of the carriage of goods on deck, that an agreement was entered into with the shipper that the goods could be carried on deck, and that the carrier shall insert in the bill of lading a statement to that effect. In the absence of such a statement, the carrier would not be able to invoke such an agreement as against a claim of the consignee or other holder of the bill of lading for value.

The carriage of containers in purpose-built cellular vessels is an entirely different proposition to the carriage of containers on the deck of a conventional dry cargo ship or bulk carrier. In the latter case, there can be hardly any question but that deck carriage of containers without express agreement and the issue of an ondeck bill of lading would be a breach of the contract of carriage and would deprive the carrier of the exemptions from, and the limitations of the Rules, but the carriage of containers on the deck of the purpose-built container ship is another matter. More and more of these large container vessels are being introduced in the carriage of goods by sea, and more and more goods are being containerised for carriage, these containers arriving at the docks for shipment in no particular order for shipment and, generally speaking, being loaded on the basis of the containers being first loaded below decks and, when the below decks are full, the balance loaded on deck. Apart from the exception of a specific container or containers requiring below-deck stowage, it would be almost impossible for the carrier to say before shipment which containers will receive under-deck stowage and which will be loaded on deck. It may be that such carriage will be held to come within Article 9(1) which provides that the carrier shall be entitled to carry the goods on deck only if such carriage is in accordance with agreement with the shipper "or with the usage of the particular trade". So far, it has been found difficult to establish whether or not a certain carriage was within the meaning of the term "the usage of the trade".

Article 9 paragraph 3 has reference to the liability of the carrier for cargo loss or damage resulting from the carriage of goods on deck. Paragraph 3 provides that where the goods have been carried on deck contrary to the provisions of paragraph (1) of Article 9 or where the carrier may not under paragraph (2) of this article invoke an agreement for carriage on deck, the carrier, notwithstanding the provisions of

114

paragraph (1) of Article 5 is liable for loss of or damage to the goods, as well as for delay in delivery resulting solely from the carriage on deck, and the extent of his liability is to be determined in accordance with the provisions of Article 6 or Article 8 of this Convention, as the case may be. Briefly stated, paragraph (1) of Article 5, which deals with the basis of liability, provides that the carrier shall be liable for loss of or damage to the goods, as well as from delay in delivery "unless the carrier proves that he, his servants and agents took all measures that could reasonably be required to avoid the occurrence and its consequences." The effect of Article 9 paragraph (3) is therefore to deprive the carrier of the benefit of Article 5(1) in the case of carriage of goods on deck without the agreement of the shipper. In other words, the carrier cannot escape the consequences of the carriage on deck without agreement of the shipper, by proving that all proper measures to avoid the damage had been taken. To summarise, it would seem that the carriage of goods on deck without agreement means, under the Hamburg Rules, that the carrier's liability is as provided for in Article 6 and 8. Article 6 has reference to the limits of liability, and Article 8 describes the circumstances in which the carrier is not entitled to limit liability, including an act or omission done with intent to cause such damage. Article 9 paragraph (4) provides that the carriage of goods on deck contrary to express agreement for carriage under deck is deemed to be an act or omission of the carrier within the meaning of Article 8. In other words, carriage on deck without agreement deprives the carrier of the right to limit liability.

Article 10 — Liability of the carrier and actual carrier

1. Where the performance of the carriage or part thereof has been entrusted to an actual carrier, whether or not in pursuance of a liberty under the contract of carriage by sea to do so, the carrier nevertheless remains responsible for the entire carriage according to the provisions of this Convention. The carrier is responsible, in relation to the carriage performed by the actual carrier, for the acts and omissions of the actual carrier and of his servants and agents acting within the scope of their employment.

2. All the provisions of this Convention governing the responsibility of the carrier also apply to the responsibility of the actual carrier for the carriage performed by him. The provisions of paragraphs 2 and 3 of article 7 and of paragraph 2 of article 8 apply if an action is brought against a servant or agent of the actual carrier.

3. Any special agreement under which the carrier assumes obligations not imposed by this Convention or waives rights conferred by this Convention affects the actual carrier only if agreed to by him expressly and in writing. Whether or not the actual carrier has so agreed, the carrier nevertheless remains bound by the obligations or waivers resulting from such special agreement.

4. Where and to the extent that both the carrier and the actual carrier are liable, their liability is joint and several.

5. The aggregate of the amounts recoverable from the carrier, the actual carrier and their servants and agents shall not exceed the limits of liability provided for in this Convention.

6. Nothing in this article shall prejudice any right of recourse as between the carrier and the actual carrier.

Article 10 of the Hamburg Rules is a completely new Article, one effect of which is to remove a grievance which has long existed with cargo interests concerning their rights of recovery in respect of cargo loss or damage when the vessel concerned is not actually owned by the parties who issued the bill of lading. In countless cases where a dispute has arisen over the question of the liability of the carrier for cargo loss or damage, cargo interests have sought to protect themselves against the requirement under the Hague Rules that proceedings must be commenced within twelve months from the date of the delivery of the goods or the date upon which they should have been delivered, otherwise the claim will be time-barred. The common practice to avoid the need for the commencement of proceedings is to obtain an extension of time from the carrier and all too often this has led to the cargo interests losing all rights of recovery of their loss or damage from the carrier.

"Carrier" is defined in the Hague Rules (Article 1a) as "including the owner or the charterer who enters into a contract of carriage with a shippper". This provision raises for consideration the question of whether any person other than the owner of the vessel or the charterer can be a carrier and who is liable as the "carrier" when vessels are chartered. The Committee felt that in order to remove any doubt on the matter, the definition of "carrier" might be clarified to include the owner, the charterer or any other person who enters into a contract of carriage with a shipper. It is around the second point that the troubles have really centred, in connection with whether proceedings may be commenced against a charterer whenever there is a demise charter or whenever the charterer contracts in his own name with the shipper and issues a bill of lading. The trouble has arisen where a vessel has been time-chartered or is on a voyage charter and a bill of lading is issued with the name of the charterers heading that document when it contains what is commonly known as a "demise" clause. Most bills of lading contain such clauses to the effect that if the ship is now owned by, or chartered by demise to the shipping company or line by which the bill of lading is issued, the bill of lading shall take effect as a contract with the shipowner or demise charterer and not with the charterer who has dealt directly with the shipper. The Committee commented that injustice has often been caused to the shipper or consignee when courts in some countries have held that a shipper or consignee cannot sue the owner of the ship because he is not considered to be the "carrier", and charterers have been permitted to evade liability because they were not considered to be "carriers" either. Cargo owners expecting a shipping line to carry their goods find instead that, by the use of demise clauses, the bill of lading terms allow the line to substitute another carrier, and find that the line has not agreed to carry their goods at all, but merely to find a suitable carrier. In the result, shipping lines using bills of lading on their own forms and with their own headings escape liability for cargo loss or damage because they believed that the shipping line issuing the bill of lading was the real carrier. Unfortunately, this does not become apparent until after the time limit has expired, when it is too late to either sue or obtain an extension of time from the actual owner of the carrying vessel.

Article 10 of the Hamburg Rules goes a long way towards remedying this situation. Paragraph 2 of Article 10 provides that—All the provisions of this Convention governing the responsibility of the carrier also apply to the responsibility of the actual carrier for the carriage performed by him. The provisions of paragraphs 2 and 3 of Article 7 and of paragraph 2 of Article 8 apply if an action is brought against a servant or agent of the actual carrier.

Paragraph 2 of Article 7 provides that if an action is brought against a servant or agent of the carrier, such servant or agent, if he proves that he acted within the scope of his employment, shall be entitled to avail himself of the defences and limits of liability which the carrier is entitled to invoke under this Convention. Paragraph 3 of Article 7 provides that the aggregate of the amounts recoverable from the carrier and any persons referred to in paragraph 2 of this Article, shall not exceed the limits of liability provided for in the Convention. Paragraph 2 of Article 8 provides that notwithstanding the provisions of paragraph 2 of Article 7, a servant or agent of the carrier shall not be entitled to the benefit of the limitation of liability if it is proved that the loss, damage or delay in delivery resulted from an act or omission of such servant or agent, done with intent to cause such loss, damage or delay or recklessly and with knowledge that such loss, damage or delay would probably result.

Paragraph 3 of Article 10 provides that any special agreement under which the carrier assumes obligations not imposed by the Convention or waives rights conferred by this Convention affects the actual carrier only if agreed to by him expressly and in writing. Whether or not the actual carrier has so agreed, the carrier nevertheless remains bound by the obligations or waivers resulting from such special agreement. Paragraph (4) of Article 10 provides that where and to the extent that both the carrier and the actual carrier are liable, their liability is joint and several. Paragraph (5) of Article 10 states that the aggregate of the amounts recoverable from the carrier, the actual carrier and their servants and agents shall not exceed the limits of liability provided for in the Convention and paragraph (6) of Article 10 provides that nothing in this Article shall prejudice any right of recourse as between the carrier and the actual carrier.

Another facet of the problem is the case of the vessel named in the bill of lading being concerned with only part of the carriage. In other words, there may be the case of transhipment of the cargo at a port en route to final destination.

Article 11 — Through carriage

1. Notwithstanding the provisions of paragraph 1 of Article 10, where a contract of carriage by sea provides explicitly that a specified part of the carriage covered by the said contract is to be performed by a named person other than the carrier, the contract may also provide that the carrier is not liable for loss, damage or delay in delivery caused by an occurrence which takes place while the goods are in the charge of the actual carrier during such part of the carriage. Nevertheless, any stipulation limiting or excluding such liability is without effect if no judicial proceedings can be instituted against the actual carrier in a court competent under paragraph 1 or 2 of Article 21. The burden of proving that any loss, damage or delay in delivery has been caused by such an occurrence rests upon the carrier.

2. The actual carrier is responsible in accordance with the provisions of paragraph 2 of Article 10 for loss, damage or delay in delivery caused by an occurrence which takes place while the goods are in his charge.

Presently it is the practice to include in bills of lading a clause giving the liberty to tranship the cargo at another port or ports for carriage to final destination and, provided that the provision in the bill of lading giving the carrier this liberty is reasonable, there is nothing in the Hague Rules to prevent this. Furthermore, the Rules are applicable from the time of the loading of the goods into the carrying vessel and until discharge therefrom, and it is the practice of carriers to provide in their bills of lading that their liability ceases on discharge from the carrying vessel.

It is sometimes customary in a particular trade for the original carrying vessel to tranship at a certain port for the final leg of the voyage and, if this is provided for in the bill of lading terms and conditions, such a provision would not offend the Rules. But if the original carrying vessel, for her own convenience deviates from the contractural voyage for the purpose of perhaps transhipping her cargo or part of her cargo in order to take other cargo to a destination other than that stated in the bill of lading, then such a transhipment would be regarded as a deviation from the contractural voyage and the carrier would lose the right of the exclusions and benefits of the Rules because of the breach of contract. The liberty to tranship has been held to be sufficiently wide to cover the discharge of the cargo into lighters to complete the voyage and a clause in the bill of lading giving the liberty to tranship could not be said to offend the Rules. Bills of lading providing for transhipment to final destination are commonly referred to as "through bills of lading" and provided that the provision for transhipment is reasonable and can be classed as "proper carriage", such provision in such bills of lading may be regarded as not offending the Rules.

Paragraph 2 of Article 11 provides that the actual carrier is responsible in accordance with the provisions of paragraph 2 of Article 10 for loss, damage or delay in delivery caused by an occurrence which takes place while the goods are in his charge. Article 10 paragraph 1, provides that where the performance of carriage or part thereof has been entrusted to an actual carrier, whether or not in pursuance of a liberty under the contract of carriage by sea to do so, the carrier nevertheless remains responsible for the entire carriage according to the provisions of this Convention. The carrier is responsible in relation to the carriage performed by the actual carrier, for the acts and omissions of the actual carrier and of his servants and agents acting within the scope of their employment.

Paragraph 2 of Article 10 referred to in Article 11, provides that all the provisions of this Convention governing the responsibility of the carrier also apply to the responsibility of the actual carrier for the carriage performed by him. The provisions of paragraphs 2 and 3 of Article 7 and of paragraph 2 of Article 8 apply if an action is brought against a servant or agent of the actual carrier.

Article 11 deals with a different situation than that contemplated in Article 10, which deals with the liability of the "carrier" and the "actual carrier" making it clear that their respective liabilities are joint and several and in the case of loss, damage or delay in delivery of cargo, it would seem that the cargo claimant may claim against both. Article 11, on the other hand has provided that in contracts under which the carrier of goods by sea agrees to carry the goods but provides in his contract for the right to tranship the goods into another vessel at some stage or another for the completion of the voyage, and stipulating that he, the carrier, will not be responsible for loss, damage or delay occurring during the on-carriage, such liability to be that of the on-carrier.

Whilst Article 11 seems to provide that in cases of transhipment the contracting carrier can exclude his liability from the part of the carriage performed by the on-carrier, this is subject to the proviso that a through bill of lading must actually name the carrier who is to take over the goods from the original carrier. This provision could have the effect of restricting the use of what are commonly termed through bills of lading, for the reason that in many cases it may not be possible for the contracting carrier to name the carrier responsible for the carriage of the goods to ultimate destination after transhipment.

The intention and effect of the provision in Article 11 which provides that any stipulation limiting or excluding the liability of the contracting carrier in respect of the carriage performed by a named person other than the carrier, is without effect if no judicial proceedings can be instituted against the actual carrier, is somewhat difficult to follow or to understand what circumstances the framers of the Hamburg Rules had in mind when drafting this provision.

Both Article 10 and Article 11 have no counterpart in the Hague Rules.

PART III. LIABILITY OF THE SHIPPER

Article 12 — General rule

The shipper is not liable for loss sustained by the carrier or the actual carrier, or for damage sustained by the ship, unless such loss or damage was caused by the fault or neglect of the shipper, his servants or agents. Nor is any servant or agent of the shipper liable for such loss or damage unless the loss or damage was caused by fault or neglect on his part.

There are a number of references to the shipper in the Hague Rules, and before proceeding further with the provisions of Part III of the Hamburg Rules, it would be helpful just to look at these. Article III paragraph 5 of the Hague Rules provides that the shipper shall be deemed to have guaranteed to the carrier the accuracy at the time of shipment of the marks, number, quantity, and weight, as furnished by him, and the shipper shall indemnify the carrier against all loss, damage, and expenses arising or resulting from inaccuracies in such particulars. The right of the carrier to such indemnity in no way limits his responsibility and liability under the contract of carriage to any person other than the shipper. Under the provisions of Article IV paragraph 2(i) of the Hague Rules, it is provided that neither the carrier nor the ship shall be responsible for loss or damage arising or resulting from act or omission of the shipper or owner of the goods, his agent or representative. Under Article IV paragraph 3, it is provided that the shipper shall not be responsible for the loss or damage sustained by the carrier or the ship arising or resulting from any cause without the act, fault or neglect of the shipper, his agents or servants. With these present Rules in the background, it will be possible to examine the Hamburg Rules and to understand the nature of the deletion of the old Rules and the introduction of the new.

The Hamburg Rules relative to the liability of the shipper, contained in Part III, Article 12, is a new introduction having no counterpart in the Hague Rules as they presently exist. It is provided in Article III paragraph 5 of the Hague Rules that the shipper shall be deemed to have guaranteed to the carrier the accuracy at the time of shipment of the marks, number, quantity, and weight as furnished by the shipper. The new Hamburg Rule makes no such provision and also omits the indemnity contained in the present rule that the shipper shall indemnify the carrier against all loss, damages, and expenses arising or resulting from inaccuracies in such particulars, but reintroduces this in Article 17,

120

as will be seen later. In the new rule, there is substituted a provision to the effect that the shipper shall not be liable for loss or damage sustained by the carrier or actual carrier, except in the case that such loss or damage was caused by the fault or neglect of the shipper, his agents or servants. It is also provided that no servant or agent of the shipper shall be liable for such loss or damage unless the loss or damage was caused by fault or neglect on his part. The new rule also replaces Article IV paragraph 2(i) of the Hague Rules which provides that neither the carrier nor the ship shall be responsible for loss or damage arising or resulting from act or omission of the shipper or owner of the goods, his agent or representative.

Article 13 — Special rules on dangerous goods

1. The shipper must mark or label in a suitable manner dangerous goods as dangerous.

2. Where the shipper hands over dangerous goods to the carrier or an actual carrier, as the case may be, the shipper must inform him of the dangerous character of the goods and, if necessary, of the precautions to be taken. If the shipper fails to do so and such carrier or actual carrier does not otherwise have knowledge of their dangerous character:

(a) the shipper is liable to the carrier and any actual carrier for the loss resulting from the shipment of such goods, and

(b) the goods may at any time be unloaded, destroyed or rendered innocuous, as the circumstances may require, without payment of compensation.

3. The provisions of paragraph 2 of this article may not be invoked by any person if during the carriage he has taken the goods in his charge with knowledge of their dangerous character.

4. If, in cases where the provisions of paragraph 2, subparagraph (b), of this article do not apply or may not be invoked, dangerous goods become an actual danger to life or property, they may be unloaded, destroyed or rendered innocuous, as the circumstances may require, without payment of compensation except where there is an obligation to contribute in general average or where the carrier is liabile in accordance with the provisions of Article 5.

Article 13 of Part III of the Hamburg Rules contains special rules on dangerous goods, which, whilst bearing some similarity to the rule contained in Article IV paragraph 6 of the Hague Rules, has at the same time been redrafted with additional provisions.

The Hague Rules provide that goods of an inflammable, explosive or dangerous nature to the shipment whereof the carrier, master or agent of the carrier has not consented, with knowledge of their nature and character may at any time before discharge be landed at any place or destroyed or rendered innocuous by the carrier without compensation, and the shipper of such goods shall be liable for all damages and expenses directly or indirectly arising out of or resulting from such shipment. It is also provided in Article IV paragraph 6 that if any such goods shipped with such knowledge and consent shall become a danger to the ship or cargo, they may in like manner be landed at any place or destroyed or rendered innocuous by the carrier without liability on the part of the carrier except to general average, if any. Article 13 of the Hamburg Rules provides in paragraph (1) that the shipper must mark or label in a suitable manner dangerous goods as dangerous. This is an additional requirement over and above the present rule. Paragraph (2) of Article 13 also provides a new requirement and states that where the shipper hands over dangerous goods to the carrier or an actual carrier, as the case may be, the shipper must inform him of the dangerous character of the goods and, if necessary of the precautions to be taken. If the shipper fails to do so and such carrier, or actual carrier, does not otherwise have knowledge of their dangerous character, (a) the shipper is liable to the carrier and any actual carrier for all loss resulting from the shipment of such goods, and (b) the goods may at any time be unloaded, destroyed or rendered innocuous, as the circumstances may require, without payment of compensation. The words "such carrier or actual carrier does not otherwise have knowledge of their dangerous character", may prove difficult of interpretation in that they pose the question as to what sort of knowledge the carrier or actual carrier should possess. Another question posed by this Article concerns the words "the shipper shall inform him of the dangerous character of the goods". The question seems to be one of whether the adequate labelling of the package or packages, when dangerous goods are so packed, is sufficient notice to the carrier of the dangerous nature of the contents, or will the shipper be required specifically to notify the carrier in writing. The requirement that the shipper must, if necessary, give notice of the precautions, implies a notice in writing.

Paragraph (3) of Article 13 provides that the provisions of paragraph 2 of this Article may not be invoked by any person if during the carriage he has taken the goods in his charge with knowledge of their dangerous character. This would seem to contemplate, amongst other things, that where the shipper has failed to give the carrier the required notice of the dangerous nature of the goods and the carrier has taken the goods aboard the vessel with knowledge of their dangerous character, then the provisions of this paragraph become void.

Paragraph (4) of Article 13 provides that if, in cases where the provisions of paragraph 2, sub paragraph (b) of this Article do not apply or may not be invoked, dangerous goods become an actual danger to life or property, they may be unloaded, destroyed or rendered innocuous, as the circumstances may require, without payment of compensation except where there is an obligation to contribute in general average or where the carrier is liable in accordance with the provisions of Article 5. This latter Article has reference to the basis of the carrier's liability.

The phrase "dangerous goods" has, of course, a very wide coverage and embraces goods that are neither packed nor bagged, as for instance certain concentrates, such as copper-ore concentrates. Some time ago such a cargo was shipped aboard the vessel *Erwin Schroder* at Newcastle, N.B., and whilst the vessel was proceeding through the Gulf of St. Lawrence she ran into heavy weather and the cargo began to shift, causing the vessel to roll heavily. The concentrates were shipped with too great a moisture content, with the result that the vibration of the vessel's engines, and the action of the seas against the vessel, caused the concentrates to liquefy to the extent that the roll of the ship resulted in the concentrates moving from their fixed position in a mass from one side of the vessel to the other. The master put in to Halifax as a port of refuge and commenced to discharge the cargo to be reloaded after the holds had been fitted with shifting boards to prevent further shifting of the cargo. The cargo owners sued the shipowners for breach of contract but the owners of the vessel relied upon Article IV paragraph 6 of the Hague Rules, on the grounds that the concentrates were dangerous goods within the meaning of the Rule, with which the Court was in full agreement.

PART IV. TRANSPORT DOCUMENTS

Article 14 — Issue of bill of lading

1. When the carrier or the actual carrier takes the goods in his charge, the carrier must, on demand of the shipper, issue to the shipper a bill of lading.

2. The bill of lading may be signed by a person having authority from the carrier. A bill of lading signed by the master of the ship carrying the goods is deemed to have been signed on behalf of the carrier.

3. The signature on the bill of lading may be in handwriting, printed in facsimile, perforated, stamped, in symbols, or made by any other mechanical or electronic means, if not inconsistent with the law of the country where the bill of lading is issued.

Part IV of the Hamburg Rules is a new introduction covering transport documents, in which the present requirements of the Hague Rules have been completely redrafted. The Hague Rules, require in Article III paragraph 3, that after receiving the goods into his charge, the carrier, or the master or agent of the carrier, shall, on demand of the shipper issue to the shipper a bill of lading showing among other things (a) the leading marks necessary for identification of the goods as the same are furnished in writing by the shipper before the loading of such goods starts, provided such marks are stamped or otherwise shown clearly upon the goods if uncovered, or on the cases or coverings in which such goods are contained, in such a manner as should ordinarily remain legible until the end of the voyage; (b) either the number of packages or pieces, or the quantity, or weight, as the case may be, as furnished in writing by the shipper: (c) the apparent order and condition of the goods. The Article then states that no carrier, master or agent of the carrier, shall be bound to state or show in the bill of lading any marks, number quantity or weight which he has reasonable ground for suspecting not accurately to represent the goods actually received, or which he has no reasonable means of checking. Article III paragraph 4 then provides that such a bill of lading shall be *prima facie* evidence of the receipt by the carrier of the goods as therein described. Article III paragraph 7 then provides that, after the goods are loaded, the bill of lading to be issued by the carrier, master or agent of the carrier to the shipper shall, if the shipper so demands, be a "shipped" bill of lading provided that if the shipper shall have previously taken up any document of title to such goods, he shall surrender the same as against the issue of the "shipped" bill of lading, but at the option of the carrier such a document of title may be noted at the port of shipment by the carrier, master, or agent with the name or names of the ship or ships upon which the goods have been shipped and the date or dates of shipment, and when so noted the same shall for the purpose of this Article be deemed to constitute a "shipped" bill of lading.

Part IV of the Hamburg Rules contains three articles covering transport documents, namely Article 14 which deals with the issue of the bill of lading, Article 15 which concerns the matter of the contents of the bill of lading. Article 16 which deals with reservations and evidentiary effect, Article 17 which deals with the matter of guarantees by the shipper and Article 18 which concerns documents other than bills of lading. Article 14 paragraph (1) provides that when the carrier or the actual carrier takes the goods in his charge, the carrier must, on demand of the shipper, issue to the shipper a bill of lading. Paragraph (2) provides that the bill of lading may be signed by a person having authority from the carrier, and that a bill of lading signed by the master of the ship carrying the goods is deemed to have been signed on behalf of the carrier. Paragraph 3 provides that the signature on the bill of lading may be in handwriting, printed in facsimile, perforated, stamped, in symbols, or made by any other mechanical or electronic means, if not inconsistent with the law of the country where the bill of lading is issued. As will be seen, all of this is completely new.

Article 15 — Contents of bill of lading

1. The bill of lading must include, inter alia, *the following particulars:*

(a) the general nature of the goods, the leading marks necessary for identification of the goods, an express statement, if applicable, as to the dangerous character of the goods, the number of packages or pieces, and the weight of the goods or their quantity otherwise expressed, all such particulars as furnished by the shipper;

(b) the apparent condition of the goods;

(c) the name and principal place of business of the carrier;

(d) the name of the shipper;

(e) the consignee if named by the shipper;

(f) the port of loading under the contract of carriage by sea and the date on which the goods were taken over by the carrier at the port of loading;

(g) the port of discharge under the contract of carriage by sea;

(h) the number of originals of the bill of lading, if more than one;

(i) the place of issuance of the bill of lading;

(j) the signature of the carrier or a person acting on his behalf;

(k) the freight to the extent payable by the consignee or other indication that freight is payable by him;

(l) the statement referred to in paragraph 3 of Article 23;

(m) the statement, if applicable, that the goods shall or may be carried on deck;

(n) the date or the period of delivery of the goods at the port of discharge if expressly agreed upon between the parties; and

(o) any increased limit or limits of liability where agreed in accordance with paragraph 4 of Article 6.

2. After the goods have been loaded on board, if the shipper so demands, the carrier must issue to the shipper a "shipped" bill of lading which, in addition to the particulars required under paragraph 1 of this article, must state that the goods are on board a named ship or ships, and the date or dates of loading. If the carrier has previously issued to the shipper a bill of lading or other document of title with respect to any of such goods, on request of the carrier, the shipper must surrender such document in exchange for a "shipped" bill of lading. The carrier may amend any previously issued document in order to meet the shipper's demand for a "shipped" bill of lading if, as amended, such document includes all the information required to be contained in a "shipped" bill of lading.

3. The absence in the bill of lading of one or more particulars referred to in this article does not affect the legal character of the document as a bill of lading provided that it nevertheless meets the requirements set out in paragraph 7 of Article 1.

It is required by paragraph 1 of this article that the bill of lading must include, *inter alia*, the following particulars:

(a) the general nature of the goods, the leading marks necessary for identification of the goods, an express statement, if applicable, as to the dangerous character of the goods, the number of packages or pieces, and the weight of the goods or their quantity otherwise expressed, all such particulars as furnished by the shipper. It will be noted that this new rule imposes a duty to set out in the bill of lading all of the details without the Hague Rules alternative of "either" the number of packages or pieces, or the quantity, or weight as furnished in writing by the shipper. Omitted from the new rule is the provision in the Hague Rules that the bill of lading should show the leading marks necessary for the identification of the goods "as the same are furnished in writing by the shipper before the loading of such goods starts, provided such marks are stamped or otherwise shown clearly upon the goods if uncovered, or on the cases or coverings in which such goods are contained, in such a manner as should remain legible until the end of the voyage".

Article 15 paragraph I sub-paragraph (b) of the Hamburg Rules provides that the bill of lading sets forth the apparent condition of the goods. The word "order" in the Hague Rules is omitted. There then continues a catalogue of provisions not provided for in the Hague Rules as they presently exist. Sub-paragraph (c) of the new Convention rule provides that the bill of lading shall set forth the name and principal place of the business of the carrier. This is an important provision for the benefit of the shipper or the consignee of the goods in the event that the goods shall suffer loss or damage during transit. In paragraph (d) it is required that the bill of lading sets the name of the shipper, and in paragraph (e) it is provided that the bill of lading shall bear the name of the consignee if named by the shipper. There then follows in paragraph (f) the requirement that the bill of lading states the port of loading under the contract of carriage and also the date on which the goods were taken over by the carrier at the port of loading. The requirement that the bill of lading states the date on which the goods were taken over by the carrier at the port of loading is a most significant provision. Paragraph (g) requires that the bill of lading shall state the port of discharge under the contract of carriage, and paragraph (h) demands that the bill of lading shall set forth the number of originals of the bill of lading, if more than one. Paragraph (i) requires a statement of the place of issuance of the bill of lading, and paragraph (j) requires the signature of the carrier or a person acting on his behalf. Paragraph (k) makes the important provision that the bill of lading shall state the freight to the extent payable by the consignee or other indication that freight is payable by him. Paragraph (l) requires that the statement referred to in paragraph 3 of Article 23 of the Convention shall be set forth in the bill of lading— *i.e.* that when a bill of lading or any other document evidencing the contract of carriage is issued, it shall contain a statement that the carriage is subject to the provisions of the Convention which nullify any stipulation derogating therefrom to the detriment of the shipper or the consignee paragraph (m) provides that, the statement, if applicable, that the goods shall or may be carried on deck. (n) the date or period of delivery of the goods at the port of discharge is expressly agreed upon between the parties. This is again an entirely new innovation and it remains to be seen the manner in which it will become operative, but it seems clear that in the drafting of the paragraph, questions arising out of deviation and delay have been considered. (o) any increased limits of liability where agreed in accordance with paragraph 4 of Article 6. It will be noted that the provision in the Hague Rules that a declaration of the nature and value of the goods in the bill of lading "shall be *prima facie* evidence, but shall not be binding or conclusive on the carrier" has been dropped.

Paragraph 2 of Article 15 has the effect of amending various provisions in the Hague Rules contained in Article III paragraph 7 of those Rules.

Paragraph 3 of Article 15 goes on to provide that the absence in the bill of lading of one or more particulars referred to in Article 15 does not affect the legal character of the document as a bill of lading, provided that it nevertheless meets the requirements set out in paragraph 7 of Article 1. Paragraph 7 states that "Bill of Lading" means a document which evidences a contract of carriage and the taking over or loading of the goods by the carrier, and by which the carrier undertakes to deliver the goods against the surrender of the document. A provision in the document that the goods are to be delivered to the order of a named person, or to order, or to bearer, constitutes such an undertaking. Paragraph 2 gives effect to a practice sometimes commonly used of issuing a bill of lading after the goods have been received for shipment but have not actually been shipped, and when in such circumstances a bill of lading is demanded it will presumably still be regarded as a "received for shipment" bill of lading and will become a shipped bill of lading when the goods are actually received on board the vessel when the bill of lading will no doubt be stamped with some such provision as "shipped on board".

Article 16 — Bills of lading: reservations and evidentiary effect

1. If the bill of lading contains particulars concerning the general nature, leading marks, number of packages or pieces, weight or quantity of the goods which the carrier or other person issuing the bill of lading on his behalf knows or has reasonable grounds to suspect do not accurately represent the goods actually taken over or, where a "shipped" bill of lading is issued, loaded, or if he had no reasonable means of checking such particulars, the carrier or such other person must insert in the bill of lading a reservation specifying these inaccuracies, grounds of suspicion or the absence of reasonable means of checking.

2. If the carrier or other person issuing the bill of lading on his behalf fails to note on the bill of lading the apparent conditions of the goods, he is deemed to have noted on the bill of lading that the goods were in apparent good condition.

3. Except for particulars in respect of which and to the extent to which a reservation permitted under paragraph 1 of this article has been entered:
(a) the bill of lading is prima facie *evidence of the taking over or, where a "shipped" bill of lading is issued, loading, by the carrier of the goods as described in the bill of lading; and*
(b) proof to the contrary by the carrier is not admissible if the bill of lading has been transferred to a third party, including a consignee, who in good faith has acted in reliance on the description of the goods therein.

4. A bill of lading which does not, as provided in paragraph 1, subparagraph (k) of article 15, set forth the freight or otherwise indicate that freight is payable by the consignee or does not set forth demurrage incurred at the port of loading payable by the consignee, is prima facie *evidence that no freight or such demurrage is payable by him. However, proof to the contrary by the carrier is not admissible when the bill of lading has been transferred to a third party, including a consignee, who in good faith has acted in reliance on the absence in the bill of lading of any such indication.*

Article III paragraph 3 of the Hague Rules provides that no carrier, master or agent of the carrier, shall be bound to state or show in the bill of lading any marks, number, quantity or weight which he has reasonable ground for suspecting not accurately to represent the goods actually received, or which he has no reasonable means of checking. This rule is amended in the Hamburg Rules in Article 16 paragraph 1. The effect of this amendment is clear; namely, that from a position that exists at present in which the carrier need not show in the bill of lading any marks, number, quantity or weight which he has reasonable ground for suspecting not accurately to represent the goods actually received, or which he has no reasonable means of checking, the carrier, under the Hamburg Rules, will now have the obligation of inserting in the bill of lading a reservation specifying such inaccuracies, grounds of suspicion or absence of reasonable means of checking. This new rule imposes upon the carrier a new burden, for if he fails to comply with the requirement it will be deemed that the goods were as described in the bill of lading.

Article 16, paragraphs 2 and 3 of the Draft Convention seem to confirm this position, paragraph 2 providing that if the carrier, or other person issuing the bill of lading on his behalf, fails to note on the bill of lading the apparent condition of the goods, he is deemed to have noted on the bill of lading that the goods were in apparent good condition. Paragraph 3 of Article 16 provides that, except for particulars in respect of which and to the extent to which a reservation permitted under paragraph 1 of this Article has been entered: (a) the bill of lading is *prima facie* evidence of the taking over or, where a "shipped" bill of lading is issued, loading, by the carrier of the goods as described in the bill of lading; and (b) proof to the contrary by the carrier is not admissible if the bill of lading has been transferred to a third party, including any consignee who in good faith has acted in reliance on the description of the goods therein.

Paragraph 4 of Article 16 is an entirely new introduction to the Rules which concerns freight and demurrage at the port of loading and has the effect of affording considerable protection to the consignee who might otherwise find himself liable for such items. It will be recalled that Article 15 paragraph 1(k) of the Hamburg Rules provides that the bill of lading shall set forth the freight to the extent payable by the consignee or other indication that freight is payable by him. Article 16 paragraph 4 provides that a bill of lading which does not, as provided for in paragraph 1 subparagraph (k), set forth the freight or otherwise indicate that freight shall be payable by the consignee or does not set forth demurrage incurred at the port of loading payable by the consignee, is *prima facie* evidence that no freight or such demurrage is payable by him. However, proof to the contrary by the carrier is not admissible when the bill of lading has been transferred to a third party, including a consignee, who in good faith has acted in reliance on the absence in the bill of lading of any such indication. The provision with regard to freight is obviously a valuable addition to the Rules for the consignee, and no such protection is presently afforded under the Rules as they exist, but the effect of the provision with regard to demurrage, whilst again affording the consignee protection, is somewhat difficult to fully determine, as demurrage is commonly associated with contracts of carriage evidenced by charter-parties and such documents usually provide for periods of laytime and demurrage normally at both loading and discharging ports, the calculation of demurrage usually being determined after the completion of discharge.

Article 17 — Guarantees by the shipper

1. The shipper is deemed to have guaranteed to the carrier the accuracy of particulars relating to the general nature of the goods, their marks, number, weight and quantity as furnished by him for insertion in the bill of lading. The shipper must indemnify the carrier against the loss resulting from inaccuracies in such particulars. The shipper remains liable even if the bill of lading has been transferred by him. The right of the carrier to such indemnity in no way limits his liability under the contract of carriage by sea to any person other than the shipper.

2. Any letter of guarantee or agreement by which the shipper undertakes to indemnify the carrier against loss resulting from the issuance of the bill of lading by the carrier, or by a person acting on his behalf, without entering a reservation relating to particulars furnished by the shipper for insertion in the bill of lading, or to the apparent condition of the goods, is void and of no effect as against any third party, including a consignee, to whom the bill of lading has been transferred.

3. Such letter of guarantee or agreement is valid as against the shipper unless the carrier or the person acting on his behalf, by omitting the reservation referred to in paragraph 2 of this article, intends to defraud a third party, including a consignee, who acts in reliance on the description of the goods in the bill of lading. In the latter case, if the reservation omitted relates to particulars furnished by the shipper for insertion in the bill of lading, the carrier has no right of indemnity from the shipper pursuant to paragraph 1 of this article.

4. In the case of intended fraud referred to in paragraph 3 of this article the carrier is liable, without the benefit of the limitation of liability provided for in this Convention, for the loss incurred by a third party, including a consignee, because he has acted in reliance on the description of the goods in the bill of lading.

The liability of the shipper to the carrier is covered in the Hamburg Rules in Part III Article 12, which has already been discussed, and we now reach Article 17 of Part IV of the Hamburg Rules which deals with the shipper's guarantees to the carrier. The Hague Rules provide for this guarantee in Article III paragraph 5, which provides that the shipper shall be deemed to have guaranteed to the carrier the accuracy at the time of shipment of the masks, number, quantity, and weight, as furnished by the shipper. It is also provided that the shipper shall indemnify the carrier against all loss, damages, and expenses arising or resulting from inaccuracies in such particulars, but the right of the carrier to such indemnity in no way limits his responsibility and liability under the contract of carriage to any person other than the shipper. Article 17 of the Hamburg Rules follows this existing wording very closely in paragraph 1 of this article, and provides that the shipper is deemed to have guaranteed to the carrier the accuracy of particulars relating to the general nature of the goods, their marks, number, weight and quantity as furnished by him for insertion in the bill of lading. The Article also provides for a similar indemnity to the carrier and states that the shipper must indemnify the carrier against the loss resulting from inaccuracies in such particulars, providing also that the shipper remains liable even if the bill of lading has been transferred by him. Paragraph 1 of Article 17 also provides that the right of the carrier to such indemnity in no way limits his liability under the contract of carriage to any person other than the shipper. This indemnity by the shipper is extremely wide, indemnifying the carrier against "all loss resulting from inaccuracies in such particulars". In the case of inaccuracies in the weight of a package or unit, the carrier may in the first place suffer a loss because inadequate freight has been charged, but beyond this there are a host of other liabilities that the carrier may incur as a result of reliance upon the weight of a package or unit as furnished by the shipper in the bill of lading. The carrier may be led into trouble by declaring that weight to other parties such as a lighterage company who has supplied a lighter inadequate to receive a package or unit of the actual weight. In one such case the lighter capsized with the consequent loss of the goods already on board. The loading gear may be insufficient to lift safely a package or unit having a much greater weight than that declared by the shipper, causing the package or unit to be dropped and resulting in damage to the ship and other cargo. Another type of liability the carrier may suffer as a result of inaccuracy in the statement as regards weight could arise out of port or customs fines, etc., apart from expenses that the carrier may be caused. One final comment on Article 17 paragraph 1 of the Hamburg Rules namely that it will be observed that there is no mention of indemnity from the consignee, the shipper only being involved and, further, the consignee will not, it would seem, suffer from any limitation

130

of liability which such inaccuracies in declarations of particulars in bills of lading might give rise to so far as the shipper is concerned.

Article 17 contains three further paragraphs, paragraph 2 stating that any letter of guarantee or agreement by which the shipper undertakes to indemnify the carrier against loss resulting from the issuance of the bill of lading by the carrier, or by a person acting on his behalf, without entering a reservation relating to particulars furnished by the shipper for insertion in the bill of lading, or to the apparent condition of the goods, is void and of no effect as against any third party, including a consignee, to whom the bill of lading has been transferred. This provision is a new introduction into the rules and, in so drafting, the UNCTAD Committee no doubt had in mind the generally condemned practice of some carriers to issue clean bills of lading against a letter of indemnity from the shipper indemnifying the carrier against the consequences of so doing. It may be that the goods have suffered loss or damage before shipment, such as goods having been exposed for example to rain, the results of which may be clearly seen on the packages or units. If the bill of lading is claused for example to the effect that the packages are wet-stained, the bank would probably refuse to accept the documents and refuse to advance the cash that shipment with cleans bills of lading would entitle the shipper to. Should the carrier issue a clean bill of lading, this is tantamount to a fraud, for the consignee has bought the goods in reliance upon the bill of lading providing evidence of the apparent order and condition of the goods. The consignee would have a claim against the carrier because the bill of lading being clean and the goods being discharged in a damaged condition, the carrier would then settle the claim and claim against the shipper under the letter of indemnity, without the consignee having any knowledge of the transaction between the shipper and the carrier. But the consignees, instead of receiving goods in sound condition will have suffered a loss of trade because of the damaged condition. Article 17 paragraph 3 goes on to provide, however, that such a letter of guarantee or agreement is valid as against the shipper unless the carrier or the person acting on his behalf, by omitting the reservation referred to in paragraph 2 of this article, intends to defraud a third party, including a consignee, who acts in reliance on the description of the goods in the bill of lading. If, in the latter case, if the reservation omitted relates to particulars furnished by the shipper for insertion in the bill of lading, the carrier has no right of indemnity from the shipper pursuant to paragraph 1 of this article.

Paragraph 4 of Article 17 states that in the case of intended fraud referred to in paragraph 3 of this article, the carrier is liable, without the benefit of the limitation of liability provided for in this Convention, for the loss incurred by a third party, including a consignee, because he has acted in reliance on the description of the goods in the bill of lading.

When such guarantees or agreements, such as letters of indemnity, are accepted by the carrier in exchange for a clean bill of lading, it is tantamount to fraud, and the Courts have declined to acknowledge the terms of a letter of indemnity or to give the carrier the right to sue under such document, on the grounds that it is a fraudulent document. A number of delegations to the Conference took the view that paragraphs 2, 3 and 4 of Article 17 should be deleted.

Article 18 — Documents other than bills of lading

Where a carrier issues a document other than a bill of lading to evidence the receipt of the goods to be carried, such a document is prima facie *evidence of the conclusion of the contract of carriage by sea and the taking over by the carrier of the goods as therein described.*

In connection with this article it is of interest to look at the ruling of Mr. Justice Devlin in the case of *Pyrene Company Ltd. v. Scindia Steam Navigation Company Ltd*, when he said, amongst other things, that where a contract of carriage was concluded and it was contemplated that a bill of lading would in due course be issued in respect of it, that contract was from its creation "covered" by a bill of lading (within the meaning of Article I(b) of the Hague Rules) and was therefore from its inception a contract of carriage to which the Hague Rules applied.

The Hamburg Rules apply to contracts of carriage by sea and are defined in Article 1(6) as any contract whereby the carrier undertakes against payment of freight to carry goods by sea from one port to another. Bill of lading is defined in Article 1(7) as a document which evidences a contract of carriage by sea. It remains to be seen how Article 18 fits in with Article 1 but it would seem to have the effect of making it clear that the Hamburg Rules will apply from the time that the carrier acknowledges the receipt of the goods to be carried. However, it has also to be remembered that Article 1(6) also provides that in the case of a contract which involves carriage by sea and also carriage by some other means it is deemed to be a contract of carriage by sea only in so far as it relates to the carriage by sea.

PART V. CLAIMS AND ACTIONS

Article 19 — Notice of loss, damage or delay

1. Unless notice of loss or damage, specifying the general nature of such loss or damage, is given in writing by the consignee to the carrier not later than the working day after the day when the goods were handed over to the consignee, such handling over is prima facie *evidence of the delivery by the carrier of the goods as described in the document of transport or, if no such document has been issued, in good condition.*

2. Where the loss or damage is not apparent, the provisions of paragraph 1 of this article apply correspondingly if notice in writing is not

132

given within 15 consecutive days after the day when the goods were handed over to the consignee.

3. If the state of the goods at the time they were handed over to the consignee has been the subject of a joint survey or inspection by the parties, notice in writing need not be given of loss or damage ascertained during such survey or inspection.

4. In the case of any actual or apprehended loss or damage the carrier and the consignee must give all reasonable facilities to each other for inspecting and tallying the goods.

5. No compensation shall be payable for loss resulting from delay in delivery unless a notice has been given in writing to the carrier within 60 consecutive days after the day when the goods were handed over to the consignee.

6. If the goods have been delivered by an actual carrier, any notice given under this article to him shall have the same effect as if it had been given to the carrier, and any notice given to the carrier shall have effect as if given to such actual carrier.

7. Unless notice of loss or damage, specifying the general nature of the loss or damage, is given in writing by the carrier or actual carrier to the shipper not later than 90 consecutive days after the occurrence of such loss or damage or after the delivery of the goods in accordance with paragraph 2 of Article 4, whichever is later, the failure to give such notice is prima facie *evidence that the carrier or the actual carrier has sustained no loss or damage due to the fault or neglect of the shipper, his servants or agents.*

8. For the purpose of this Article, notice given to a person acting on the carrier's or the actual carrier's behalf, including the master or the officer in charge of the ship, or to a person acting on the shipper's behalf is deemed to have been given to the carrier, to the actual carrier or to the shipper, respectively.

Article III paragraph 6 of the Hague Rules provides that unless notice of loss or damage and the general nature of such loss or damage be given in writing to the carrier or his agent at the port of discharge before or at the time of the removal of the goods into the custody of. the person entitled to delivery thereof under the contract of carriage, or, if the loss or damage be not apparent within three days, such removal shall be *prima facie* evidence of the delivery by the carrier of the goods described in the bill of lading. The notice in writing need not be given if the state of the goods has at the time of their receipt been the subject of a joint survey or inspection.

Article 19 paragraph (1) of the Hamburg Rules provides that — unless notice of loss or damage, specifying the general nature of such loss or damage, is given in writing by the consignee to the carrier not later than the working day after the day when the goods were handed over to the consignee, such handing over is *prima facie* evidence of the delivery by the carrier of the goods as described in the document of transport or, if no such document has been issued, in good condition. The important words here are "when the goods were handed over to the consignee", and in the case of cargo loss or damage, the consignee will need to take particular care to determine at what point he, or his agents, did take delivery within the meaning of this new rule.

Article 19 paragraph (2) provides that where the loss or damage is not apparent, the provisions of paragraph (1) of this Article shall apply correspondingly if notice in writing is not given within 15 consecutive days after the day when the goods were handed over to the consignee. In connection with these two sub paragraphs of Article 19, the emphasis is on the words *prima facie* but in any event, nothing in these paragraphs seem to have changed the position that, regardless of whether notice of loss or damage is notified to the carrier within the period laid down, any loss or damage in the goods will need to be proved by the consignee. On the other hand, there still remains the obligation on the carrier to deliver the goods in the same apparent order and condition as described in the bill of lading. If the goods are in fact delivered by the carrier in the same apparent order and condition as described in the bill of lading, then the onus will remain with the consignee to prove loss or damage during the sea transit, whether or not notice of loss or damage is given within the prescribed period. Article 19 contains four further sub-paragraphs nos. 3, 4, 5 and 6. In considering these sub-paragraphs it is necessary to have in mind the provisions of sub-paragraphs 1 and 2. Sub-paragraph (3) provides that — if the state of the goods at the time that they were handed over to the consignee has been the subject of joint survey or inspection by the parties, notice in writing need not be given of loss or damage ascertained during such survey or inspection. This provision follows very much on the lines of Article III paragraph 6 of the Hague Rules, but there is a subtle difference in that the latter provides that notice in writing need not be given if the state of the goods has at the time of their receipt been the subject of joint survey or inspection, whereas Article 19 sub-paragraph 3 provides that the notice in writing need not be given "of loss or damage ascertained during such survey or inspection". This amendment gives an entirely different effect to the existing Rule in that, whereas a joint inspection or survey of the goods presently eliminates entirely the necessity of giving notice in writing, the amendment does not have this effect and, if, for example, other damage is found after the joint inspection, the consignee will presumably be required to give notice of loss or damage within the required period, extended under the Hamburg Rules to 15 days. The words *prima facie* in sub-paragraph (1) of Article 19 are of special significance, for even though notice of loss, damage or delay be not given within the required period it will still be open to the consignee to show the loss, damage, or delay has taken place during the period that the goods were in the care and custody of the carrier.

Article 19 sub-paragraph (4) provides that — in the case of any actual or apprehended loss or damage the carrier and the consignee must give all reasonable facilities to each other for inspecting and tallying the goods. This provision is identical with the provision contained in Article III paragraph 6 of the existing Rules.

Paragraph 5 of Article 19 provides that — no compensation shall be payable for loss resulting from delay in delivery unless a notice has been given in writing to the carrier within 60 consecutive days after the day when the goods were handed over to the consignee. This is an entirely new Rule having no counterpart in the Hague Rules and is extremely important in that, although up to now the Hamburg Rules have been made applicable to claims arising out of loss of goods, damage to goods and loss arising out of delay, this particular Rule now separates loss by reason of delay and places it in a separate category, seemingly discharging the carrier from all liability unless a notice has been given in writing to the carrier within 60 consecutive days after the day when the goods were handed over to the carrier. Article 19 paragraph 6 provides that — if the goods have been delivered by an actual carrier, any notice given under this Article to him shall have the same effect as if it had been given to the carrier, and any notice given to the carrier shall have effect as if given to such actual carrier. This provision is made clear if the reader will refer to Article 1 of Part 1 of the Hamburg Rules which deals with definitions. Sub-paragraph (1) of Article 1 states that "carrier" means any person by whom or in whose name a contract of carriage of goods by sea has been concluded with a shipper, whilst sub-paragraph (2) states that "actual carrier" means any person to whom the performance of the carriage of the goods, or part of the carriage, has been entrusted by the carrier, and any other person to whom such performance has been entrusted. With these definitions in the background, the importance of Article 19 sub-paragraph 6 can be well understood, relieving as it does the consignee of the burden of discovering who is the proper party on whom the claim should be made. The Hague Rules do not contain any such provision and neither do they include a definition of "actual carrier", the word "carrier" having also been revised so as to include any person by whom or in whose name a contract of carriage of goods by sea has been concluded with a shipper.

Paragraph 7 is an additional provision having no counterpart in the Hague Rules. The overall effect and object of this paragraph is difficult to determine immediately but seems aimed at a limitation of time in respect of a claim against the shipper by the carrier because perhaps by reason of damage done to the ship by the cargo. But it might perhaps extend to a claim on the shipper in respect of damage or loss suffered by the cargo for which the carrier has to pay, or perhaps damage done to other cargo. Special note has to be taken of the words "is *prima facie* evidence". Paragraph 8 is a new provision also having no counterpart in the Hague Rules extending extra facilities to the cargo owner in giving notice of loss or damage. Unquestionably of great value to the cargo owner.

Article 20 — Limitation of actions

1. Any action relating to carriage of goods under this Convention is time-barred if judicial or arbitral proceedings have not been instituted within a period of two years.

2. The limitation period commences on the day on which the carrier has delivered the goods or part thereof or, in cases where no goods have been delivered, on the last day on which the goods should have been delivered.

3. The day on which the limitation period commences is not included in the period.

4. The person against whom a claim is made may at any time during the running of the limitation period extend that period by a declaration in writing to the claimant. This period may be further extended by another declaration or declarations.

5. An action for indemnity by a person held liable may be instituted even after the expiration of the limitation period provided for in the preceding paragraphs if instituted within the time allowed by the law of the State where proceedings are instituted. However, the time allowed shall not be less than 90 days commencing from the day when the person instituting such action for indemnity has settled the claim or has been served with process in the action against himself.

Article 20 of Part V of the Hamburg Rules deals with the important matter of limitation of actions, and is a complete re-draft of the present Rule contained in Article III paragraph 6 of the Hague Rules, which provides that, in any event, the carrier and the ship shall be discharged from all liability in respect of loss or damage unless suit is brought within one year after delivery of the goods or the date when the goods should have been delivered. At the time the Committee were examining the need for revising the Hague Rules, the conclusion was reached that Article III paragraph 6 was not clear as to whether the one-year limitation period begins to run from delivery or discharge of the goods, when those operations occur at different times. The view was taken that if the Rules were amended to apply to the entire period during which the goods are in the carrier's custody, then the time limit would begin to run from delivery and the uncertainty would be resolved. On the other hand, if the Rules could not be amended in this way, the Committee thought that it would still be useful to amend Article III paragraph 6 to clarify that delivery means the moment when the consignee receives, or shall receive, the goods. It was also thought that Article III paragraph 6 might be amended further to state that it would be sufficient for suit to be brought in any jurisdiction having a reasonably close connection with the contract of carriage, such as the country of shipment or destination, and that the cargo claimant would not be restricted to bringing suit in a particular jurisdiction.

This Hague Rules provision states, amongst other things, that "in any event" suit must be brought "within one year after the delivery of the goods or the date when the goods should have been delivered", and when the Rule was being considered for amendment the Committee had certain questions in mind: (a) What constitutes "delivery" in order to start the one-year period running, particularly bearing in mind the variations of the one-year period in some countries. (b) Does "brought within one year" mean brought anywhere within one year, or brought before a particular court within that time? (c) Does the word "suit" include arbitration? (d) What is the significance of the phrase "in any event"? (e) May the parties extend the time limit by agreement?

The question of delivery has been dealt with earlier in a different context and it now arises in connection with the deliberations of UNCTAD on this present problem. The time limitation period begins to run upon "delivery" or "when the goods should have been delivered". In considering this matter, it was felt that the use of the word "delivery" instead of "discharge" appears to be intentional because "discharge" is used elsewhere in the Rules. "Delivery" would ordinarily mean the moment when the consignee receives the goods from the party competent to deliver them but some courts have held that the time limitation period begins to run before that time. There was the further uncertainty as to whether a suit in one country stops the running of the one-year period in another country.

What does the word "suit" mean? In this connection, the question arose as to whether arbitration proceedings are to be considered "suits" for the purposes of the one-year time limitation. The Committee felt that if this were so, the result could be harsh for consignees when the bill of lading has been issued under a charter-party containing an arbitration clause. In such cases, the charter-party is usually incorporated into the bill of lading by reference, and the consignee does not know of its contents. In the result, the consignee might well commence legal proceedings within one year but later discover that his legal suit has failed because he did not in the first place arbitrate, and then find that his application for arbitration has also failed because he did not in the first place appoint an arbitrator within one year. The question also arose as to whether the word "suit", if taken to exclude arbitration, (and the parties in fact submit to arbitration), means that the parties have thereby waived the requirement that suit must be brought within one year. It will be seen from Articles 20, 21 and 22 of Part V of the Hamburg Rules, that these matters have been taken care of, when redrafting, at length, Article III paragraph 6.

Article 20 carries the title "Limitation of Actions" and is divided into five sections. Paragraph (1) provides that — any action relating to the carriage of goods under the Convention is time-barred if judicial or arbitral proceedings have not been instituted within a period of two years. The period allowed in the Hague Rules is one year and in this connection, it will be recalled that under the terms of the Gold Clause Agreement shipowners would grant cargo interests an extension of one year beyond the one-year time limitation contained in Article III paragraph 6 of the Hague Rules, subject to certain matters having been complied with, namely proper notice of loss to the carrier of the loss or damage within the twelve-month period contained in the Rules. This amendment seems to have resulted from a recognition that the twelve-month period for the commencement of "suit" was too short to allow proper negotiation of claims between the parties.

Paragraph (2) of Article 20 provides that — the limitation period commences on the day on which the carrier has delivered the goods or part thereof or, in cases where no goods have been delivered, on the last day on which the goods should have been delivered. Paragraph (3) provides that — the day on which the limitation period commences is not included in the period. Paragraph (4) provides that — the person against whom a claim is made may at any time during the running of the limitation period extent that period by a declaration in writing to the claimant. This period may be further extended by another declaration or declarations. This has the effect of recognising the need for making extensions of time legally valid. Paragraph (5) provides that — an action for indemnity by a person held liable may be instituted even after the expiration of the limitation period provided for in the preceding paragraphs if instituted within the time allowed by the law of the State where proceedings are instituted. However, the paragraph continues with the provision that — the time allowed shall not be less than 90 days commencing from the day when the person bringing such action for indemnity has settled the claim or has been served with process in the action against himself.

Article 21 — Jurisdiction

1. In judicial proceedings relating to carriage of goods under this Convention the plaintiff, at his option, may institute an action in a court which, according to the law of the State where the court is situated, is competent and within the jurisdiction of which is situated one of the following places:

(a) the principal place of business or, in the absence thereof, the habitual residence of the defendant; or

(b) the place where the contract was made provided that the defendant has there a place of business, branch or agency through which the contract was made; or

(c) the port of loading or the port of discharge; or

(d) any additional place designated for that purpose in the contract of carriage by sea.

2. (a) Notwithstanding the preceding provisions of this article, an action may be instituted in the courts of any port or place in a Contracting State at which the carrying vessel or any other vessel of the same ownership may have been arrested in accordance with applicable rules of the law of that State and of international law. However, in such a case, at the petition of the defendant, the claimant must remove the action, at his choice, to one of the jurisdictions referred to in paragraph 1 of this article for the determination of the claim, but before such removal the defendant must furnish security sufficient to ensure payment of any judgement that may subsequently be awarded to the claimant in the action.

(b) All questions relating to the sufficiency or otherwise of the security shall be determined by the court of the port or place of the arrest.

3. No judicial proceedings relating to carriage of goods under this Convention may be instituted in a place not specified in paragraph 1 or 2 of this article. The provisions of this paragraph do not constitute an obstacle to the jurisdiction of the Contracting States for provisional or protective measures.

4. (a) Where an action has been instituted in a court competent under paragraph 1 or 2 of this article or where judgement has been delivered by such a court, no new action may be started between the same parties on the same grounds unless the judgement of the court before which the first action was instituted is not enforceable in the country in which the new proceedings are instituted;

(b) for the purpose of this article the institution of measures with a view to obtaining enforcement of a judgement is not to be considered as the starting of a new action;

(c) for the purpose of this article, the removal of an action to a different court within the same country, or to a court in another country, in accordance with paragraph 2(a) of this article, is not to be considered as the starting of a new action.

5. Notwithstanding the provisions of the preceding paragraphs, an agreement made by the parties, after a claim under the contract of carriage by sea has arisen, which designates the place where the claimant may institute an action, is effective.

This article has no counterpart in the Hague Rules, the question of jurisdiction under those Rules being left to be decided according to national law. The Hamburg Rules, by Article 21, give the claimant a wide choice of jurisdiction and even though the contract of carriage may stipulate for jurisdiction in a particular country or courts, the claimant is not, by the Hamburg Rules denied the right of seeking optional jurisdiction. The optional jurisdictions open to the claimant are contained in paragraph 1 of Article 21, and before proceeding to the actual provisions of this article it should perhaps be mentioned that the choice of jurisdiction under the Hamburg Rules is available whether the claim is being brought against the carrier or the actual carrier.

The Hamburg Rules, by this article deal with jurisdictional matters at great length, and the framers of the Rules have obviously given much thought to the jurisdictional problems that have arisen under the Hague Rules.

Paragraph (1) provides that — in a judicial proceeding relating to the carriage of goods under the Convention the plaintiff, at his option, may institute an action in a court which, according to the law of the State (it seems that a considerable number of delegations favoured the addition of the word "Contracting" before the word "State" and this would seem reasonable because the Convention Rules will only be applicable to those States who have ratified or acceded to the Convention) where the court is situated, is competent and within the jurisdiction of which is situated one of the following: (a) The principal place of business or, in the absence thereof, the habitual residence of the defendant; or (b) the place where the contract was made provided that the defendant has there a place of business, branch or agency through which the contract was made; or (c) the port of loading or the port of discharge; or (d) any additional place designated for that purpose in the contract of carriage by sea.

Paragraph 2 of Article 21 goes on to provide—(a) that notwithstanding these preceding provisions of Article 21, an action may be instituted in the courts of any port or place in a contracting State at which the carrying vessel or any other vessel of the same ownership may have been arrested in accordance with the applicable rules of law of that State and of international law. It is provided, however, that—in such a case, at the petition of the defendant, the claimant must remove the action, at his choice, to one of the jurisdictions referred to in paragraph 1 of this Article for the determination of the claim, but before such removal the defendant must furnish security sufficient to ensure payment of any judgment that may be subsequently awarded to the claimant in the action. (b) all questions relating to the sufficiency or otherwise of the security shall be determined by the court of the port or place of the arrest.

This provision as regards the furnishing of security is of extreme importance as will be immediately apparent.

Paragraph 3 of Article 21 provides that — no judicial proceedings relating to the carriage of goods under this Convention may be instituted in a place not specified in paragraphs 1 or 2 of this Article. It is provided also that — the provisions of this paragraph do not constitute an obstacle to the jurisdiction of the contracting States for provisional or protective measures. Paragraph 4 of Article 21 provides (a) that where an action has been instituted in a court competent under paragraph 1 or 2 of this article or where judgment has been delivered by such a court, no new action shall be started between the same parties on the same grounds unless the judgment of the Court before which the first action was instituted is not enforceable in the country in which new proceedings are instituted (b) that — for the purpose of this article the institution of measures with a view to obtaining enforcement of a judgment is not to be considered as the starting of a new action (c) that for the purpose of this article the removal of an action to a different area within the same country or to a court in another country, in accordance with paragraph 2(a) of this article, is not to be considered as the starting of a new action. Paragraph 5 of Article 21 provides that notwithstanding the provisions of the preceding paragraphs, an agreement by the parties, after a claim under the contract of carriage has arisen, which designates the place where the claimant may institute an action is effective.

These provisions rule out the doubt as to the rights of carriers to stipulate in bills of lading for any dispute arising out of the contract of carriage to be determined by the courts of a country irrelevant to the port or ports of loading or discharge, or irrelevant to the country from which the goods are shipped or that in which they are discharged, but perhaps making provision in the contract of carriage as evidenced by the bills of lading for any dispute to be determined in the courts of the country of ownership of the vessel. Article 21 lays down mandatory rules as to the court or courts where the cargo claimants may, at their option, bring legal proceedings to enforce their claim.

It would seem that this wide choice of jurisdiction is applicable whether the claim be against the "carrier" or the "actual carrier" and also it would seem that it applies in the case of a claim by the carrier against the shipper.

Article 22 — Arbitration

1. Subject to the provisions of this article, parties may provide by agreement evidenced in writing that any dispute that may arise relating to carriage of goods under this Convention shall be referred to arbitration.

2. Where a charter-party contains a provision that disputes arising thereunder shall be referred to arbitration and a bill of lading issued pursuant to the charter-party does not contain a special annotation providing that such provision shall be binding upon the holder of the bill of lading, the carrier may not invoke such provision as against a holder having acquired the bill of lading in good faith.

3. The arbitration proceedings shall, at the option of the claimant, be instituted at one of the following places:

(a) a place in a State within whose territory is situated:
(i) the principal place of business of the defendant or, in the absence thereof, the habitual residence of the defendant; or
(ii) the place where the contract was made, provided that the defendant has there a place of business, branch or agency through which the contract was made; or
(iii) the port of loading or the port of discharge; or

(b) any place designated for that purpose in the arbitration clause or agreement.

4. The arbitrator or arbitration tribunal shall apply the rules of this Convention.

5. The provisions of paragraphs 3 and 4 of this article are deemed to be part of every arbitration clause or agreement, and any term of such clause or agreement which is inconsistent therewith is null and void.

6. Nothing in this Article affects the validity of an agreement relating to arbitration made by the parties after the claim under the contract of carriage by sea has arisen.

The Hague Rules make no reference to arbitration, leaving open the question as to whether arbitration proceedings constitute "a suit" within the meaning of Article III paragraph 6 of the Hague Rules.

Article 22 of the Hamburg Rules deals at great length with this problem and for those parties concerned in the field of ship chartering, shipowners and cargo interests in particular, the provisions of this Article are of extreme importance.

PART VI. SUPPLEMENTARY PROVISIONS

Article 23 — Contractual stipulations

1. Any stipulation in a contract of carriage by sea, in a bill of lading, or in any other document evidencing the contract of carriage by sea is null and void to the extent that it derogates, directly or indirectly, from the provisions of this Convention. The nullity of such a stipulation does not affect the validity of the other provisions of the contract or document of which it forms a part. A clause assigning benefit of insurance of the goods in favour of the carrier, or any similar clause, is null and void.

2. Notwithstanding the provisions of paragraph 1 of this article, a carrier may increase his responsibilities and obligations under this Convention.

3. Where a bill of lading or any other document evidencing the contract of carriage by sea is issued, it must contain a statement that the carriage is subject to the provisions of this Convention which nullify any stipulation derogating therefrom to the detriment of the shipper or the consignee.

4. Where the claimant in respect of the goods has incurred loss as a result of a stipulation which is null and void by virtue of the present article, or as a result of the omission of the statement referred to in paragraph 3 of this article, the carrier must pay compensation to the extent required in order to give the claimant compensation in accordance with the provisions of this Convention for any loss of or damage to the goods as well as for delay in delivery. The carrier must, in addition, pay compensation for costs incurred by the claimant for the purpose of excercising his right, provided that costs incurred in the action where the foregoing provision is invoked are to be determined in accordance with the law of the State where proceedings are instituted.

Paragraph (1) of Article 23 amends the provisions of Article III paragraph 8 of the Hague Rules, paragraph 8 providing that any clause, covenant or agreement in a contract of carriage relieving the carrier or the ship from liability for loss or damage to or in connection with goods arising from negligence, fault of failure in the duties and obligations provided for in Article III or lessening such liability otherwise than as provided in the Rules, shall be null and void and of no effect. At one time, considerable doubt existed as to whether a clause partially offending the Rules would be held void in its entirety or whether only that part of the clause which offended the Rules would be of no effect, leaving the balance of the clause valid. The case of *Svenska Traktors v. Maritime Agencies* partially answered this question. In that case, the bill of lading contained a clause giving the carrier the liberty to ship goods on deck, providing also that if the goods were shipped on deck the carrier would not be responsible for any loss or damage. Concerned was a consignment of tractors which the carrier shipped on deck and, during the course of the voyage, one of the tractors went overboard and was lost. When the case came before the Court, it was held that whilst part of the clause giving the liberty to ship on deck was permissible under the Rules, it was not permissible for the carrier to exempt himself from liability, in respect of loss or damage that the cargo might suffer, except as provided for in the Rules. It was held that the clause could be read disjunctively and that, therefore, although one part of the clause offended the Act and was therefore void, this did not render the whole clause invalid.

Article 23 of the Hamburg Rules now clarifies the question and provides that any stipulation in a contract of carriage by sea in a bill of lading or other document evidencing the contract of carriage by sea is null and void to the extent that it derogates, directly or indirectly, from the provisions of the Convention. Also that the nullity of such a stipulation does not affect the validity of the other provisions of the contract or document of which it forms a part. There then follows a similar provision presently contained in the Hague Rules providing that a clause assigning benefit of insurance of the goods in favour of the carrier, or any similar clause is null and void.

Paragraph 2 of Article 23 maintains the position under the Hague Rules by providing that — notwithstanding the provisions of paragraph 1 of this article, a carrier may increase his responsibilities and obligations under the Convention. Under the provisions of the Hague Rules, it is provided that, by agreement between the carrier, master or agent of the carrier and the shipper, another maximum amount than that provided for in the Rules may be fixed provided that such maximum shall not be less

143

than the sum provided for in the Rules. The amendment in the Hamburg Rules, although more concise, does not appear to alter the position materially under the provisions of Article IV paragraph 5 sub paragraph 3 of the Rules. The Carriage of Goods by Sea Act, 1924, which gave the Hague Rules statutory effect in the U.K., contains a provision to the effect that every bill of lading, or similar document of title, issued in Great Britain or Northern Ireland which contains or is evidence of any contract to which the Rules apply, shall contain an express statement that it is to have effect subject to the Rules as applied by the Act. Article 23 paragraph 3 of the Hamburg Rules introduces into the Rules the provision that — when a bill of lading or any other document evidencing the contract of carriage by sea is issued, it must contain a statement that the carriage is subject to the provisions of the Convention which nullify any stipulation derogating therefrom to the detriment of the shipper or the consignee. Thus is the provision in the Carriage of Goods by Sea Act now made mandatory on an international basis.

Paragraph (4) of Article 23 is a new introduction having no counterpart in the Hague Rules and provides that — where the claimant in respect of the goods has incurred a loss as a result of a stipulation which is null and void by virtue of Article 23, or as a result of the omission of the statement referred to in paragraph 3 of Article 23, the carrier must pay compensation to the extent required in order to give the claimant compensation in accordance with the provisions of the Convention for any loss of or damage to the goods, as well as for delay in delivery. The carrier must in addition, pay compensation for costs incurred by the claimant for the purpose of excercising his right, provided that costs incurred in the action where the foregoing provision is invoked are to be determined in accordance with the law of the State where proceedings are instituted. This provision seems to contemplate, amongst other things, a situation in which the bill of lading issued in one of the contracting States covering a voyage to a country which has not ratified the Hamburg Rules, contains a provision giving the carrier rights or exemptions from liability otherwise than as provided for in the Hamburg Rules. In such a case, the Courts of the country of destination would give effect to the contract evidenced by the bill of lading and since such contract did not incorporate the Hamburg Rules they would have no effect. Such a situation developed after the Hague Rules were passed in 1924 when, because the United Kingdom, by the Carriage of Goods by Sea Act, made the Rules effective in respect of outward shipments from the United Kingdom, bills of lading covering shipments to the U.K. not incorporating the Rules were given effect soley as to the conditions contained in the contract of carriage so evidenced. Therefore, in the event of a claim for loss or damage being pursued against the carrier in respect of cargo loss or damage, and the carrier relying on wide exemption clauses which would be rendered void under the provisions of the Rules, the Courts, unless the bill of lading stated the Rules were to apply, would have to deal with the question of carrier's liability giving effect to the exemption clauses contained in the bill of lading. This situation could develop in any country where the Hague Rules did not operate with regard to inward as well as outward shipments. This situation, however, seldom arises because most bills of lading contain a clause paramount incorporating the Rules, but Article 23 paragraph (4) of the Hamburg Rules seems to be aimed, amongst other things, at plugging the gap.

Article 24 — General average

1. Nothing in this Convention shall prevent the application of provisions in the contract of carraige by sea or national law regarding the adjustment of general average.

2. With the exception of Article 20, the provisions of this Convention relating to the liability of the carrier for loss of or damage to the goods also determine whether the consignee may refuse contribution in general average and the liability of the carrier to indemnify the consignee in respect of any such contribution made or any salvage paid.

The Hague Rules provide that nothing in the Rules shall be held to prevent the insertion in a bill of lading of any lawful provision regarding general average. Article 24 of the Hamburg Rules goes a great deal further, but maintains this Hague Rules provision.

Article 24 provides that nothing in the Convention shall prevent the application of provisions in the contract of carriage by sea or national law regarding the adjustment of general average. Thus is the Hague Rules provision maintained. However, the Hamburg Rules contain an additional provision in paragraph 2 of Article 24, a provision which has no counterpart in the Hague Rules. This paragraph provides that — with the exception of Article 20, (this article deals with the question of time limitation for the commencement of proceedings against he carrier) the provisions of the Hamburg Rules relating to the liability of the carrier for loss of or damage to the goods also determine whether the consignee may refuse contribution in general average and the liability to indemnify the consignee in respect of any such contribution made or any salvage paid.

It would seem that cargo interests may no longer be required to contribute in general average and salvage cases, when there has been a breach of the contract of carriage by sea, in the event that the carrier or his servants or agents fail to prove that all measures that could reasonably be required were taken to avoid the occurrence giving rise to the general average. From time to time one hears the cry that general average should be abolished and that the loss should lie where it falls, and perhaps the Hamburg Rules may be paving the way to such a gaol but certainly they will place the cargo interests in a stronger position.

145

Article 25 — Other conventions

1. This Convention does not modify the rights or duties of the carrier, the actual carrier and their servants and agents, provided for in international conventions or national law relating to the limitation of liability of owners of seagoing ships.

2. The provisions of Articles 21 and 22 of this Convention do not prevent the application of the mandatory provisions of any other multilateral convention already in force at the date of this Convention relating to matters dealt with in the said articles, provided that the dispute arises exclusively between parties having their principal place of business in States members of such other convention. However, this paragraph does not affect the application of paragraph 4 of Article 22 of this Convention.

3. No liability shall arise under the provisions of this Convention for damage caused by a nuclear incident if the operator of a nuclear installation is liable for such damage:

(a) under either the Paris Convention of July 29, 1960 on Third Party Liability in the Field of Nuclear Energy as amended by the Additional Protocol of January 28, 1964 or the Vienna Convention of May 21, 1963 on Civil Liability for Nuclear Damage, or
(b) by virtue of national law governing the liability for such damage, provided that such law is in all respects as favourable to persons who may suffer damage as either the Paris or Vienna Conventions.

4. No liability shall arise under the provisions of this Convention for any loss of or damage to or delay in delivery of luggage for which the carrier is responsible under international convention or national law relating to the carriage of passengers and their luggage by sea.

5. Nothing contained in this Convention prevents a Contracting State from applying any other international convention which is already in force at the date of this Convention and which applies mandatorily to contracts of carriage of goods primarily by a mode of transport other than transport by sea. This provision also applies to any subsequent revision or amendment of such international convention.

Article 25 provides that this Convention does not modify the rights or duties of the carrier, the actual carrier and their servants and agents, provided for in international conventions or national law relating to the limitations of liability of owners of sea-going ships. When the Hague Rules were given the force of law in the United Kingdom by the passing of the Carriage of Goods by Sea Act, 1924, the Act contained a provision that nothing in the Act shall affect the operation of sections 446 to 450, both inclusive, 502 and 503 of the Merchant Shipping Act, 1894, as amended by any subsequent enactment, or the operation of any other enactment for the time being in force limiting the liability of seagoing ships. Sections 446 to 450 deal with the carriage of dangerous goods, the marking of the packages, the duties of the shipper and the rights of the master to dump such goods etc. Section 502 of the Act provides that the owner of a British sea-going ship shall not be liable to make good to any extent whatever any loss or damage happening without his actual fault or privity in the following cases: (i) where any goods, merchandise or other things whatsoever taken in or put on board his ship are lost or damaged by reason of fire on board his ship; (ii) where any gold, silver, diamonds, watches, jewels, or precious stones taken in or put on board his ship, the true nature and value of which have not, at the time of shipment, been declared by the owner or shipper thereof to the owner or master of the ship, in the bills of lading or otherwise in writing, are lost or damaged by reason of any robbery, embezzlement, making away with, or secreting thereof.

Section 503 of the Merchant Shipping Act deals with the question of limitation of liability, and gives effect to international law, and provides that where all or any of the following occurrences take place without the fault or privity of the owners of a British or foreign ship (a) where any loss of life or personal injury is caused to any person being carried in the ship; (b) where any damage or loss is caused to any goods, merchandise, or other things whatsoever on board the ship; (c) where any loss of life or personal injury is caused to any person carried in any other vessel by reason of the improper navigation of the ship; (d) where any loss or damage is caused to any other vessel, or to any goods, merchandise, or other things whatsoever on board any other vessel, by reason of the improper navigation of the ship; be liable to pay damages beyond certain amounts. The amounts vary from time to time because of increases agreed at international conventions. Paragraph (1) of Article 25 of the Hamburg Rules clearly contemplates these and many other local and international laws since adopted to be included in any enactment passed by the maritime nations to give effect to the Hamburg Rules.

Paragraph 2 of Article 25 provides that — the provisions of Articles 21 and 22 of this Convention do not prevent the application of the mandatory provisions of any other multilateral Convention already in force at the date of this Convention relating to matters dealt with in the said articles, provided that the dispute arises exclusively between parties having their principal place of business in States which are members of such other convention. However, this paragraph does not affect the application of paragraph 4 of Article 22 of this Convention.

Paragraph 3 of Article 25 provides that no liability shall arise under the provisions of the Convention for damage caused by nuclear incident if the operator of a nuclear installation is liable for such damage (a) under either the Paris Convention of July 29, 1960 on Third Party Liability in the field of nuclear energy as amended by the Additional Protocol of January 28, 1964 or the Vienna Convention of May 21, 1963 on Civil Liability for nuclear damage, or (b) by virtue of national law governing the liability for such damage, provided that such law is in all respects as favourable to persons who may suffer damage as are either the Paris or Vienna Conventions. Paragraph 4 of Article 25 provides that — no liability shall arise under the provisions of the Convention for any loss of, or damage to or delay in delivery of luggage for which the carrier is responsible under any international convention or national law relating to the carriage of passengers and their luggage by sea.

Paragraph 5 provides that — nothing contained in this Convention prevents a Contracting State from applying any other international convention which is already in force at the date of this Convention and which applies mandatorily to contracts of carriage of goods primarily by a mode of transport other than transport by sea. This provision also applies to any subsequent revision or amendment of such international convention.

This Rule seemingly has in mind such conventions as the C.M.R. and C.I.M. Conventions applicable to international carriage of goods by road and rail. Also presently, contemplated in the international field is legislation governing the carriage of passengers and luggage by sea, and the object of this provision would seem to be that the Hamburg Rules shall not affect the deliberations and decisions of international forums who produce legislation on these liabilities. However, if luggage is carried under a contract evidenced by a bill of lading then the Hamburg Rules will presumably apply, since there is no exclusion, other than the above. In other words, if the luggage is carried under the terms of the contract for the carriage of the passenger, as is normally the case, the terms of the Hamburg Rules will not apply, but paragraph 4 of Article 25 seems to leave a gap, for the reason that it provides that no liability shall arise under the terms of the Hamburg Rules for which the carrier is responsible under any international Convention or national law, whereas presently there is no international law.

So far as national laws are concerned both in the United States and the United Kingdom there exist national laws relative to the question of liability for loss of or damage to luggage. However, this liability will no doubt in the future become the subject of an international convention.

Article 26 — Unit of account

1. The unit of account referred to in Article 6 of this Convention is the Special Drawing Rights as defined by the International Monetary Fund. The amounts mentioned in Article 6 are to be converted into the national currency of a State according to the value of such currency at the date of judgement or the date agreed upon by the parties. The value of a national currency, in terms of the Special Drawing Right, of a Contracting State which is a member of the International Monetary Fund is to be calculated in accordance with the method of valuation applied by the International Monetary Fund in effect at the date in question for its operations and transactions. The value of a national currency in terms of the Special

Drawing Right of a Contracting State which is not a member of the International Monetary Fund is to be calculated in a manner determined by that State.

2. Nevertheless, those States which are not members of the International Monetary Fund and whose law does not permit the application of the provisions of paragraph 1 of this article may, at the time of signature, or at the time of ratification, acceptance, approval or accession or at any time thereafter, declare that the limits of liability provided for in this Convention to be applied in their territories shall be fixed as:

12,500 monetary units per package or other shipping unit or 37.5 monetary units per kilogramme of gross weight of the goods.

3. The monetary unit referred to in paragraph 2 of this article corresponds to sixty-five and a half milligrammes of gold of millesimal fineness nine hundred. The conversion of the amounts referred to in paragraph 2 into the national currency is to be made according to the law of the State concerned.

4. The calculation mentioned in the last sentence of paragraph 1 and the conversion mentioned in paragraph 3 of this article is to be made in such a manner as to express in the national currency of the Contracting State as far as possible the same real value for the amounts in Article 6 as is expressed there in units of account. Contracting States must communicate to the depositary the manner of calculation pursuant to paragraph 1 of this article, or the result of the conversion mentioned in paragraph 3 of this article, as the case may be, at the time of signature or when depositing their instruments of ratification, acceptance, approval or accession, or when availing themselves of the option provided for in paragraph 2 of this article and whenever there is a change in the manner of such calculation or in the result of such conversion.

Article 26 refers to the unit of account contained in Article 6 and has relation to the limits to liability of the carrier in respect of cargo loss or damage. The limit of liability of the carrier under the Hague Rules is £100 per package or unit (gold value) or, in the case of parties to the Gold Clause agreement, £200. The limits under the Hague/Visby Rules are 10,000 Poincare francs per package or unit or 30 Poincare francs per kilo, whichever is the higher. Under the provisions of Article 6 of the Hamburg Rules the carrier may limit his liability to an amount equivalent to 835 units per package or other shipping unit or 2.5 units of account per kilogramme of gross weight of the goods lost or damaged, whichever is the higher. Converted into sterling at the time of the Final Act of the United Nations Conference on the Carriage of Goods by Sea in 1978 when the Hamburg Rules were passed, 835 Special Drawing Rights approximated to £555 and 2.5 Special Drawing Rights to £1.66. In the result the limit of liability has been increased by approximately 25% over the Hague/Visby Rules limits.

PART VII. FINAL CLAUSES

Article 27 — Depositary

The Secretary-General of the United Nations is hereby designated as the depositary of this Convention.

Article 28 — Signature, ratification, acceptance, approval, accession

1. This Convention is open for signature by all States until 30 April, 1979 at the Headquarters of the United Nations, New York.

2. This Convention is subject to ratification, acceptance or approval by the signatory States.

3. After 30 April, 1979, this Convention will be open for accession by all States which are not signatory States.

4. Instruments of ratification, acceptance, approval and accession are to be deposited with the Secretary-General of the United Nations.

Article 29 — Reservations

No reservations may be made to this Convention.

Article 30 — Entry into force

1. This Convention enters into force on the first day of the month following the expiration of one year from the date of deposit of the 20th instrument of ratification, acceptance, approval or accession.

2. For each State which becomes a Contracting State to this Convention after the date of the deposit of the 20th instrument of ratification, acceptance, approval or accession, this Convention enters into force on the first day of the month following the expiration of one year after the deposit of the appropriate instrument on behalf of that State.

3. Each Contracting State shall apply the provisions of this Convention to contracts of carriage by sea concluded on or after the date of entry into force of this Convention in respect of that State.

Article 31 — Denunciation of other conventions

1. Upon becoming a Contracting State to this Convention, any State party to the International Convention for the Unification of Certain Rules relating to Bills of Lading signed at Brussels on 25 August, 1924 (1924 Convention) must notify the Government of Belgium as the depositary of the 1924 Convention of its denunciation of the said Convention with a declaration that the denunciation is to take effect as from the date when this Convention enters into force in respect of that State.

2. Upon the entry into force of this Convention under paragraph 1 of Article 30, the depositary of this Convention must notify the Government of Belgium as the depositary of the 1924 Convention of the date of such entry into force, and of the names of the Contracting States in respect of which the Convention has entered into force.

3. The provisions of paragraphs 1 and 2 of this article apply correspondingly in respect of States parties to the Protocol signed on 23 February, 1968 to amend the International Convention for the Unification of Certain Rules relating to Bills of Lading signed at Brussels on 25 August, 1924.

4. Notwithstanding Article 2 of this Convention, for the purposes of paragraph 1 of this article, a Contracting State may, if it deems it desirable, defer the denunciation of the 1924 Convention and of the 1924 Convention as modified by the 1968 Protocol for a maximum period of five years from the entry into force of this Convention. It will then notify the Government of Belgium of its intention. During this transitory period, it must apply to the Contracting States this Convention to the exclusion of any other one.

Article 32 — Revision and amendment

1. At the request of not less than one-third of the Contracting States to this Convention, the depositary shall convene a conference of the Contracting States for revising or amending it.

2. Any instrument of ratification, acceptance, approval or accession deposited after the entry into force of an amendment to this Convention, is deemed to apply to the Convention as amended.

Article 33 — Revision of the limitation amounts and unit of account or monetary unit

1. Notwithstanding the provisions of Article 32, a conference only for the purpose of altering the amount specified in Article 6 and paragraph 2 of Article 26, or of substituting either or both of the units defined in paragraphs 1 and 3 of Article 26 by other units is to be convened by the depositary in accordance with paragraph 2 of this article. An alteration of the amounts shall be made only because of a significant change in their real value.

2. A revision conference is to be convened by the depositary when not less than one-fourth of the Contracting States so request.

3. Any decision by the conference must be taken by a two-thirds majority of the participating States. The amendment is communicated by the depository to all the Contracting States for acceptance and to all the States signatories of the Convention for information.

4. Any amendment adopted enters into force on the first day of the month following one year after its acceptance by two-thirds of the Contracting States. Acceptance is to be effected by the deposit of a formal instrument to that effect, with the the depositary.

5. After entry into force of an amendment a Contracting State which has accepted the amendment is entitled to apply the Convention as amended in its relations with Contracting States which have not within six months after the adoption of the amendment notified the depositary that they are not bound by the amendment.

6. Any instrument of ratification, acceptance, approval or accession deposited after the entry into force of an amendment to this Convention, is deemed to apply to the Convention as amended.

Article 34 — Denunciation

1. A Contracting State may denounce this Convention at any time by means of a notification in writing addressed to the depositary.

2. The denunciation takes effect on the first day of the month following the expiration of one year after the notification is received by the depositary. Where a longer period is specified in the notification, the denunciation takes effect upon the expiration of such longer period after the notification is received by the depositary.

DONE at Hamburg, this thirty-first day of March one thousand nine hundred and seventy-eight, in a single original, of which the Arabic, Chinese, English, French, Russian and Spanish texts are equally authentic.

IN WITNESS WHEREOF the undersigned plenipotentiaries, being duly authorized by their respective Governments, have signed the present Convention.

ANNEX II

COMMON UNDERSTANDING ADOPTED BY THE UNITED NATIONS CONFERENCE ON THE CARRIAGE OF GOODS BY SEA

It is the common understanding that the liability of the carrier under this Convention is based on the principle of presumed fault or neglect. This means that, as a rule, the burden of proof rests on the carrier but, with respect to certain cases, the provisions of the Convention modify this rule.

This common understanding was seemingly agreed because there was some doubt as to whether Article 5, which deals with the basis of liability and provides that the carrier is liable for loss resulting from loss of or damage to the goods, as well as delay in delivery, if the occurrence which caused the loss, damage or delay took place while the goods were in his charge as defined in Article 4, unless the carrier proves that he, his agents or servants took all measures that could reasonably be required to avoid the occurrence and its consequences, was in effect intended to impose strict liability upon carriers or whether the intention was that liability should depend upon fault. For this reason Annex II was introduced into the Rules.

SECTION IV

Review of Bill of Lading clauses not specifically covered by the Hague Rules but considered by UNCTAD in the drafting of the Hamburg Rules.

Liberty clauses generally

Many bills of lading contain a number of so called "liberty" clauses, purporting to grant the carrier rights and immunities which he would otherwise not enjoy, but which in fact are invalid because they conflict with the Hague Rules. Investigations disclose that such clauses may mislead cargo owners into dropping valid claims, and may prolong negotiation over claims which might otherwise have been settled promptly, so encouraging unnecessary litigation. The recommendation of the Committee was to end the practice of including invalid clauses in bills of lading and to include in the Rules specific references to many commonly used invalid clauses as examples of those excluded by the Rules.

Freight and Refrigeration

Reference was made to two examples of frequently invalid liberty clauses namely "freight clauses" and "refrigeration clauses". A freight clause is one which states that the freight shall be earned and payable regardless of whether the vessel and goods are lost, and if there is a loss for which the carrier is legally responsible, then such a clause is invalid as a lessening of the carrier's liability in violation of the provisions of Article III (8) of the Rules. Refrigeration clauses are those which attempt to relieve the carrier from liability for defective functioning of the refrigeration machinery, again a clause lessening the liability of the carrier otherwise than as provided for in the Rules.

Jurisdiction

Another point made was that carriers often insert "jurisdiction clauses" specifying that any dispute arising under a bill of lading shall be decided in a particular country, or that a particular country's law should apply to such disputes. The validity of jurisdiction clauses is non-uniform and uncertain, and at present the Rules are silent on the subject. There should, say the Committee, be contained in the Rules a uniform rule on jurisdiction, it being both certain and fair to stipulate that jurisdiction lies either in the country of shipment or that of desination, at the option of the party claiming the loss.

Transhipment

One final matter upon which UNCTAD took some serious views was the matter of "transhipment clauses" which often state that each carrier along route is to be responsible for the goods only while they are in his possession. They point out that if valid such clauses raise problems (a) because the extent of the carriers' liabilities is difficult to determine precisely (b) because goods might be transhipped at a port where the Hague Rules are not in force, with the result that the Rules may not apply to the non-carriage period (c) the transhipment clause may state that each individual carrier's bill of lading is to apply while the goods are in the carrier's hands. A further question is whether jurisdiction clauses in each bill of lading along the route are valid, for if they are a cargo owner might have to sue different carriers in different jurisdictions. UNCTAD recommend that these problems be solved by stipulating in the Rules that the original carrier shall be responsible for the entire through transit, and that the Rules shall apply to the entire transit.

Problem clauses

The provisions of the Hague Rules do not pretend to cover all aspects of ocean carriage, and much is left to the mutual agreement between the parties to the contract of carriage provided that the clauses or covenant in the bill of lading do not contravene the Rules. The Committee took the view that in addition to the specific provision of the Hague Rules, there were a number of standard bill of lading clauses which raised problems and required special consideration.

In the consideration of such clauses and in regard to their recommendations the Committee had in mind two standards, namely Article III paragraph 8 of the Rules which nullifies any clauses lessening the liability of the carrier otherwise than as provided in the Rules, and general considerations of fairness in the balance of rights and duties between the parties to a contract of affreightment.

Jurisdiction clauses in particular

Commonly contained in bills of lading are so termed "Jurisdiction Clauses" such as (1) "Any dispute arising under this bill of lading shall be decided in the country where the carrier has his principal place of business, and the law of such country shall apply". (2) "The contract evidenced by this bill of lading shall be governed . . . law and any dispute determined in . . . or at the option of the carrier at the port of destination according to . . . law to the exclusion of the jurisdiction of the Courts of any other country". The latter is more usually found in liner bills of lading, while Clause (1) has been severely criticised by many Courts and authorities on grounds that it should be unthinkable that a receiver had to discover the principal place of business of an unknown carrier in order to exercise his rights against him.

With reference to contracts of carriage evidenced by bills of lading, ever since the introduction of the Hague Rules into the Statute Books of the maritime nations disputes and litigation have arisen. In 1927 a dispute arose under a bill of lading, which was governed by the Carriage of Goods by Sea Act, and which contained a clause providing that all claims arising under that contract of carriage should be determined at the port of destination. The English Court, before whom the proceedings had been commenced for the recovery of the damage and loss suffered by the goods during course of transit, decided that the clause was not a clause tending to lessen the liability of the carrier, and the action commenced by the cargo claimants in this country was set aside.

Another case, amongst many others concerning the matter of jurisdiction, concerned bills of lading that were issued in Palestine covering a cargo of oranges to the U.K. An action was brought against the owners of the carrying vessel, the proceedings being commenced in the U.K. for the recovery of the alleged short delivery of part of the consignment. The bill of lading provided that wherever signed it was to be construed by English law, but the Palestine Carriage of Goods by Sea Ordinance provided not only that every bill of lading issued in Palestine shall contain an express statement that it should have effect subject to the Hague Rules applied by the Ordinance, but also provided that it should be effective notwithstanding the omission of such an express statement. The Appeal Court in London held that the bills of lading in the hands of indorsees were governed by the Ordinance and that the laws of Palestine could not be evaded by an illegal declaration that the bills of lading were to be construed by English law.

When Australia gave effect to the Hague Rules it was provided in the Australian Act that all parties to any bill of lading relating to the carriage of goods from any place in Australia to any place outside Australia shall be deemed to have intended to contract according to the laws in force at the place of shipment. Any stipulation or agreement to the contrary, or purporting to oust or lessen the jurisdiction of the Courts of the Commonwealth or of a State in respect of the bill of lading or document, shall be null and void, and of no effect. It is also provided that any stipulation or agreement, whether made in the Commonwealth or elsewhere, purporting to oust or lessen the jurisdiction of the Courts of the Commonwealth or of a State in respect of any bill of lading or document relating to the carriage of goods from any place outside Australia to any place in Australia shall be illegal, null and void and of no effect.

However, other countries, including the U.K. and the U.S. have no such provisions and problems frequently arise when a foreign shipowner carrying goods to another country requires, by his bill of lading conditions, that any dispute arising under the bill of lading shall be settled in the country of the origin of the shipment, or of the country of the ownership of the vessel, or at destination, in the owner's option. Such clauses have in cases become burdensome, in that, for example a consignee in the U.K. might be compelled by such a clause to pursue his

156

claim for the recovery of cargo loss or damage in some remote country, despite the fact that the shipowner may be domiciled in the U.K. Such cases have also arisen in the United States when a foreign shipowner has delivered the goods to the consignee in the United States in a damaged condition, the shipowners replying to the claim in the United States to the effect that under the clause in the bill of lading such claims must be determined in the country of shipment or ownership of the vessel.

The Committee's findings disclose that carriers usually attempt to avoid confrontation with courts and jurisprudence that may operate against their interests, by inserting "jurisdiction" clauses in their bills of lading specifying that a particular court, or the law of a particular country should exclusively determine any disputes that may arise from the bill of lading, as partially illustrated above.

The Hague Rules are silent on the matter of jurisdiction clauses. However, some countries, in giving effect to the Rules, have included provisions concerning jurisdiction, but the courts of thoe countries having no jurisdiction provisions may invoke Article III paragraph 8 of the Rules at their discretion. This rules that the jurisdiction clause is invalid if the court should consider that the change might have the effect of reducing the rights of the cargo owner.

Among those countries whose laws are silent on jurisdiction clauses, there are differences in the manner in which the courts exercise their discretion to accept or refuse jurisdiction. Some Courts will not enforce clauses which attempt to grant exclusive jurisdiction to a foreign court. In rejecting such a clause one court stated that to require a consignee, claiming damages in the sum of $26,000, to travel 4,200 miles to a court with a different legal system and language would, in practical effect, decrease the carrier's liability, and, therefore, the Court invoked Article III paragraph 8 of the Rules. The Court observed that in such cases the jurisdiction clause allows carriers to secure lower settlements than would be possible if cargo owners were allowed to sue in the most convenient forum. In their deliberations the Committee took particular note of this situation, noting also that other courts tend to recognise jurisdiction clauses contained in bills of lading only if they are satisfied that the foreign courts will apply the Hague Rules as enacted in their maritime law. It has to be noted that courts are more willing to recognise such clauses on the basis of freedom of contract and they will generally stay proceedings in cases where there is a foreign jurisdiction clause, and will only allow them to proceed when satisfied that it is just and proper to do so. It was suggested that if jurisdiction were required to be either in the country of shipment or that of the delivery of the goods "at the option of the claimant" there might be certainty as well as fairness to cargo owners. It was also felt that this would be fair to carriers as it is arguable that, by agreeing trade between the two ports, they implied acceptance of the probability of submitting to the jurisdiction of either port. However, at least at the present time, carriers make no such provision and include generally, in bills of lading, jurisdiction clauses to suit their convenience, and when optional, generally provide that the decision is at the option of the carrier. There was opportunity at the time of the Brussels Convention of 1968, when the amended Hague Rules were agreed, to ease the jurisdiction problem by making the Rules applicable to both outward and homeward shipments, as in the case of United States and certain other countries, but the scope of the Rules was not so extended.

Transhipment clauses in particular

Now, to pass on to the problem of "transhipment clauses" such clauses being contained in virtually all cargo liner bills of lading which provide, amongst other things, that each carrier along a route is to be responsible for the goods only while they are in his possession. The Committee commented that, if valid, such clauses raise problems because (a) carrier's extent of the different liability is difficult to determine precisely: (b) goods might be transhipped at a port where the Hague Rules are not in force, with the result that the Rules may not apply to the non-carriage period: (c) the transhipment clause may state that each individual carrier's bill of lading is to apply while the goods are in such carrier's hands. This also raises the question whether jurisdiction in each bill of lading along the route would be valid, so that the cargo owner might have to sue different carriers in different jurisdictions.

It was thought that these problems might be resolved by amending Rules to make the original carrier responsible for the whole transit, and to make the Rules apply during the entire period. This approach is in fact applied by an Australian bill of lading which provides, amongst other things, that the goods or part thereof may be carried by the named vessel or other vessels, whether belonging to the line or others and should circumstances in the opinion of the carrier, master or agent, render transhipment desirable or expedient may be transhipped at any port or ports, place or places whatsoever, and while in course of transhipment may be placed or stored in craft or ashore and may be reshipped or forwarded by land and/or water and/or air at carrier's option and expense, all as part of the contract voyage and all the provisions of the bill of lading continue to apply. Although in some quarters the view has been expressed that P. & I. insurers were concerned at the potential liability imposed upon shipowners and carriers by such clauses, it is believed that such insurers are not unduly worried at the problems involved.

In making their recommendation that the Rules be amended so as to apply during the entire period of the transit, the view was taken that it should be made clear that even when a transhipment clause is valid, certain conditions must be satisfied by the carrier in order to effect the carriage "properly and carefully" within the meaning of Article III paragraph 2 of the Rules, and that this would go a long way to bring certainty into the transhipment process.

The proposals of UNCTAD with regard to these conditions was intended, amongst other things, to provide that (1) transhipment is reasonable and proper in the circumstances; (2) wherever applicable, the carrier notifies the cargo owner of the transhipment so as to enable him to insure any new risks which might be involved through the substitution of another ship for the original ship; (3) the carrier shall exercise due care for the goods during the transhipment; (4) wherever applicable, the carrier continues to excercise due care and diligence to forward the goods as soon as possible and will not be excused if he delays the transhipment in order to avoid paying a high freight rate for forwarding the goods: (5) in appropriate circumstances the carrier would deliver the goods at his own risk or expense, or these may be shared with the cargo owner.

The Rules, as amended, should, in the opinion of the Committee also make it clear that the original carrier must seek indemnity from the on-carrier to satisfy a claim for loss or damage occurring while the goods are in the custody of the on-carrier. In fact many shipowners who are container operators currently do this voluntarily.

On this issue of transhipment clauses the comment was made that the primary interest of the cargo owner would appear to be to hold a bill of lading which would ensure that, unless he has otherwise agreed, the transhipment of his goods cannot be effected under terms less favourable than those in his original contract of carriage. The carrier, on the other hand, would wish to be protected against the sole burden of risk and expense of caring for and forwarding cargo under unavoidable and unreasonable circumstances.

Reference was made in connection with the above to Article III paragraph 2 of the Hague Rules and also Article V of the 1968 amendments to the Hague Rules, and it might be appropriate here to provide the details of these Rules for the benefit of the reader. Article V provides, so far as these notes are concerned, that the carrier is at liberty to surrender in whole or in part all or any of his rights and immunities or to increase any of his responsibilities and obligations under the Rules, provided that such surrender or increase shall be embodied in the bill of lading issued to the shipper. Article III paragraph 2 provides that subject to the provisions of Article IV, the carrier shall properly and carefully load, handle, stow, carry, keep, care for, and discharge the goods carried.

Clauses incorporating terms of charter-parties into bills of lading

The main argument advanced in support of incorporating clauses is that the practice, if effective, would lead to simplicity in documentation. In the case of charter-parties, the bill of lading should correspond with the charter-party, and to achieve this purpose it is convenient to state that "all terms of the charter-party" (or similar words) are to be considered to be part of the bill of lading.

It is thought that by this method the bill of lading becomes a shorter document than the usual liner bill of lading. It is often put forward that the bill of lading should include all the relevant provisions, but it is virtually impossible to prepare a satisfactory tramp bill of lading in advance because the clauses can only be drafted when the charter-party contents are known. It obviously saves time to use incorporating clauses, and by using them the parties to the contract avoid the possibility of prejudicing their position by deciding beforehand which of the charter-party terms should be repeated in the bill of lading. It was pointed out, however, that the incorporation of charter-party terms into bills of lading also entails certain disadvantages.

There are many disadvantages of incorporating clauses, among which is the fact that the parties to the bill of lading may have some difficulty in ascertaining their legal position. It might be difficult to determine which of the clauses of a lengthy charter-party are incorporated, and frequently the charter-party is not at hand when the bill of lading contract is concluded, or when the bill of lading is transferred. The bill of lading governs the rights and responsibilities of the shipowner and the bill of lading holder, and the shipowner should not, therefore, it was thought have any claims or defences which do not appear in some way from the document.

In contracts of sale the buyer may be forced to accept a bill of lading. It may be agreed in the sale contract that the buyer shall pay upon presentation of the bill of lading, but even if this is not done the seller has the right in some instances, *e.g.* if the sale is made c.i.f., f.o.b., to oblige the buyer to pay on presentation of the bill of lading. If "Incoterms" apply, the charter-party has to be presented with the bill of lading, but otherwise this may not be so. In the case of *Finska Cellulosaforeningen* v. *Westfield Paper Company* some years ago, it was held that even if the charter-party is referred to in the bill of lading the buyer will not necessarily be entitled to a copy of it if its terms are well known in the trade.

When goods are sold afloat, the prospective buyer is free to refuse to become a party to an agreement if he thinks that a reference to a charter-party is likely to become dangerous, in which case it can be argued that the effect of the incoporating clause is to reduce the transferability of the bill of lading. Also under the "Uniform Customs and Practice for Documentary Credits", unless specifically authorised in the credit, a bill of lading which is issued under and subject to the conditions of a charter-party will be rejected. The effect of an incorporating clause would, therefore, have the effect of restricting the use of bills of lading as documents of credit.

The shipping committee brought out these points, and commented also that if the bill of lading is regarded in the light of commercial requirements under a sale contract, an incorporating clause may have some restrictive effects. However, if the bill of lading is treated as a contract of carriage, an incorporation clause is convenient for carriers, for carriers naturally wish to reduce their risks under the bill of lading to equal those undertaken in the charter-party.

The question arose as to what was required to improve the present situation so that the receiver does not suffer injustice and there is no delay of commercial transactions. In this connection it was recommended that the following points be taken into account in future transactions: (a) When the bill of lading is issued by the carrier, a copy of the charter-party should be attached to the bill of lading. (b) When a bill of lading is tendered under a sale contract, a copy of the charter-party should be presented with the bill of lading under "Incoterms". (c) Any demurrage incurred at the loading port should be endorsed on the bill of lading. (d) If there is a total time for loading or discharging, the time taken in loading should be endorsed on the bill of lading. (e) Any deadfreight or possible deadfreight should be endorsed on the bill of lading. (f) Cesser clauses should be invalid. (g) Regarding arbitration clauses in charter-parties, the Committee took the view that either Article III paragraph 6 of the Hague Rules should be amended to provide that "suit" would not include arbitration proceedings, or this Article could be amended to provide that the presence of an arbitration clause would not operate so as to debar cargo owners from bringing "suit" if in fact they had commenced legal proceedings of some kind within the one year time limitation period contained in Article III paragraph 6. (h) The "Uniform Customs and Practice for Documentary Credits" should be amended to provide that bills of lading subject to the conditions of a charter-party are authorised so long as they meet the requirements such as those in (a) to (e) above.

In fact virtually all charter-parties contain arbitration clauses, but on the other hand bills of lading issued under charter-parties, seldom, if ever, contain such clauses. Questions have arisen over the extent to which charter-party arbitration clauses are binding on receivers through incorporating clauses in bills of lading.

The Courts have tended to look closely at the wording of arbitration clauses in determining whether they are binding upon receivers, and so a clause providing that "all disputes under this charter shall be referred to arbitration" has been held not to be sufficient to bind the receiver. In the case of *The Phonizien* (1 Lloyd's Report 150, 1966) it was held that such a clause was not effective for a dispute arising under the bill of lading, even though the dispute was between the charterer and the shipowner instead of a third party receiver and the shipowner.

On the other hand a clause providing that "any dispute arising out of this charter or any bill of lading issued hereunder shall be referred to arbitration" has been held to be sufficient.

Attention was drawn to a further problem which arises if the time limit in the charter-party arbitration clause is shorter than that of the Hague Rules in cases where there is a bill of lading to which the Rules apply. The Hague Rules would, for example, apply to a bill of lading issued under a charter-party whenever such bill of lading has been transferred by the charterer to another person. Application of a shorter time limit would violate Article III paragraph 8 of the Rules, which provides that any clause, covenant or agreement in a contract of carriage relieving the carrier or the ship from liability for loss or damage to or in connection with goods arising from negligence, fault or failure in the duties and obligations provided in Article III, or lessening such liability otherwise than as provided in the Rules, shall be null and void and of no effect. It is, however, uncertain whether the effect would be to void the whole arbitration clause or only the provision for a shorter time limit, this having the effect of the lessening of the carrier's liability otherwise than as provided for in the Rules.

It was the view of the Committee that an English Court would nullify only the provision for a shorter time limit, allowing the remainder of the arbitration clause to stand. Reference was made to certain law cases in this connection. In one case in the United States it was held that such a conflict was for the arbitrators to resolve and not the Court. In that case *Lowry & Co.* v. *Le Moyne D'Iberville, etc.* the claimant was the transferee of bills of lading covering sugar cargoes, and the action was brought to recover damages to shipments which were carried from French ports to New York and other American ports.

Briefly, the facts were that a French Corporation entered into a charter-party at Paris for the carriage of the sugar, the charter-party containing a provision by way of an addendum: "Clauses 16 to 33 both included as attached as well as . . . Centrocon strike and arbitration clauses to be deemed fully incorporated in this charter-party and form part of same." The Centrocon clause provides, amongst other things that "all disputes . . . arising out of this contract shall . . . be referred to the final arbitrament of two arbitrators carrying on business in London . . ." On receipt of the shipments of sugar from the shipper, bills of lading were issued providing that "All conditions and exceptions are as per charter-party . . ." It was argued before the Court that the claimant was bound by the Centrocon clause and that by its failure to give notice of claim and to appoint an arbitrator within three months of final discharge, as required by the clause, the claim was waived.

The Court ruled that the cargo damaged claimant's failure to comply with the bill of lading requirement by appointing its arbitrator within three months after the goods were discharged could constitute a waiver, not only of remedy of arbitration, but also of its claim for damages. Such a provision, said the Court, was not invalidated by the Carriage of

Goods by Sea Act. However, the Court added, simultaneous incorporation of one year time for suit clause (as provided for in the Hague Rules) in the bill of lading resulted in ambiguity which the arbitrators should interpret.

Liens for deadfreight

Passing now to matters of liens for deadfreight. The Committee found that in some countries it has been held that a clause in a charter-party granting the carrier a lien for deadfreight could be enforced against the receiver under an incorporating clause in the bill of lading. The comment was made that it is somewhat difficult to justify the receiver paying for the charterers' failure to supply cargo. A lien for demurrage in a charter-party can be enforced against the receiver if the charter-party is incorporated into the bill of lading by the usual incorporating clause. Such a lien is effective against the receiver for demurrage at the loading port as well as the discharging port, and the fact that the amount of demurrage incurred at the loading port is not endorsed on the bill of lading will not affect this result.

In connection with these matters reference was made to the case of *Fidelitas Shipping Company* v. *V O Exportchleb*. The case was concerned with, amongst other things, the question as to whether a bill of lading gave the shipowners a lien for the full amount of the demurrage incurred at port of loading. The bills of lading provided that "All terms and conditions as per charter-party". Clause 13 of the bill of lading provided "The carrier shall have a lien upon the goods for and until the payment of freight and all other charges and expenses due under the contract of carriage . . ." The Court ruled that the lien provided for in clause 13 of the bill of lading covered loading port demurrage, and that, even if the lien given by the bill of lading did not cover port of loading demurrage, then that might be imported from the charter-party without inconsistency between the two documents.

Conclusions on incorporating clauses

The view was taken that problems arising from the incorporation of charter-party terms into bills of lading require considerable reflection since they affect also the terms of the sale, and the freedom of contractual relationships. It appears, generally speaking, that the consequential effects of the charter-party and the bill of lading should be kept quite separate, and the holder of the bill of lading, if he is not also the charterer, should not be subject to liabilities arising from the charter-party which he has not expressly agreed to accept.